Covered Calls and LEAPS— A Wealth Option

Covered Calls and LEAPS— A Wealth Option

A Guide for Generating Extraordinary Monthly Income

JOSEPH HOOPER
AARON ZALEWSKI

John Wiley & Sons, Inc.

Published by John Wiley & Sons, Inc., Hoboken, New Jersey.
Published simultaneously in Canada.

For general information on our other products and services or for technical support, please contact our Customer Care Department within the United States at (800) 762-2974, outside the United States at (317) 572-3993 or fax (317) 572-4002.

Wiley also publishes its books in a variety of electronic formats. Some content that appears in print may not be available in electronic books. For more information about Wiley products, visit our web site at www.wiley.com.

Library of Congress Cataloging-in-Publication Data:

Hooper, Joseph, 1943–
    Covered calls—A wealth option : a guide for generating extraordinary monthly income / Joseph Hooper And Aaron Zalewski.
        p. cm.
    Includes bibliographical references and index.
    ISBN-13 978-0-470-04470-4 (cloth/dvd : alk. paper)
    ISBN-10 0-470-04470-5 (cloth/dvd : alk. paper)
    1. Options (Finance) 2. Stock options. I. Zalewski, Aaron, 1980–
II. Title. III. Title: Covered calls.
    HG6024.A3H66 2006
    332.63'2283—dc22
        2006015461

Printed in the United States of America.

10 9 8 7 6 5 4 3 2

Contents

Foreword

Brilliant book. Anyone who has read any of my work knows that I believe buying, holding, and praying is not an optimal financial strategy. Joseph Hooper and Aaron Zalewski have done an excellent job making a complex subject simple enough for someone like me to understand.

As most of us know, investors invest for two basic things: capital gains and cash flow. Most people invest for capital gains, which is simply buying something and hoping the price goes up. Investing for cash flow is investing for a steady stream of income. Of the two, investing for cash flow requires the most skill. Anyone can deceive themselves by thinking, "The price will go up in the future." Or anyone can be suckered into a sales pitch that goes: "Prices have gone up over the past five years . . . so you better buy now."

The reason I love this book is because the authors have made investing for cash flow simple. I like the analogy in their Preface of planting trees and growing a forest to be cut down as an example of investing for *capital gains* versus planting fruit trees to harvest and replenish on a regular basis as the example of investing for *cash flow*. Obviously, the more savvy investors invest for both capital gains and cash flow. They want a forest and the fruit. They want money today and tomorrow.

Regardless, even if you never plan on investing in stocks or covered calls, this is an excellent book for anyone who wants to look into the mind of a professional investor. You see, the investment strategy discussed in this book does not apply only to stocks. This investment strategy works for real estate as well. Rarely do I buy a stock or piece of real estate without first knowing that I will receive cash flow and capital gains. In other words, this book is not about an asset class but more about a class of investor that likes to win, not gamble.

ROBERT KIYOSAKI
Author of *Rich Dad, Poor Dad*

Preface

One can think of the accumulation of a stock portfolio through time as the cultivation of a forest full of trees. Traditional Street mentality encourages investors to plant trees throughout their working lives and rely on appreciating markets to grow the forest over the long term.

Once our working lives are finished and active income ceases, the Street then encourages investors to begin cutting down the forest to provide income in retirement. The *hope* is that the forest has grown large enough over time to withstand the depletion in retirement. In our experience, this level of growth is a rarity for the average American.

What the Street has overlooked is that simple and very conservative cultivation can transform the forest into an orchard of fruit-bearing trees. Fruit-bearing trees generate cash income on a monthly basis. For investors who want to grow their assets, rather than eating the fruit each month, the fruit can be left to fall on fertile soils to grow more trees and thus to *compound* the growth of the forest through time. For investors who are in retirement, the fruit can be picked each month as cash income for living expenses—without liquidating stocks in the portfolio and destroying the forest that they depend on to live.

Correct application of the covered call technique is the vehicle by which stocks are converted to cash flow generating assets.

OPTIONS ARE NOT JUST A HIGH RISK/HIGH RETURN INSTRUMENT

Options are without doubt the most misunderstood, misrepresented, and poorly implemented financial tool in the world. When asked about options, most people (including those "in the know" like financial planners, stockbrokers, and accountants) will tell you that "they're high-risk, high-return instruments."

It is astonishing that even those who are financially educated seem unaware that options can be used to *minimize* or even *eliminate* risk in a stock portfolio. In fact, options were originally not devised for use as a speculative instrument. They were originally used in the agricultural industry to *reduce* risk by locking in future sales prices before harvest. Regardless of this original intent, options maintain the label of "high risk, high return."

The high-risk, high-return label derives its origins from the speculative use of options. Speculators use options to bet on the direction of the markets for the potential of very high returns. However, with these high returns come very high risk, and the vast majority of speculators fail over the long term. If you ever attempt to speculate with options, there is a very high chance that you, too, will be unsuccessful over the long term.

What evidence do we have that the vast majority of speculators fail over the long term? Well, if just 10 percent of the world's speculators were making regular 50–100 percent returns per trade over the long term (as is the goal of a speculator), then the world would be full of multi, multimillionaires who made overnight fortunes trading options. Clearly, this is not the reality. However, this get-rich-quick ideal continues to be perpetuated by the endless hope of investors seeking a quick and easy solution to their financial woes.

Options markets are a zero-sum game. Someone wins only when someone else loses. If most speculators lose in the long run, who are the winners? Apart from the market makers and the small portion of speculators who win over the long term, money flows each and every month into the hands of *option writers*. Option writers are the people who are selling option contracts to the speculators.

What we want to teach you has nothing to do with the risky practice of speculating with options—this is not high-risk, high-return trading. In fact, covered calls are almost the complete opposite. In this book we show you a way to use options to make consistent, steady profits that you can rely on to pay your mortgage and put food on your table or to compound your investment capital through time into significant accumulations of wealth.

JOSEPH HOOPER
AARON ZALEWSKI

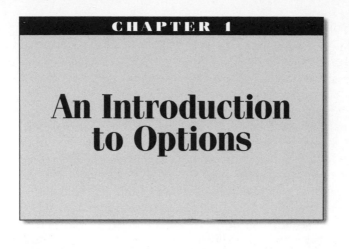

CHAPTER 1

An Introduction to Options

MARKET BASICS

This section is written specifically for the stock market novice. It is aimed at those who have never bought a stock before or those who have very little understanding of the most basic functions of stock and option markets.

What Is the Stock Market?

From the perspective of a private investor, the *stock market* provides a venue for the buying and selling of stock of publicly listed companies. If you want to buy fruit, you go to the fruit market. If you want to buy stocks, you buy them through the stock market—it is as simple as that. Other common terms for the stock market include:

- Share market
- Equity market
- Simply "the market"

From the perspective of a company, listing on the stock market provides access to a large amount of investment capital that would not otherwise be available to an unlisted company. The market provides companies with the ability to seek investment funds from retail investors as well as institutional investors (fund managers, banks, etc.) who invest on behalf of others. Access to this public market capital enables a listed company to significantly extend its potential funding base upon which it can expand and grow its business in the future.

What Is a Share?

A *share* represents a portion of ownership of a company. Public companies are very large and, in most instances, are not owned by just one person or entity. Many thousands of different people or entities own stock in large listed public companies.

A share literally entitles its owner to a portion of a company's earnings (as dividends) and a claim on the company's assets in the event of bankruptcy (priority given to creditors). Through the election of company directors, stockowners are also entitled to participate in deciding the future direction of the company.

Most adults are already stockowners. Some of these stockowners are active investors who buy and sell stocks based on their own research or on the advice of their peers or professional advisers such as a stockbroker. Other stockowners gain exposure to the stock market through mutual funds where money is pooled and invested by a professional fund manager.

How Are Stocks Bought and Sold on the Stock Market?

Think of the stock market like a fruit market. Let's assume you want to buy 10 bananas. You need to go to the fruit market and see who is selling bananas and at what price. Store owners are entitled to sell their bananas at whatever price they see fit. Obviously they don't want to make the price too high or their fruit won't sell, or too low because then they are not making as much money as they could.

You find three different stores selling bananas:

Asking Price, 10 Bananas

Store 1	$1.40
Store 2	$1.47
Store 3	$1.60

You obviously want to buy your bananas as cheaply as possible. If you think $1.40 is reasonable, you might simply buy them from store 1 at that price. If you are only prepared to pay $1.35, then you might "bid" to buy them at $1.35. The manager at store 1 may agree to this price as it's not far away from his asking price. If you both agree on a price, the bananas will sell.

Buying stocks on the stock market works exactly the same way! Let's assume you want to buy 100 shares of General Electric (GE). You look up the price at the stock market by calling your stockbroker (or going to your broker's online site). You are presented with the market for GE stock. It looks Table 1.1.

TABLE 1.1 The Market for GE Stock

Buyers (Bid)		Sellers (Ask)	
Number of Shares	Bid Price	Ask Price	Number of Shares
2,000	$25.00	$25.20	5,000
5,000	$24.80	$25.40	400
400	$24.20	$26.00	1,000

If you want to buy 100 shares, you need to buy them by reaching an agreement on price from someone who wants to sell them. The sellers put into the market how many shares they want to sell and at what price (the "ask" price). You obviously want to buy the stock as cheaply as possible, so the seller asking the lowest price is always at the top of the list. He or she is offering 5,000 shares for sale at a price of $25.20.

You now have two options:

1. If you think $25.20 is a reasonable price, you can simply put in a bid to buy 100 shares of GE at $25.20 and your order will be filled.
2. If you think $25.20 is not a reasonable price, you can put in a bid for less.

Let's assume you think $25.10 is a reasonable price. You enter this bid price into the market and the market will then look like Table 1.2. Your bid is now at the top of the column because you are the current highest bidder. If the seller at $25.20 (or any other seller) thinks that $25.10 is a reasonable price, he or she may change the order to $25.10 and the stock will trade. Or a new seller might come into the market enticed by your bid of $25.10 and your stock may trade.

What Is a Stock Code or Symbol?

All stocks that trade on public markets are represented by an individual *stock code* or *symbol*. No two stocks have the same stock code.

TABLE 1.2 Entering a Bid into the Market

Buyers (Bid)		Sellers (Ask)	
Number of Shares	Bid Price	Ask Price	Number of Shares
100	$25.10	$25.20	5,000
2,000	$25.00	$25.40	400
5,000	$24.80	$26.00	1,000
400	$24.20		

While these terms can be used interchangeably, in the United States, the term *symbol* is used. U.S. stock symbols consist of one letter to five letters. For example, Citigroup is represented by the symbol C, Wal-Mart is represented by the symbol WMT, and Shire Pharmaceuticals is represented by the symbol SHPGY.

Option contracts in the United States are also represented by symbols/ tickers, which are generally five letters long. As with stocks, no two option contracts have the same symbol.

What Makes Stock Prices Go Up and Down?

Many factors influence the price at which a company's stock trades, the most important factor being a company's future earnings. Various *fundamental* factors combine to influence a company's future earnings. You will become very familiar with fundamental factors as they are of particular interest to financial analysts and also gain significant exposure in the financial press. Common fundamental factors that affect the future earnings potential of a company include:

- Company-related issues such as increases or decreases in sales, increases or decreases in the cost of doing business, and changes in asset position, management team, business model, or perceived business risk.
- Industry-related issues such as the financial performance of competitors or introduction of significant legislation.
- Economic-related issues such as the economic growth rate of economies in which the business operates, currency fluctuations, and interest rate or inflation rate changes.

If a fundamental factor changes and causes the market to think that a company's future earnings will be higher (lower) than previously expected, the stock price will adjust upward (downward) accordingly.

Other influences on stock prices that you should be aware of are *technical* factors. Technical analysis is the study of stock price charts through time. There are many investors and traders in the financial markets who make buy and sell decisions based solely on technical analysis because they believe that all fundamental factors are represented in the price charts they analyze.

We discuss both fundamental and technical factors in more depth later in this book.

What Is a Stockbroker?

Stockbrokers provide access to the stock market by entering buy and sell orders into the market on behalf of investors. Stockbrokers also hold accounts on behalf of investors where electronic records of stocks, options, and cash held are kept.

A brokerage account is just like a bank account except it holds stocks and options as well as cash. To set up a brokerage account, contact a broker (via phone or online), fill out the paperwork, and deposit money into your account. For the type of investing you are going to be doing, it is best to use a discount broker with the lowest possible transaction costs and fast executions.

Do not use a boutique broker (one who provides advice), even if you currently use one. They are expensive and, from this point on, you will not need their advice. You will make your own decisions and the returns you will generate may be many times what the best broker can do for you in the best year!

The brokerage industry is constantly evolving with new online players entering the market and existing brokerage houses regularly making changes to trading platforms and commission structures. The current industry best brokers for using the covered call technique can be found at www.compoundstockearnings.com/brokers. We strongly advise you to use one of these recommended brokers because trading platforms and transaction costs have a very dramatic effect on profitability.

What Are the Dow Jones Industrial Average, S&P 500, and NASDAQ?

The Dow Jones Industrial Average (the Dow), S&P 500, and NASDAQ are stock market *indexes*. A stock market index is used to represent the performance of a group of stocks rather than just a single stock. Apart from some exceptions (such as the Dow), indexes are generally constructed on a market value weighted basis. Consequently, the movements of larger companies have a greater impact on the performance of the index than do movements of smaller companies.

Some of the world's most significant stock market indexes are listed in Table 1.3.

TABLE 1.3 Major Stock Market Indexes

Index Name	Market	Composition
Dow Jones Industrial (Dow)	U.S.—NYSE	30 stocks on New York Stock Exchange (NYSE)
NASDAQ Composite	U.S.—NASDAQ	All NASDAQ stocks; heavy in technology
S&P/ASX 200	Australia	200 largest and most liquid companies
Financial Times Stock Exchange (FTSE)	London	100 largest companies; often called "Footsie"
DAX	Germany	30 major companies
Hang Seng	Hong Kong	33 largest companies
Nikkei	Tokyo	225 largest companies

What Are Options and How Do They Trade?

An *option* is a financial instrument and contract. An option gives the holder the right, but not the obligation, to buy or sell a financial asset at a certain price up to a certain date. An important distinction is "the right, but not the obligation." The holder of the option does not have to exercise the right under the contract if it is not in his or her favor to do so.

Options (like futures) are known as *derivative securities* simply because their value is *derived* from the value of other more basic variables. For example, an IBM stock option is a derivative security because its value depends on the price of IBM stock. The derivative asset is also referred to as the *underlying* asset. In this case, the underlying asset is IBM stock.

Options are available on many financial assets including stocks, futures, and commodities. Most options are exchange traded, meaning they are traded on public markets, just like stocks are traded on stock exchanges.

There are two basic types of stock options:

1. A *call option* gives the holder the right, but not the obligation, to *buy* a stock at a certain price up to a certain date. Call options are used by speculators who expect an *increase* in the price of the underlying asset.

2. A *put option* gives the holder the right, but not the obligation, to *sell* a stock at a certain price up to a certain date. Put options are used by speculators who expect a *decrease* in the price of the underlying asset.

The covered call technique involves the use of call options *only*.

Options trade exactly the same way that stocks do. There are investors who want to buy options and there are investors who want to sell, or write, options. When these two investors reach an agreement on price, the contract trades. This trade happens in exactly the same way as previously described in the section on "how stocks are bought and sold on the stock market."

All exchange-traded options have certain standard characteristics. Take this description of a contract as an example:

General Electric September 2005 $30.00 Call Option

Company name All exchange-traded options relate to a specific publicly listed company (or financial asset). In this case the contract relates to stock in *General Electric* (GE).

Expiration date	All options have an expiration date. In this case the option expires in *September 2005*.
Strike or exercise price	All options have a specific *strike* or *exercise* price. These two terms are used interchangeably. If you own this contract you have the right to buy GE stock at a price of *$30.00*.
Type	All options are either a call option or a put option. A call option provides the right to buy the stock. A put option provides the right to sell the stock. This contract is a *call option*.

If you owned the GE September 2005 $30.00 call option, you would have the right, but not the obligation, to buy GE stock at $30.00 per share up to the expiration date of September 2005.

Unlike stocks, options are referred to as *contracts*. In the United States, a standard contract relates to 100 shares in the underlying stock—this number changes depending on which country the option is listed in. Thus, if you buy four GE September 2005 $30 calls, you own four *contracts*. Each contract relates to 100 shares, so in this instance, you own the right to buy 400 shares.

What Basic Options Terminology Do You Need to Know?

Long and Short Positions   An investor who has an overall buy position in a stock or option contract is said to be *long*. If you currently do not own GE stock and you purchase 500 GE shares, you are *long* 500 GE shares. If you purchase four GE September 2005 $30 calls and have no existing position in that contract, you are *long* four GE September 2005 $30 calls.

Conversely, an investor who has an overall sell position in an option contract is said to be *short*. If you currently do not own GE stock and you sell 400 GE shares, you are *short* 400 shares. If you sell three GE September 2005 $30 calls and have no existing position in that contract, you are said to be *short* three September 2005 $30 calls.

Table 1.4 shows each position classified as either long or short. It assumes that the investor has no existing position in any stock or option contract.

Opening and Closing Transactions   An *opening transaction* is one where an option buyer or seller establishes a new position or increases an existing position as either a buyer or a seller. For example, if John buys one

TABLE 1.4 Comparison of Long and Short Positions

Position	Long	Short
Buy 300 GE shares	X	
Sell 12 WMT calls		X
Buy 4 HD calls	X	
Buy 8 JPM calls	X	
Sell 1 CD call		X

GE September 2005 $30 call, he is said to be "buying to open"—he has opened a new position. John may also elect to sell one GE September 2005 $30 call. In this case he would be "selling to open" if he was not already long in the identical contract. The effect of an opening transaction is that the number of contracts the investor is exposed to is increased.

A *closing transaction* is one where an option buyer makes an offsetting sale of an identical option or an option seller makes an offsetting purchase of an identical option. For example, if John is long one GE September 2005 $30 call and then sells one GE September 2005 $30 call, he would be "selling to close" because he has now closed out his position in that option contract and has no further rights or obligations under the contract. The effect of a closing transaction is that the number of contracts the investor is exposed to is decreased.

Alternatively, if John holds a short position of one GE September 2005 $30 call and then buys one GE September 2005 $30 call, he would likewise be "buying to close" because he has now closed out his position in that option contract and has no further rights or obligations under the contract. Again, the effect of a closing transaction is that the number of contracts the investor is exposed to is decreased.

Table 1.5 shows transactions categorized as either an opening or closing.

The important concept to understand is that an option buyer or seller can, at any time, close an open position by performing an equal and opposite transaction with the identical contract. Whether the transaction is closed for a profit or loss depends on the option's price at the time that the closing transaction is executed. This action is very similar to closing a traditional stock investment—the investor can sell the stock and close the position at any time, but whether the stock can be sold for a profit or loss depends on the current market price at the time.

TABLE 1.5 Classification of Transactions

Current Position	Next Transaction	Buy to Open	Buy to Close	Sell to Open	Sell to Close
Long 100 GE shares	Buy 100 GE shares	X			
Long 100 GE shares	Sell 100 GE shares				X
Long 300 GE shares	Buy 100 GE shares	X			
Short 200 GE shares	Buy 200 GE shares		X		
No position	Buy 2 GE calls	X			
No position	Sell 2 GE calls			X	
Short 2 GE calls	Buy 2 GE calls		X		
Long 2 GE calls	Sell 2 GE calls				X

In the Money, Out of the Money, and At the Money   Option market participants have coined the phrases in, out, and at the money to describe an option's strike price in relation to the stock price.

An *in-the-money* option is one that has intrinsic value, where the owner of the option stands to profit by exercising his or her right under the contract. For a call option to be in the money, the stock price must be higher than the strike price. For example, a $15.00 call option is in the money when the stock price is greater than $15.00.

An *out-of-the-money* option is one that has no intrinsic value, where the owner of the option does not stand to profit by exercising his or her right under the contract. For a call option to be out of the money, the stock price must be lower than the strike price. For example, a $15.00 call option is out of the money when the stock price is below $15.00.

An *at-the-money* option is one where the stock price is trading at or very close to the exercise price. For example, a $15.00 call option would be considered at the money if the stock price was $15.00. In practical terms, market participants also describe an option as at the money when the stock price is close to the exercise price of the option. So, if an option's strike price was $15.00 and the stock price was $14.80 to $15.20, it would be deemed as being at the money.

Table 1.6 shows options classified as being either in, at, or out of the money.

Physical Settlement Versus Cash Settlement   There are two types of settlement styles for exchange-traded options: physical settlement and cash settlement. *Physical-settlement* options give the owner the right to receive physical delivery of the underlying asset when the option is exercised.

TABLE 1.6　Classification as In, At, or Out of the Money

Contract	Stock Price	In	At	Out
GE Jan 07 $35 Call	$35.75	X		
WMT Sep 05 $45 Call	$48.20	X		
C Jan 06 $50 Call	$50.02		X	
JPM Aug 05 $30 Call	$24.10			X
HON Jan 07 $50 Call	$40.45			X
ABT Sep 05 $45 Call	$44.90		X	

Cash-settlement options give the owner the right to receive a cash payment based on the difference between the underlying asset price at the time of the option's exercise and the exercise price of the option. The majority of stock options are physically settled while index options are cash settled.

American Versus European Expiration　An American-style option may be exercised at any time prior to its expiration. A European-style option may be exercised only on its expiration date. The majority of stock options traded on U.S. and international options exchanges are American-style options. Our covered call technique involves the use of American-style options only.

Option Expiration Dates　In the U.S. market, virtually all standardized option contracts expire on the third Friday of each month; they *do not* expire on the last day of the month. For example, if you hold a November option contract, this contract will expire on the third Friday of November, not at the end of November.

The Options Clearing Corporation　The Options Clearing Corporation (OCC) guarantees that all market participants fulfill their obligations under the terms of options contracts. This is a very important function of an options market, particularly in terms of guaranteeing that options writers are capable of fulfilling their potentially large exposures.

Apart from keeping a record of all short and long positions, the OCC ensures that when purchasing an option the buyer must pay for it in full and the writer of an option must maintain an adequately funded margin account to cover his or her exposure at all times.

The clearinghouse allows the options market to function. Without it, the risk of counterparties defaulting on their obligations under an option contract would stifle the market.

Standardized Options and Option Chain　Exchange-traded options are almost always *standardized*. Standardized options have set parameters in terms of the amount of an underlying asset a contract relates to, the expiration date, the exercise price, the multiplier, and the option style. Investors cannot alter the standardized characteristics of an exchange-traded option to suit their own needs—they must work within the standardized parameters provided by the options exchange. The most important function of standardization is to assist in the formation of liquid secondary markets where buyers of options can close out positions by selling an identical contract and sellers/writers can close out positions by buying an identical contract.

An option chain is a list of all standardized options available for a particular stock or index. Table 1.7 shows an option chain for the U.S.-listed banking group JP Morgan. Take a moment to study it and note the different strike prices and expiration dates available.

If you wanted to buy or sell a call option on JP Morgan, you would have to select an option contract from this option chain. You are not able to select contract specifications that do not appear in the standardized option chain. Note that for simplicity only call options appear on this option chain; the same option chain is also available for put options.

How Do Speculators Use Options to Trade the Market?

While we don't use options to speculate on the future direction of a stock or market, many investors do use options for this purpose. It is essential that you understand how a speculative trade works in order for you to understand options markets.

Example of Using a Call Option to Speculate   GE stock is currently trading at $30.00. John thinks GE stock is going to go up in the next three months. It's now June, so John decides to buy a September $30.00 call option (note that he does not have to choose a strike price equal to the current stock price). John now has the right, but not the obligation, to buy GE stock at a price of $30.00 up to September. For this right John pays the *premium* of $1.00 per share. The *premium* is the price the option buyer pays to the option seller.

So let's assume John's hunch is right. It's now July and GE stock is $35.00. John has the right to buy GE stock for only $30.00. He can *exercise* this right, buy the stock at $30.00, and immediately sell it in the market for $35.00 (the current stock price). John has paid a premium of $1.00 per share for this right. His profit appears as follows:

Share sell price – Share buy price – Option price = Profit per share
$35.00   – $30.00   – $1.00   = $4.00

TABLE 1.7   JP Morgan Option Chain Example—Stock Price, $39.38

Strike	Symbol	Bid Price	Ask Price	Delta	Strike	Symbol	Bid Price	Ask Price	Delta
September					**Mar-05**				
27.50	JPMIY	11.80	12.00	1.00	27.50	JPMCY	11.90	12.10	0.98
30.00	JPMIF	9.30	9.50	1.00	30.00	JPMCF	9.50	9.70	0.97
32.50	JPMIZ	6.80	7.00	1.00	32.50	JPMCZ	7.20	7.40	0.92
35.00	JPMIG	4.40	4.50	1.00	35.00	JPMCG	5.20	5.30	0.81
37.50	JPMIU	1.95	2.05	0.91	37.50	JPMCU	3.30	3.50	0.63
40.00	JPMIH	0.30	0.35	0.33	40.00	JPMCH	1.90	2.05	0.44
42.50	JPMIV	0.00	0.05	—	42.50	JPMCV	0.90	1.05	0.26
45.00	JPMII	0.00	0.05	—	45.00	JPMCI	0.35	0.45	0.14
47.50	JPMIW	0.00	0.05	—	47.50	JPMCW	0.10	0.20	0.06
50.00	JPMIJ	0.00	0.05	—	50.00	JPMCJ	0.00	0.10	—
October					**Jan-06**				
27.50	JPMJY	11.90	12.00	1.00	20.00	WJPAD	19.30	19.50	0.95
30.00	JPMJF	9.40	9.50	1.00	25.00	WJPAE	14.40	14.60	0.94
32.50	JPMJZ	6.90	7.00	1.00	30.00	WJPAF	10.10	10.20	0.87
35.00	JPMJG	4.40	4.60	0.97	35.00	WJPAG	6.30	6.50	0.68
37.50	JPMJU	2.20	2.25	0.79	37.50	WJPAU	4.80	4.90	0.56
40.00	JPMJH	0.55	0.65	0.39	40.00	WJPAH	3.40	3.60	0.44
42.50	JPMJV	0.05	0.10	0.10	42.50	WJPAV	2.40	2.55	0.33
45.00	JPMJI	0.00	0.05	—	45.00	WJPAI	1.55	1.70	0.23
47.50	JPMJW	0.00	0.05	—	47.50	WJPAW	1.00	1.10	0.16
50.00	JPMJJ	0.00	0.05	—	50.00	WJPAJ	0.60	0.70	0.11
December					**Jan-07**				
30.00	JPMLF	9.40	9.60	0.99	25.00	VJPAE	14.40	14.90	0.88
32.50	JPMLZ	7.00	7.20	0.97	30.00	VJPAF	10.60	10.80	0.78
35.00	JPMLG	4.80	4.90	0.89	35.00	VJPAG	7.20	7.30	0.61
37.50	JPMLU	2.80	2.95	0.69	40.00	VJPAH	4.60	4.80	0.43
40.00	JPMLH	1.30	1.40	0.42	45.00	VJPAI	2.70	2.90	0.27
42.50	JPMLV	0.50	0.55	0.20	50.00	VJPAJ	1.50	1.60	0.16
45.00	JPMLI	0.10	0.15	0.07					
47.50	JPMLW	0.00	0.10	—					
Jan-05									
25.00	JPMAE	14.30	14.50	0.99					
30.00	JPMAF	9.40	9.60	0.98					
32.50	JPMAZ	7.10	7.30	0.95					
35.00	JPMAG	4.90	5.10	0.85					
37.50	JPMAU	3.00	3.20	0.66					
40.00	JPMAH	1.55	1.65	0.43					
42.50	JPMAV	0.60	0.70	0.23					
45.00	JPMAI	0.15	0.25	0.10					
47.50	JPMAW	0.05	0.10	0.04					
50.00	JPMAJ	0.00	0.05	—					

So what would have happened if John's hunch were wrong and GE stock actually fell? John has the right, but not the obligation, to buy GE stock at $30.00. If the stock is less than $30.00, he would not exercise this right and would just let the option expire. If this were the case, he would lose the $1.00 premium he paid for the contract. It is important to realize that this $1.00 is the most John could possibly lose on this trade.

The maximum loss of an option buyer is the premium paid (the cost of the option).

> *Premium:* The price of an option; the amount of money the buyer pays for the rights and the seller receives for the obligations granted by the contract. Expressed on a per share basis.

Example of Using a Put Option to Speculate   A put option works very similarly to a call option; however, investors buy a put option when they think the price of a stock is going to *fall*. Let's look at an example.

It's now September and GE is trading at $35.00. John thinks that the price of GE stock is going to fall. So he decides to buy a December $35.00 put option. He now has the right, but not the obligation, to *sell* GE stock at a price of $35.00 up to December. For this right John pays, for example, $1.00 per share.

The price of GE stock then falls to $30.00 per share. John has the right to sell GE stock at $35.00. He would, therefore, go into the market and buy GE stock for $30.00 and then exercise his right to sell GE stock at $35.00. His profit would look like this:

Share sell price − Share buy price − Option price = Profit per share
$35.00 $30.00 $1.00   = $4.00

So what would have happened if John's hunch were wrong and GE stock actually rose? John has the right, but not the obligation, to sell GE stock at $35.00. If the stock is more than $35.00, he would not take up this right to sell and would just let the option expire. If this were the case, he would lose the $1.00 he paid for the contract. It is important to realize that this $1.00 is the most John could possibly lose on this trade.

Again, the maximum loss of an option buyer is the premium paid (the cost of the option).

Options Trading in the Real World   Now you understand the rationale and logic behind an options trade, but trading in the real world is a little different!

In the real world, speculators very rarely exercise their option contracts in order to take profits from a trade. Take the first example where John has the right to buy GE stock at $30.00 and the stock is trading at

$35.00. If John wants to realize a profit on this trade, it is highly unlikely that he would exercise this option. It is more profitable for John to just *sell his call option to someone else* in the market (sell to close).

Remember, John paid $1.00 per share for the right to buy GE stock at $30.00. If GE stock quickly jumped up to $35.00, he would actually be able to sell his call option for around $6.00. This $6.00 market value comprises $5.00 exercisable value and $1.00 of remaining time value. Both exercisable (intrinsic) value and time value are discussed in detail later in "How Are Option Prices Determined?"

John's profit would look like this:

Option sell price − Option buy price = Profit per share
$6.00   − $1.00   = $5.00

So John would make $5.00 per share by *selling* the call option, compared to only $4.00 per share if he *exercised* the call option, because exercising options results in a *loss of time value* (discussed in "How Are Option Prices Determined?"). By exercising the option, John will realize the $5.00 exercisable value in the contract ($35.00 stock price minus $30.00 strike price), but will forgo the remaining time value in the contract ($1.00).

> *Time Value:* The portion of an option's price that exceeds the exercisable value.

Due to this loss of time value, option traders very rarely exercise options in order to take profits from a trade! Options are traded just like stocks, and profits and losses are made, for the most part, by buying and selling the option itself, not by exercising it. So, it is important to remember:

> *Option traders very rarely exercise their options more than two weeks before expiration. In practicality, the vast, vast majority of option contracts are exercised on the third Friday of expiration. Exercising options early results in a loss of time value to the option buyer. Instead, option traders simply buy and sell the option contract just like buying and selling stocks.*

Why Speculate with an Option Instead of a Stock?

Why speculate with an option instead of a stock? The simple answer is *leverage*. Options provide a much greater return potential than investing in the stock itself (albeit with higher risk). If a stock moves up 5 percent, an

TABLE 1.8 Comparison of Investing in Stocks Versus Options

Scenario	Type of Investment	Stock Price	Total Invested	Price	Number of Units	Sell Price	Profit
A	Shares	$30.00	$10,000	$30.00	333	$32.00	$667 or 7%
B	Options	$30.00	$10,000	$ 1.00	100	$ 1.80	$8,000 or 80%

investor will make more money if he has $10,000 invested in call options rather than if he has $10,000 invested in stock itself.

Here's an example. John thinks GE stock is going to rise by $2.00 and wishes to invest $10,000 on his hunch. He has two alternatives:

1. Buy GE stock.
2. Buy call options on GE stock.

Let's look at the two scenarios.

Scenario 1 GE stock is currently trading at $30.00. With his $10,000 John can buy 333 shares ($10,000/$30.00 per share). If GE goes up to $32.00 as he expects, John will make $2.00 per share profit, or a total of $666 on his $10,000 investment. This is a return of 6.7 percent. Not bad.

Scenario 2 GE stock is currently trading at $30.00. With his $10,000 John decides to buy GE call options. He buys the $30.00 call option for $1.00 per share. In the United States, each contract relates to 100 shares so he can buy 100 contracts [$10,000/($1.00 per share × 100 shares per contract)]. If GE stock increases by $2.00, his call option contract is likely to be worth around $1.80 per share. John will make $0.80 per share × 100 shares per contract × 100 contracts = $8,000. This is a return of 80 percent.

Table 1.8 gives a comparison of the two scenarios.

The preceding example shows that with the same dollar investment in the same company and the same move in the stock price, John made an extra 73 percent return on his investment and an extra $7,333 by buying GE options rather than GE stock. This extra bang for your buck, known as *leverage*, attracts speculators to the use of option contracts. Options are leveraged instruments. But beware! The leverage works both ways. John could have lost most, if not all, of his money if the stock price went down $2.00 rather than up!

Leverage is why options are regarded by the vast majority as risky. Options are, without doubt, very risky when used to speculate. After all, can

John, or you, or I see into the future and know which way a stock is going to go? The answer is obviously no. GE could just as easily have gone down and John could have lost most, if not all, of his $10,000 investment. We never use an option for speculative purposes. Covered call writers *sell* options, rather than *buy* them.

How Are Option Prices Determined?

As with determining the price at which a stock sells in the market, it is supply and demand that influence the price at which an option trades. An investor attempting to buy an option must do so from an investor wanting to sell/write an option contract. Option market participants do, however, assess distinct and constantly changing variables in order to determine the price at which an option trades—its market value.

The liquidity of the options market is a significant contributor to the consistency of bid and ask prices representing fair market value. In less liquid markets—those with fewer participants, fewer market makers, and a lower volume of options trades—it is more likely that bid and ask spreads will be larger and that investors need to take more caution in assessing bid and ask prices for fair market value. Your covered call activity will likely be conducted in the options market of the United States, which is the world's largest and most liquid options market. As such, the bid and ask prices or the market for contracts you trade will generally represent a reasonable approximation of fair market value.

Liquidity: Market liquidity refers to the ability to quickly buy or sell a stock or option without causing a significant movement in the price.

Mathematical formulas such as the Black-Scholes and binomial pricing models have been developed to calculate an option's theoretical value. The shortcomings of these models in terms of encompassing the scope of variables and uncertain outcomes of financial markets and their resulting detachment from market reality have been well documented. Stock options' market prices will inconsistently resemble the theoretical value as determined by models such as the Black-Scholes. As such, option traders and investors generally do not spend time calculating academic values for contracts—the market is the primary driver of value determination.

What it all boils down to is this: If you're investing in the U.S. market (or a developed overseas market), it is highly likely that the prices at the bid and ask are reasonable approximations of fair value.

That being said, six independent factors are very important when determining the value of a stock option. It is essential for you to understand these factors and how they interact and influence the price of an option contract. This knowledge will allow you to understand how the price of the contract will change with changes in the underlying stock price, with lapses in time, and so on. These six important factors are:

1. The current stock price.
2. The exercise price of the contract.
3. The time to expiration.
4. The volatility of the stock price.
5. Risk-free rate (interest rates).
6. Dividends expected on the stock during the life of the option.

To be successful in the business of writing covered calls, you need to have a good understanding of factors 1, 2, and 3 and to a lesser extent, factor 4. Be aware of points 5 and 6; however, an in-depth understanding of these factors is very academic and not essential to your success as an option writer.

Factor 1: The Current Stock Price   As discussed previously, an investor who purchases a call option is speculating that the price of the underlying stock is going to increase. The payoff to this investor will be the difference between the exercise price and the stock price. This difference is known as *intrinsic value*, which is simply what the option owner can make if he or she exercises the option and sells the stock in the market. That is, if he or she has the right to buy the stock at $35.00, and the stock price is $40.00, the intrinsic value is $5.00. If the stock price moves up again to $45.00, the intrinsic value is $10.00. It makes sense that an option contract with $10.00 of intrinsic value should be worth more than a contract with only $5.00 of intrinsic value.

Thus, call option prices increase as the stock price increases and more intrinsic value is added to the contract. Put options are the opposite, so put option prices increase as the stock price decreases. Table 1.9 shows the relationship between option price and intrinsic value.

TABLE 1.9   Intrinsic Value

Call Strike $35.00

Stock price	$35.00	$40.00	$45.00
Call value	$ 1.00	$ 5.60	$10.20

Put Strike $35.00

Stock price	$25.00	$30.00	$35.00
Put value	$10.20	$ 5.40	$ 1.10

Factor 2: The Exercise Price of the Contract   The exercise price of the contract has an influence on intrinsic value similar to changes in the stock price. Let's assume an investor has a $35.00 call option and the stock price is currently $40.00. We now know that this contract has $5.00 worth of intrinsic value. Let's assume the same investor also has a $30.00 call option on the same stock. The $30.00 call option has $10.00 of intrinsic value and obviously, then, it has to be worth more!

Thus, call options increase in price the lower the exercise price is. Put options are the opposite, so they increase in price the higher the exercise price is. Table 1.10 shows the relationship between option price and exercise price.

Factor 3: The Time to Expiration   Up to this point, we have discussed only intrinsic value. Hopefully, you have been looking at the pricing examples provided for factors 1 and 2 and wondering why the option price is greater than the intrinsic value. The option price is greater because the other portion of value in an option contract is *time value*.

Intrinsic value + Time value = Option value

The longer an option has to expiration, the greater its time value. John thinks GE stock is going to rise from the current price of $35.00. He decides to buy a $35.00 strike call. Remember, John wants GE to increase in price so that the *intrinsic value* of his contract will increase. If John has six months until his contract expires, that gives him a lot of time for GE stock to increase. However, if John purchases a contract with only one month to expiration, he does not have much time for GE stock to move in his favor.

Thus, the more time a contract has to expiration, the more it is worth. Each day that goes by, the price/value of each and every option contract decreases because there is less time to expiration. Options are, therefore, known as *decaying assets*.

TABLE 1.10   Exercise Price

Stock Price $35.00			
Call strike price	$35.00	$30.00	$25.00
Call value	$ 1.10	$ 6.00	$10.40

Stock Price $35.00			
Put strike price	$35.00	$40.00	$45.00
Put value	$ 1.00	$ 5.70	$10.60

TABLE 1.11 How Time Value Affects Options Price

Strike $35.00

Expiration date	June	July	Sep	Dec
Option price	$0.50	$1.00	$1.30	$1.50

Table 1.11 shows how time affects an option's price (assume it is early June).

A very important point to understand in options pricing is that time decay is not linear! (See Figure 1.1.) Contracts that expire in one or two months have a significantly higher level of time decay than contracts that expire in one or two years. *The majority of an option's time value is lost in the weeks leading up to expiration.*

The covered-call method of investing actually utilizes the decay in time value to your advantage. You will make money from the decay in the speculators' assets.

Factor 4: The Volatility of the Stock Price   Option contracts are worth more on a stock that is volatile than on a stock that is less volatile. *Volatility* is technically defined in terms of standard deviation; however, for our purposes volatility can be thought of simply as a measure of how uncertain we are about a stock's future price movements. As volatility increases, the chance that a stock will make a significant move upward or downward increases.

If you were the owner of stock in a company, these two extreme outcomes tend to offset one another. However, if you are the owner of a call or a put, while your potential loss is limited to the amount invested, your potential profit can be many times over your original investment from significant price swings in the appropriate direction.

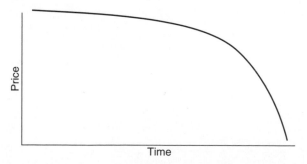

FIGURE 1.1   Example of the rapid decay of time value toward the end of an option's life.

TABLE 1.12 Effect of Volatility on Price

	Stock Price	Call Strike	Expiration	Option Price
Stable stock	$30.00	$30.00	Mar-06	$1.00
Volatile stock	$30.00	$30.00	Mar-06	$1.30

So, all else being equal, a more volatile stock will have higher option prices (see Table 1.12). Additionally, options prices will adjust upward or downward to significant changes in a stock's volatility levels.

Factor 5: Risk-Free Rate (Interest Rates) The effect of interest rates on option prices is very academic and perhaps only meaningfully noticeable over the longer term where significant interest rate changes occur. Therefore, this brief discussion of that effect is included for completeness rather than necessity. Understanding this effect will not have any significant influence on your success as an option writer.

As interest rates increase, (1) the present value of future cash flows received by the holder of the option decreases and (2) the expected growth rate of stock prices tend to increase. In the case of calls, effect (1) tends to decrease option prices and effect (2) tends to increase prices. In the case of puts, both (1) and (2) have negative effects on prices.

Factor 6: Dividends Expected on the Stock During the Life of the Option Dividends have the effect of reducing the stock price on the ex-dividend date (the date the dividend on a stock is paid). The price reduction, in turn, decreases the value of call options and increases the value of put options. A high proportion of companies you are likely to invest in will pay dividends. Worrying about insignificant pricing influences such as dividends creates headaches, not better returns. So forget about them, and leave the squabbling to the academics.

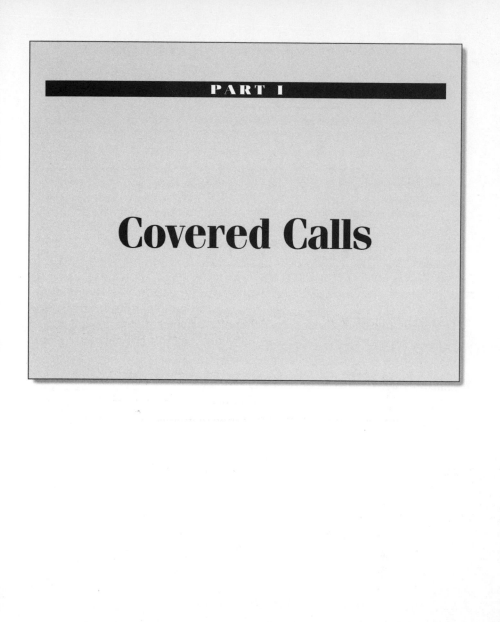

PART I

Covered Calls

COVERED CALL PROCESS FLOWCHART

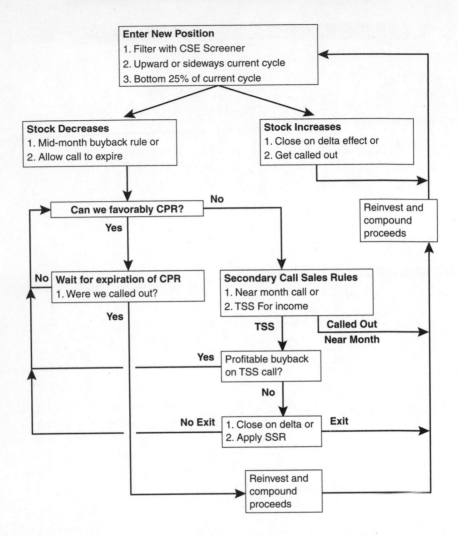

Each step in the covered call investing process is shown in the flowchart above—from entering new positions, to managing positions for income, to advanced defensive techniques. Investors familiar with our covered call method know that there is a specific technique to address every situation that may occur in the markets. Each situation that can be presented to a covered call investor can be handled through the use of a specific management technique. Part I of this book will elaborate, expand on, and provide an example of each step presented in the covered call process flowchart. You may wish to revisit the flowchart at the beginning of each new topic so you can gain an understanding of where a particular rule or technique is applied in the overall investment process.

CHAPTER 2

An Introduction to Covered Calls

OPTION SELLERS/WRITERS

In Chapter 1 we discussed only the intentions of speculators who are buying options to bet on the movement of the market, buyers of calls who are anticipating an upward move in the stock price, and buyers of puts who are anticipating a downward move in the stock price. We also stated that for every buyer of an option contract, there is also a seller/writer of that contract (the terms *seller* and *writer* can be used interchangeably). So who are the sellers of options and what are their objectives?

There are basically three types of sellers of options:

1. Sellers who are closing existing long positions.
2. Sellers who are opening short uncovered positions.
3. Sellers who are opening short covered positions.

Long Position: An overall buy position in a stock or option.

Short Position: An overall sell position in a stock or option.

Sellers Who Are Closing Existing Long Positions

Sellers who are closing existing long positions are generally traders who are speculating in the market. Closing a long position is exactly the same as someone who has bought stock and is now trying to sell it for a profit or loss. The seller holds a long position (has bought an option) and is now hoping to realize a profit or loss on the position by selling the option to close.

For example, when GE stock was trading at $34.00, a speculator bought to open a GE $35.00 call option for $1.00 in anticipation of the stock price rising. Let's assume the speculator correctly picked the direction of the market and the stock price is now $36.00. This speculator can sell to close the GE $35.00 call at $1.50 and realize a $0.50 profit. Alternatively, if the price of GE stock declined, the speculator could sell this contract for something less than $1.00 and would realize a loss.

Selling to Close: Closing a long stock or option position.

Sellers Who Are Opening Short Uncovered Positions

In most financial markets, you can sell something that you don't already own. Such a transaction is possible through *short selling*. The objective of short selling is to buy the share or contract back (buy to close) at a lower price than you sold it for. Let's look at an example.

Buying to Close: Closing a short stock or option position.

John sells a GE $35.00 call option for $1.20. He will immediately get the $1.20 premium of the contract deposited in his brokerage account by the option buyer. John wants the stock price to drop so that the call price also drops and he can buy the contract back (buy to close) and make a profit. Let's assume the stock price drops and John buys the contract back (buy to close) for $1.00. He has made the difference of $0.20.

This transaction is an example of selling an uncovered call. Selling an uncovered call is simply selling a call option without owning the underlying stock or another covering option, which prevents a loss if the stock price increases (we discuss this in the following section, "Sellers Who Are Opening Short Covered Positions"). If you sell a call option without owning the underlying stock or another covering option you are said to be "uncovered" or "naked." Selling naked calls is one of the most risky activities any investor can do in the markets—the profit and loss potential is simply not stacked in the naked seller's favor. Let's look at the example of John selling a GE $35.00 call option for $1.20 and see what his profit and loss potential looks like.

Profit   Remember, John sold this option, so someone has the right, but not the obligation, to buy GE stock from John for $35.00. When he sold the contract, John received the premium of $1.20 from the option buyer. The maximum possible profit that John can make from this trade is restricted to the price he received for selling the option, which is $1.20. The best outcome for John is that the stock price plummets, the call is way out of the money, and the contract expires worthless. In this instance, he would keep the $1.20 he sold the contract for. However, it is more likely that John will buy the contract back at some time in the future for something less than he sold it for. Remember, John has to buy the option back in order to close his position. Otherwise, if the contract finishes in the money, the buyer will exercise his option and John may need to deliver GE stock.

Loss   We understand now that the most John can make from this trade is $1.20. But, believe it or not, he has the potential to lose an *unlimited* amount of money, because the stock price can theoretically go up to any value. Let's assume GE stock goes up to $45.00. There are two scenarios here:

1. The buyer of the option may exercise his or her contract and John will need to deliver GE stock at $35.00. GE stock is available in the market at $45.00. So John will have to take the $10.00 loss.

2. John sees the share price soaring and decides to cut his losses. He will buy to close the contract so that he has no further obligation under the contract. If the stock is at $45.00, he'll have to pay around $11.00 to buy back the call. In this case he would lose $1.20 – $11.00 = $9.80.

Summary   In any case, John stands to make a maximum of $1.20 and lose a potentially unlimited amount on this trade. Business and markets are all about risk and return. You should now understand that selling naked calls is a very bad business proposition. Even though people still sell naked calls, our advice is that you do not ever, under any circumstances, sell naked calls. Doing so is categorically the quickest and easiest way to lose your money in the options markets.

Sellers Who Are Opening Short Covered Positions

Sellers who open short covered positions are executing covered calls. These are the smart sellers and this is the sort of selling that will regularly put money into your account with very, very low risk. These types of sellers are also selling option positions to open. However, the distinction is that these sellers also own the underlying stock (or another option contract) and are thus *covered* in the event the stock price increases.

Remember in the preceding example where John sold a $35.00 call option for $1.20? He made money when the stock price declined, as the option expired worthless and he kept the premium. However, the problem with this transaction was that, in the event the stock price increased, John stood to experience a substantial loss. In the event the stock price increased to, for example, $45.00, the speculator would exercise the call. John would be forced to buy the stock at the current market price of $45.00, only to immediately deliver the stock to the speculator at a price of $35.00—a $10.00 loss. This problem of suffering a large loss in the event the stock price increases can be easily remedied by *owning* the underlying stock before selling the call option.

If John already owned GE stock before selling the call, he would not be concerned about the stock price rising as he could simply deliver the stock he already owned. John is therefore covered in the event the stock price increases after selling the call—he will not be forced to buy the stock at a higher price in the market and then immediately sell it at a loss to the speculator.

So if John already owned the stock before selling the call, he would make money if the stock price goes up, he would also keep the premium if the stock price goes down. This is an example of selling a covered call, which is discussed at length later in this book.

Selling or writing covered calls is perhaps the safest and most consistent way to make money in the financial markets and also involves less risk than owning stock. If you're not convinced, here's another example. Let's assume it is June and GE stock is trading at $34.50. John decides he'd like to buy GE stock and sell a covered call against it. Let's assume he elects to sell the June $35.00 call and receives a premium of, for example, $0.70 straight into his brokerage account. There are two possible things that can now happen to John.

1. He gets called out. Remember, John has sold a GE June $35.00 call. So someone else has the right to buy his GE stock for $35.00 up until the third Friday of June (remember that the third Friday of the month is the expiration date for U.S. option contracts). Getting *called out* means that the person who bought the GE June $35.00 contract has decided to exercise the contract and wants to buy John's stock, because GE stock has gone up and it is worth more than $35.00. John is contractually obligated to oblige.

So John delivers (or sells) his stock at a price of $35.00 to the option buyer and this money gets deposited into his account. This transaction is good, because John only paid $34.50 for his stock and thus has made $0.50 per share on the call out. John has also received a premium of $0.70 from the option buyer, which he also gets to keep. So he's made a total of $1.20 per share in just one month! Based on a share price of $34.50, that's a monthly return of around 3.5 percent. If he makes that return each month, he'll make 41 percent on his money per year (uncompounded). If he's really smart and reinvests his earnings and uses the power of compounding, his 3.5 percent per month turns into an amazing 51 percent per year!

2. He doesn't get called out. Again, John's fate rests in the hands of the investor who bought the option he sold. If the stock price at the end of the month is below the $35.00 strike price of the option, then it is not in the option buyer's interest to exercise the contract, so John won't get called out. In this situation, the contract would simply expire and John would keep the $0.70 he received for selling the option. That's a return of 2.0 percent in a month or 24 percent per year (uncompounded).

John would be left with his GE stock at the end of June and would simply sell another call for July and start all over again.

You should now be starting to realize the power of covered calls. You should also be starting to understand that selling covered calls actually decreases the risk of stock ownership because you are continually generating cash flow from your stock investment and effectively lowering your cost in the stock.

Think of selling covered calls as investing in real estate. You are literally renting your stock out each month and getting cash flow in return. Would you buy an investment property and not rent it out while you wait to sell it? Of course not! You would be leaving thousands of dollars on the table each month for no reason. Similarly, if you own stocks (which almost everyone does) and are not selling covered calls against these stocks, you are also leaving thousands of dollars on the table each month!

COVERED CALLS: THE RIGHT MIND-SET

To be a successful covered call writer, you must recognize from the outset what your objectives are and the mind-set you require in order to achieve them.

Compound Interest

Our objective is to generate consistent monthly cash flow from our assets. We can then reinvest this cash flow each month to compound our investment capital and generate extraordinary long-term returns.

Compound interest is *the* way to accumulate wealth. Whether in business, real estate, financial markets, or any other financial pursuit, compounding your assets is the fastest way to make them grow. Don't take our word for it. Many years ago Albert Einstein was asked what he thought was the human race's greatest invention. His reply was "compound interest." He also regarded compounded interest as "the eighth wonder of the world."

If you are not aware, there are two types of interest: simple and compound. Simple interest allows you to earn money on your principal. Compound interest allows you to earn money on your principal *and* your interest. Table 2.1 gives the example of two bank accounts, each with a starting balance of $10,000 and each earning 5 percent interest per year. However, one account earns simple interest and the other, compound interest. As you can see, the account that pays compound interest is worth significantly more at the end of the 10-year period.

Now, in the context of covered calls, compounding is many times more powerful. Remember, our objective is not to make 5 percent per year; our objective is to generate *monthly* returns of 3–6 percent for covered call transactions. We will then reinvest this return into new positions and compound our returns on a *monthly*, not a *yearly*, basis. Let's look at the $10,000 bank account again, but this time let's compound that account at a

TABLE 2.1 Simple Versus Compound Interest at 5 Percent Per Year

Time	Simple Interest	Compound Interest
Start	$10,000	$10,000
Year 1	10,500	10,500
Year 2	11,000	11,025
Year 3	11,500	11,576
Year 4	12,000	12,155
Year 5	12,500	12,763
Year 6	13,000	13,401
Year 7	13,500	14,071
Year 8	14,000	14,775
Year 9	14,500	15,513
Year 10	15,000	16,289

TABLE 2.2	Compound Interest at 4 Percent Per Month
Time	**Account Value**
Start	$ 10,000
Year 1	16,010
Year 2	25,633
Year 3	41,039
Year 4	65,705
Year 5	105,196
Year 6	168,423
Year 7	269,650
Year 8	431,718
Year 9	691,195
Year 10	1,106,626

return of just 4 percent per month and see what it looks like after 10 years. See Table 2.2

Wow, a $10,000 account has grown to over $1.1 million in 10 years! If you had started with $50,000, you would have $5.5 million at the end of 10 years. This is the power of covered calls: We are compounding returns that most investors get in a year on a monthly basis. Now, is this enough motivation for you to gradually take control of your own financial future? We should hope so!

Cash Flow Focus

We have established that generating monthly cash flow and compounding this cash flow into much larger sums of money is our objective. To achieve this objective as a covered call writer we prioritize cash flow over account market value. To be successful in this technique, you must let go of the traditional benchmarks for measuring equity portfolio performance—particularly in the short term.

The traditional benchmark that is used by the brokers and fund managers to measure a portfolio's performance is *market value*. Brokers and fund managers report to you the market value of your portfolio on a regular basis. For instance, you may have started with $100,000, and the broker bought you stock of this value. Now the combined value of your stocks has gone up and your portfolio is worth $120,000. So the broker says you have made $20,000 based on a current market valuation. While this valuation is fine if you sell today, it is just a *paper gain* and, if the market turns down, these gains can be easily lost because they have not been realized as cash.

A covered call writer should only be interested in *cash*. We do not care if the stock we purchased for $10.00 is now worth only $8.00 or $5.00 in the market. We understand and accept that stock prices of good companies go up and down.

We do not care.

We care only about how much cash (premium income) we are able to generate from a position. If you purchase a good company with real earnings at a reasonable valuation and the stock falls, it is likely that eventually the stock price will go back to where it was when you purchased it. Even if it doesn't, eventually we will make back all the money we invested in the stock by selling calls against it. We never, *ever*, sell a stock for a loss.

This advice goes against all traditional measures of portfolio performance and the "loser mentality" of "cutting your losses" that is instilled in us by brokers to increase their own revenues. We look at stock investments as you would an investment property. If you buy good property in a good position, are you afraid of not getting your money back over the long term? Do you get a weekly valuation of the property and stress if that valuation is less than what you paid for the property? No. You take a long-term view, let time run its course, and collect your rent each month. That is the mind-set of a successful covered call writer.

The stock market is the *only* market in the world where investors have developed a mind-set that it is acceptable, even advantageous, to sell a generally appreciating asset for a loss. You do not run out and sell your house or an investment property for a loss because, at some point in time, the market value happens to be down. You will only sell your investment property because, at some point in time, it happens to be *up* in value and you are getting a good price. We reiterate: The stock market is the only market in the world where people voluntarily sell generally appreciating assets for a loss because the market value just happens to be down at a particular point in time. This is a destructive financial mentality based on ignorance and fear, and it is perpetuated by the brokerage community to increase its own revenues. We *never* sell a stock for a loss, and neither should you!

History indicates that the U.S. stock market (as measured by the S&P 500) has never failed to make new highs over the long term. Figure 2.1 is a chart of the S&P 500, which measures the performance of the top 500 U.S.-listed companies, from 1930 through 2004. It is clear that good companies have historically increased in value over the long run. Over the short term, however, stocks go up and down—that's what they do. Accept this fact and do not concern yourself with the daily or monthly fluctuations in the market value of your portfolio. You must concern yourself only with generating cash flow and compounding this cash flow. This is a concept that will take time for you to gain confidence in. But history, and our experience, indicates that it works.

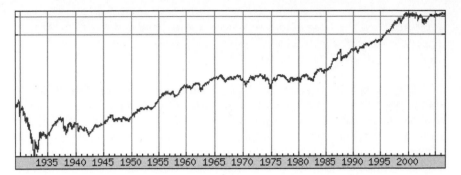

FIGURE 2.1   Value of the S&P 500 index from 1930 through 2004.

Growth Through Cash Flow   Correct application of the covered call technique provides portfolio growth through cash flow rather than speculative appreciation. A cash return of 4 percent per month equates to 48 percent cash return per year (uncompounded) or nearly 100 percent over two years (uncompounded).

> Dozens of client testimonials and recorded interviews can be found at www.compoundstockearnings.com/testimonials attesting to achieving consistent cash returns between 4 percent and 6 percent per month using the techniques outlined in this book.

The initial capital investment can be entirely liquidated by premium income in just two years. If the stocks have any value at all after two years, the investor will be ahead. It is more likely that the stocks are around breakeven, leaving the investor with his or her original capital investment *plus* the premium income. Growth through cash flow, then, is another critical mind-set for the covered call writer.

The Impact of Cash Flow Focus on Short-Term Portfolio Market Value   Understanding the impact of cash flow–focused covered call investing on short-term portfolio market value is vitally important. Investors new to the covered call technique often become discouraged when after the first several months of covered call investing, the market value of their portfolios remains relatively unchanged. Short-term stagnation of portfolio market value is the nature of this technique and should be expected by all investors.

Market Value: The value of the portfolio if it were immediately liquidated for cash at current market prices.

When using the covered call technique, growth in portfolio value should not be expected in the initial months of the investment. In the early stage of the investment, the "winning" stocks in the portfolio are capped at around a 5 percent return (monthly), yet the "losing" stocks in the portfolio (those that decrease in value) are held and can fall by more than that amount. This condition initially has a negative effect on the portfolio's market value. It is then that the management and defensive techniques outlined in Chapters 4 and 5 of this book are applied to continue to generate cash flow on these fallen positions. The overall portfolio market value then begins to increase after a period of months when the *cash flow* generated from all positions accumulates, compounds, and then outweighs the market value losses of particular stocks in the portfolio.

The traditional use of the covered call technique does not generally lead to portfolio growth as fallen stock positions become dormant and unproductive due to a lack of management and defensive techniques (an inability to continue to generate income on fallen stocks). The management and defensive techniques outlined in this book are *the difference* between great success and complete mediocrity in the business of covered calls.

We cannot overemphasize that it is important for investors to understand and expect a lack of portfolio market value growth in the initial months of using the technique. This initial lack of growth is the norm and should not be a reason for discouragement. In our experience, portfolio market value growth comes after a period of months when the cash flow generated from all positions accumulates and begins to compound. Understanding this characteristic of the technique is essential so that we can remain focused on the long-term objective of consistently generating and compounding cash flow.

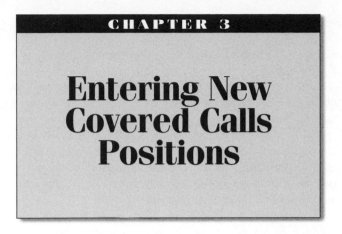

CHAPTER 3

Entering New Covered Calls Positions

This chapter details the actual process of establishing covered call positions.

SOME BASICS

SOME BASICS

Markets to Invest In

Choosing a market to invest in depends on your own personal objectives and your country of residence. If you are a non-U.S. resident and have existing stock holdings in non U.S. stocks or would like to invest only in your country of residence for whatever reason (familiarity, etc.), then you are able to write covered calls on your non-U.S. stocks. If, however, you have new funds to commit to the market or you want to make a serious commitment to the growth of your investment capital, you should invest in the U.S. market.

Base your decision on what makes you more comfortable. Even if you are a non-U.S. resident and decide to initially invest only in stocks listed in your home country, it is likely (and advisable) that you will eventually move all your covered call activity to the U.S. market. The U.S. market is incredibly large and provides significantly more opportunity, lower transaction costs, and much higher covered call returns. If you are committing new capital to the market, it is strongly advisable to invest in the U.S. market.

Some advantages of writing covered calls in the United States include:

- *More stocks to choose from.* The United States boasts the largest and most liquid stock and options market in the world. This allows U.S. covered call investors to be very selective in their investment and stock selection process, which, in turn, leads to a higher likelihood of positive investment outcomes.
- *Higher monthly covered call yields.* The U.S. market is significantly more volatile than the majority of other developed foreign markets. As volatile markets are positive for option prices, U.S. covered call investors will normally receive higher percentage returns (yields) on call sales compared to other international markets.
- *Access to information.* There are some excellent information services that allow U.S. covered call investors to research and filter all covered call opportunities for the U.S. market. These services significantly assist you in selecting companies based on the fundamental and technical criteria you should use to select companies in which to invest (discussed later).
- *U.S. option contracts relate to only 100 shares.* Generally U.S. option contracts relate to only 100 shares, whereas international option contracts may relate to more than 100 shares. During your learning period, you can invest a lot less money in a U.S. covered call transaction than in some international markets (discussed in detail later).
- *Lower transaction costs.* Due to the size of the U.S. market and the number of brokerage houses competing for your business, transaction costs are significantly less in the United States compared to most developed overseas markets. You will, therefore, be able to invest at a much lower rate of commission in the United States compared to most international markets. Saving on commissions equates to higher profits.

Disadvantages of writing covered calls in the United States include:

- *Limited market hours.* While your covered call activity should only occupy a few hours of your time per month, if you choose to invest in the United States you will need to work the hours when the U.S. market is open. If you are outside the United States, the time difference between your home country and the United States is a disadvantage for most investors.
- *Foreign exchange risk.* If your country of residence is outside the United States, it is likely that you will also need to manage foreign exchange risk as your profits will be made in U.S. dollars. While there are techniques to use that will help manage this risk (see Appendix B), it is an added consideration.

Option Contract Sizes

It is important for you to understand that, in the United States, option contracts generally relate to just 100 shares, while in foreign markets, option contracts may relate to a different number of shares. For example, in Australia, option contracts relate to 1,000 shares. The more shares an option contract relates to, the more difficult it becomes for an investor to diversify a portfolio with a smaller capital resource.

Using the example of Australia, because one option contract relates to 1,000 shares, an investor must have 1,000 shares to sell one covered call contract. This requirement makes it very difficult for covered call writers in Australia to build a diversified covered call portfolio with a smaller capital resource. Let's look at an example of one $0.50 call option sold on a $10.00 stock in both the U.S. and Australian markets.

Table 3.1 shows that if an investor wishes to write one covered call contract on a $10.00 stock in the United States, the investor need only commit US$1,000 to the stock purchase. However, if an investor wishes to write one covered call contract on a $10.00 stock in Australia, the investor needs to commit AU$10,000 (approximately US$7,500) to the stock purchase.

Thus there is a significant advantage of investing in the U.S. market, particularly in terms of the following:

- Minimizing capital investment when learning the covered call technique.
- Gaining adequate levels of diversification with limited capital resources.
- Reinvesting monthly earnings into new covered call opportunities.

The Importance of Diversification

While you might start off with just one or two stocks during the learning period, your eventual goal is to have a diversified portfolio of optionable

TABLE 3.1 Comparison of Option Contract Sizes

	U.S.	Australia
Shares bought	100	1,000
Stock price	$10	$10
Capital invested	$1,000	$10,000
Call contracts sold	1	1
Call sale price	$0.50	$0.50
Cash inflow from call	$50	$500
Uncalled return	5%	5%

stocks that you have selected because of high-yielding covered call opportunities. Investors should construct portfolios of between 10 and 20 stocks regardless of which market they choose to invest in.

The importance of diversification cannot be stressed enough. Investors *must* diversify their portfolios between different stocks and different industries—you must not find one or two or three high-yielding covered call opportunities and put all your money into just a few positions. You must spread risk across many different stocks in many different sectors. Diversification is particularly easy to achieve in the U.S. market due to its size, but is also achievable in foreign markets.

THE RULES FOR ENTERING NEW COVERED CALL POSITIONS IN THE U.S. MARKET

If you have decided to invest in the U.S. market, you should invest a small amount of money into two or three stocks while learning. To begin with, only buy 100–200 shares and concentrate on stocks with relatively low stock prices. By following these guidelines, investors can begin learning the covered call technique with a capital commitment of as little as US$1,000 to US$3,000. Once comfort is gained with the technique, investors can build a diversified portfolio of U.S. covered calls with as little as US$10,000 to US$15,000. The sky is the limit in terms of how much capital you can have effectively invested in covered calls as the U.S. market is tremendously large and liquid. And because of the large variety, investors can be very selective when entering into new covered call positions.

The eight rules, then, for entering new covered call positions in the U.S. market are:

1. You can only establish new positions on down market days. A down market day is any time when the Dow and the NASDAQ are in the red (trading lower than the close of the previous day).

2. You must always only sell the near month call when entering a transaction.

3. Use the CSE Screener (discussed in the following section) to filter through all available covered call opportunities on the U.S. market.

4. Select the highest-yielding opportunities presented by the CSE Screener.

5. Ensure that the stock is an upward moving or sideways moving stock (discussed in a later section, "Assessing Chart Positions for New Covered Call Positions").

6. Ensure that the stock adheres to the buying low rule for covered calls (discussed later in this chapter).

7. Always give priority to maintaining acceptable levels of diversification between stocks and industries—even if a stock you are already invested in presents an excellent covered call opportunity.

8. Buy the stock first and then immediately sell the call. Do not hesitate. If you buy the stock and wait for a better price for the call, you are no better than a speculator, and you will get burned!

USING THE CSE SCREENER TO SELECT U.S. COVERED CALLS

The CSE Screener is a proprietary covered call search and filter tool designed, developed, and maintained by Compound Stock Earnings. The CSE Screener allows investors to quickly and easily search the stock market for the highest-returning covered call positions that meet specific fundamental and technical requirements. The tool is tailored to accommodate the criteria and rules established in this book for selecting covered call positions.

Anyone who purchases *Covered Calls and LEAPS—A Wealth Option* is entitled to one month's complimentary access to the Covered Call Toolbox (which includes the CSE Screener) by going to www.compoundstock earnings.com/freemonth. Thus readers can actually use the tools while learning about them in this book.

Selection Parameters

Because the U.S. market is extremely large, you can be very selective in terms of the quality of the companies in which you invest. You should use the following eight parameters to filter U.S. covered call opportunities:

1. Uncalled return of minimum 4 percent.

2. Called return of minimum 4 percent.

3. Price-earnings ratio (PE) of 35 or less.

4. Market capitalization of US$500 million or more.

5. Average broker recommendation of 2.5 or less.

6. An aggregate of the brokers recommending the stock as "Strong Buy" and "Buy" greater than the number of brokers recommending the stock as "Hold."

7. A consensus earnings per share (EPS) estimate for "Next Fiscal Year" forecast to be greater than the consensus EPS estimate for "This Fiscal Year."

8. Stock trading less than 75 percent of its 52-week trading range.

Rationale Behind CSE Screener Filters

The return filters ensure that acceptable covered call yields are realized on entering the transaction. A 4 percent uncalled and called return is the minimum acceptable return when entering a new covered call transaction. In most instances, the CSE Screener will present transactions that yield returns of 4–8 percent. You should select the transaction(s) with the highest uncalled and called return.

Uncalled and Called Returns   There are two separate return calculations that you must compute and be aware of for every covered call transaction: the uncalled return and the called return.

The *uncalled return* is also known as the "percentage return" or "yield" and is simply the premium you received on the call sale divided by the cost of the stock. So if you sell a call for $1.00 and you paid $20.00 for the stock, your uncalled return is 5 percent ($1.00/$20.00). The uncalled return is the most important return in a covered call transaction because it represents your return in the worst-case scenario and is the cash return in your hand as soon as you sell the call.

The *called return* is the sum of the uncalled return plus the profit or loss you make if your call is exercised (called out) divided by your cost in the stock. If you are called out, you have to deliver the stock you own at the exercise price of the call. For example, if you own a $19.50 stock and sell a $20.00 call for $0.70 and are called out, your profit would look like this:

- You will deliver (sell) the stock at $20.00. You bought the stock for $19.50. So you make $0.50.
- You also keep the $0.70 that you sold the call for.
- In total you make $0.50 + $0.70 = $1.20.
- Called return = $1.20/$19.50 = 6.15 percent.

PE Ratio   A PE ratio of 35 or less ensures that the company you are investing in is historically profitable and its stock is not overly expensive relative to the market. You want to be investing in solid, low-PE stocks. High-PE stocks are often "priced to perfection" and their stock prices have a long way to fall if the company does not perform as expected by the market.

PE Ratio: A stock's market price divided by its earnings per share. A PE ratio of a stock is used to measure how cheap or expensive the stock price is.

Market Capitalization   Market capitalization is a measure of the value and size of a company. It is calculated by multiplying a company's stock price by the number of shares it has on issue. A market capitalization of $500 million or more ensures that the company is of a reasonable size. Investors should give preference to companies with higher market capitalization.

Broker Recommendations   An average broker recommendation of 2.5 or less ensures that the stock is rated at least an average of "buy" by the analysts who cover it. This statement does not imply that we value or follow the opinions of brokers. However, the brokerage community will be in the markets promoting the stock and the masses will be providing buying support for the stock. More importantly, the stock is not likely to go out of business in the short term.

The aggregate of the brokers recommending the stock as Strong Buy and Buy must be greater than the number of brokers recommending the stock as Hold. This criterion simply ensures that more brokers are positive on the stock than are neutral.

Broker recommendations range from Strong Buy (1) to Strong Sell (5).

Earnings per Share   A forecast consensus EPS estimate for "Next Fiscal Year" greater than the consensus EPS estimate for "This Fiscal Year" simply ensures that the brokers covering the stock believe that the company's earnings will grow next fiscal year and helps prevent investors from buying stocks that are going into a period of contracting earnings.

Earnings per Share: A company's earnings divided by the number of ordinary shares.

52-Week Trading Range   Buying the stock at less than 75 percent of its 52-week range simply ensures that you are not paying a historically high price for the stock.

52-Week Range: Refers to the lowest and highest price a company's stock has traded for during the past year.

Remember, you are a cash generator and compounder. All you are trying to do when selecting a covered call opportunity is to make sure you get a high uncalled and called return and that the company you invest in isn't going out of business in the near future. While it is nice if the stock goes up and you are called out at the end of each month, you do not really care if it goes down. You own stock in a fundamentally sound, profitable company with a reasonable PE and significant broker support, and you have not paid top dollar for the stock. Just worry about generating cash flow and let time take care of the rest.

You should be concerned only with generating and compounding cash flow. Compounding of the monthly cash return leads to portfolio growth.

Directions for Using the CSE Screener

To access the covered call search tools, you need to establish a username and password from www.compoundstockearnings.com/freemonth. Then do the following:

1. Go to www.compoundstockearnings.com/cctoolbox.
2. Enter your username and password.
3. Click Log On.
4. Click CSE Screener—Covered Calls.

The CSE Screener will automatically run the search for the best covered call positions using the eight criteria listed previously. It will then search the entire market to find all the stocks that meet the stipulated fundamental and technical criteria. It examines the option chains on these stocks to find positions with near month calls that provide both an uncalled and called return of 4 percent or more. The CSE Screener then presents the results of the search to the investor (see Figure 3.1).

The criteria for selecting covered call positions have remained substantially the same for many years. However, from time to time, the criteria have been modified to adapt to the current conditions of the market. It is very important for investors to understand that the objective of the criteria will always remain the same: to find a low PE company of reasonable size and with high broker support and forecast earnings growth that is not trading at yearly highs and that presents a very good covered call return in the near month.

While this objective never changes, the market does. The market is not static. PE ratios expand and contract with the performance of the market, volatility increases and decreases affecting covered call premiums, strong

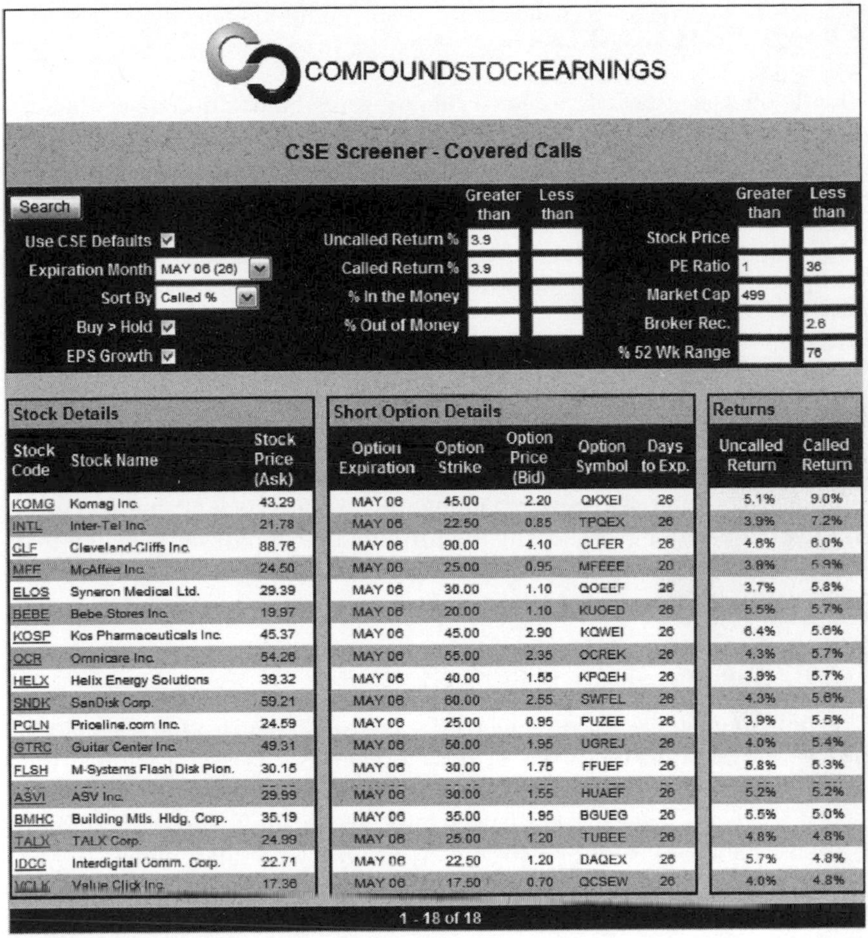

Stock Details			Short Option Details					Returns	
Stock Code	Stock Name	Stock Price (Ask)	Option Expiration	Option Strike	Option Price (Bid)	Option Symbol	Days to Exp.	Uncalled Return	Called Return
KOMG	Komag Inc.	43.29	MAY 06	45.00	2.20	QKXEI	26	5.1%	9.0%
INTL	Inter-Tel Inc.	21.78	MAY 06	22.50	0.85	TPQEX	26	3.9%	7.2%
CLF	Cleveland-Cliffs Inc.	88.76	MAY 06	90.00	4.10	CLFER	26	4.6%	6.0%
MFE	McAffee Inc.	24.50	MAY 06	25.00	0.95	MFEEE	26	3.8%	5.9%
ELOS	Syneron Medical Ltd.	29.39	MAY 06	30.00	1.10	QOEEF	26	3.7%	5.8%
BEBE	Bebe Stores Inc.	19.97	MAY 06	20.00	1.10	KUOED	26	5.5%	5.7%
KOSP	Kos Pharmaceuticals Inc.	45.37	MAY 06	45.00	2.90	KQWEI	26	6.4%	5.6%
OCR	Omnicare Inc.	54.26	MAY 06	55.00	2.35	OCREK	26	4.3%	5.7%
HELX	Helix Energy Solutions	39.32	MAY 06	40.00	1.55	KPQEH	26	3.9%	5.7%
SNDK	SanDisk Corp.	59.21	MAY 06	60.00	2.55	SWFEL	26	4.3%	5.6%
PCLN	Priceline.com Inc.	24.59	MAY 06	25.00	0.95	PUZEE	26	3.9%	5.5%
GTRC	Guitar Center Inc.	49.31	MAY 06	50.00	1.95	UGREJ	26	4.0%	5.4%
FLSH	M-Systems Flash Disk Pion.	30.15	MAY 06	30.00	1.75	FFUEF	26	5.8%	5.3%
ASVI	ASV Inc.	29.99	MAY 06	30.00	1.55	HUAEF	26	5.2%	5.2%
BMHC	Building Mtls. Hldg. Corp.	35.19	MAY 06	35.00	1.95	BGUEG	26	5.5%	5.0%
TALX	TALX Corp.	24.99	MAY 06	25.00	1.20	TUBEE	26	4.8%	4.8%
IDCC	Interdigital Comm. Corp.	22.71	MAY 06	22.50	1.20	DAQEX	26	5.7%	4.8%
VCLK	Value Click Inc.	17.36	MAY 06	17.50	0.70	QCSEW	26	4.0%	4.8%

FIGURE 3.1 Sample screenshot of the CSE Screener for covered calls.

market periods reduce the number of stocks trading below 75 percent of the 52-week range, and so on. The market is constantly evolving, and occasionally the criteria need to evolve to stay relevant to the condition of the market. When such a change is needed, the authors adapt the *default criteria* of the CSE Screener to keep investors in step with the current conditions of the markets. Therefore, it is highly recommended that investors simply use the default criteria of the CSE Screener when searching for new positions.

USING PRICE CHARTS

Simply because the CSE Screener has presented a position does not automatically qualify it as an acceptable investment. Revisit the "Rules for Entering New Covered Call Positions in the U.S. Market." The present section addresses in significant detail the two rules that relate to price charts:

- Ensure that the stock is an upward moving or sideways moving stock.
- Ensure that the stock adheres to the buying low rule for covered calls.

Judicious assessment of a stock's price cycle is critical before a new covered call position is entered into. Investors who get caught up in hype and buy when markets are going up or who panic and sell when markets are going down are categorically the losing investors in the markets. You must buy low and sell high: You must buy when markets are falling and sell when markets are rising. If you were selling any product as a business venture, you would be attempting to buy the product low and to sell it high. Financial markets are no different. The importance of these rules cannot be stressed enough.

Identifying and Assessing Price Cycles

To implement these rules, you will need to recognize that virtually all stocks move in distinct price cycles. Movements between parallel lines characterize these cycles. What you want to do is identify a *price channel* or a *price cycle* (these terms are used interchangeably). The way to identify a price channel is to draw two lines (preferably parallel) connecting the bottoms and the tops of a chart. The best source for free charts on the Internet is www.bigcharts.com. If you select "Java Chart" and then check "Draw Trendlines," you will be able to draw cycles on the chart similar to those in the following illustrations. You should always assess a stock using a 12-month chart.

Price Channel or Cycle: The price trend that a stock is trading in. Identified by the trading range between two parallel lines.

Figure 3.2 shows how stocks move. Almost all stocks cycle between parallel lines. Perhaps the most costly misunderstanding among uneducated investors is that *stocks do not go straight up or straight down*. A stock that is cycling upwards or downwards also has upward and downward movements within that cycle. Look at Figure 3.2. Regardless of the trend of the stock, the stock is moving upwards and downwards within a cycle. We repeat: Understanding this characteristic is vitally important.

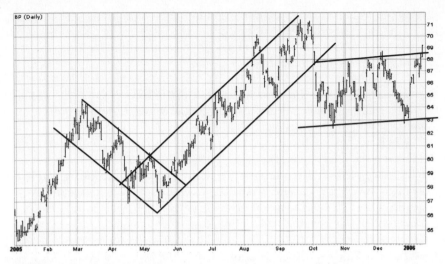

FIGURE 3.2 Example of how stocks cycle between parallel lines.

Stocks do not go straight up or straight down—they move up and down within cycles characterized by parallel lines.

Upward Cycles In an upward cycle, the tops of the cycle are getting higher and the bottoms are also getting higher. An upward cycle has higher tops and higher bottoms. See Figure 3.3.

When we have an upward cycle, start by drawing a line connecting the *bottoms* on the chart, because the buyers are in control of the market and

FIGURE 3.3 Example of an upward cycle.

driving prices higher. Then attempt to identify the top of the cycle by drawing a line that is parallel to the bottoms. *Note:* Assessing cycles is not an exact science and absolute accuracy is not a contributing factor to the success of our covered call technique.

Downward Cycles   In a downward cycle, the tops of the cycle are getting lower and the bottoms are also getting lower. A downward cycle has lower tops and lower bottoms. See Figure 3.4.

When we have a downward cycle, start by drawing a line connecting the *tops* on the chart, because the sellers are in control of the market and driving prices lower. Then attempt to identify the bottom of the cycle by drawing a line that is parallel to the tops. Again note that assessing cycles is not an exact science and absolute accuracy is not a contributing factor to the success of our covered call technique.

Horizontal Cycles   In a horizontal cycle, the tops and bottoms are not getting substantially higher or lower. A horizontal cycle has relatively stable tops and bottoms. The cycle highlighted in Figure 3.5 is a general horizontal cycle (although it does have slight upward bias).

In a horizontal cycle, the market is in consolidation and it is not important which line is drawn first. Simply try to make the two lines parallel remembering that assessing cycles is not an exact science and absolute accuracy is not a contributing factor to the success of the covered call technique.

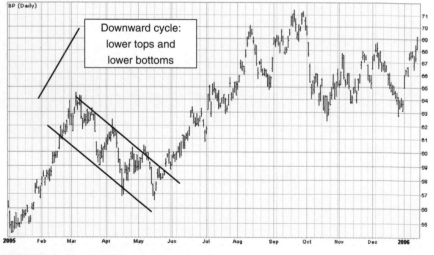

FIGURE 3.4   Example of a downward cycle.

FIGURE 3.5   Example of a horizontal cycle.

How to Look at a Price Chart

When an investor assesses a price chart, he or she must be able to answer the following four questions:

1. What is the overall trend: upwards, downwards, or sideways?
2. What are the past cycles: upwards, downwards, or sideways?
3. What is the current cycle: upwards, downwards, or sideways?
4. Where are we in the current cycle: the bottom, middle, or top?

Step 1: Identify the Overall Trend   A first glance at Figure 3.6 shows that the overall trend for this stock is upward. We know this because in a broad sense prices are increasing—significant tops and bottoms are getting higher, so the chart is generally upward moving.

Step 2: Identify the Individual Cycles   After identifying the overall trend, we are then looking to identify the individual cycles. There is normally more than one cycle on any given chart of six months' duration or greater. Remember, cycles are characterized by movements between parallel lines. See Figure 3.7.

Step 3: Identify the Current Cycle   After identifying the individual cycles, we then want to classify the current cycle, that is, the cycle the

FIGURE 3.6   Identify this trend.

stock is trading in now. To do so we need to determine if the tops and bottoms of the current cycle are getting:

- Higher (upward cycle)
- Lower (downward cycle)
- Relatively stable (horizontal cycle)

FIGURE 3.7   Identify the cycles.

FIGURE 3.8 Identify the current cycle.

Figure 3.8 shows that the current cycle of BP is horizontal with slight upward bias. Understanding the direction of the current cycle is critical.

Step 4: Identify the Position in the Current Cycle   After we have identified the current cycle, in Figure 3.8 it is horizontal with slight upward bias, we then want to understand the position of the stock in relation to the current cycle. Is the stock at the top, middle, or bottom of the current cycle? Where is the stock price in relation to the top and bottom lines of the current cycle? In Figure 3.9 we can see that the stock price is at the top of the current cycle.

Utilizing the Information   So we now understand this chart of BP (Figures 3.6 through 3.9). We know that BP is (1) in an overall upward trend, (2) currently in a horizontal cycle with slight upward bias, and (3) at the top of the current cycle.

The stock is at the top of the cycle—its bias is to head back down. When a stock is in the high point of the current cycle, its bias is to go down. When a stock is in the low point of the current cycle, its bias is to go up. These facts are so basic and fundamental, yet they are ignored by most investors and that ignorance is the single biggest reason that investors lose in the market. They are constantly on the wrong end of the cycle. They are constantly chasing the trend and having it reverse on them. The mind-set of a losing investor is to buy this stock right now, after all "it's increased from $60 to almost $70 in just one month and it's in the press as a top performer

FIGURE 3.9   Identify the stock's position in the current cycle.

last month, it's having a great run, so there must be further to go." This is the mind-set of the average losing investor. It should be abundantly clear why this investor is an expert at picking stocks that then fall in the ensuing weeks. This investor's stock selection mentality always leads to purchasing stocks at the top of the current cycle. The investor then panics when the stock starts cycling down and sells out for a loss, only to see the stock go back up a month later. The investor is completely ignorant to the fact that stocks go up and down—that is what they do.

Let's look at another example in Figure 3.10. We can quickly identify that there is no distinct overall trend. However, we can identify three distinct price cycles. The stock is currently in an upward cycle and it is at the very top of that cycle. The stock's likely move over the short term is to head back to the bottom of the rising cycle. The short-term bias for this stock is down.

On occasion, you will find charts that are harder to identify and classify in this fashion. If you do not understand a chart, *do not* invest in the stock.

Assessing Chart Positions for New Covered Call Positions

The optimal outcome for covered call investors is that the stock price rises after entering the transaction, they are called out at the end of the month,

FIGURE 3.10   Assess this chart.

and they then reinvest and compound their capital the following month. To increase the likelihood of this outcome, investors should only invest in upward moving or sideways moving stocks.

The CSE Screener filters stipulate that investments can only be made in stocks that are trading less than 75 percent of their 52-week trading range. This criterion commonly leads to stocks being presented by the CSE Screener with three distinct stock price chart types:

1. Upward moving stocks
2. Downward moving stocks
3. Sideways moving stocks

Upward Moving Stocks   In the context of covered calls, upward moving stocks can be of two types:

1. Stocks in a *generally rising cycle.*
2. Stocks that have had significant price declines in the preceding months and are *currently in an upward cycle.* A stock is currently in an upward cycle if it has (a) substantially broken through the upper line of the declining price cycle and (b) established a new rising price cycle (a cycle with higher tops and higher bottoms).

Type 1 upward moving stocks are generally upward moving within an upward cycle. However, they are not trading at or near their highs for the year. See Figures 3.11, 3.12, and 3.13 for examples.

Type 2 upward moving stocks have had significant price declines in the preceding months and are *now rising*. The most important factors in

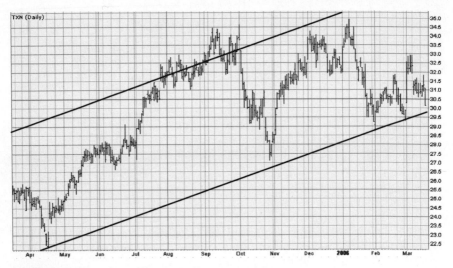

FIGURE 3.11 Generally upward moving stock.

FIGURE 3.12 Generally upward moving stock.

FIGURE 3.13 Generally upward moving stock.

determining whether the stock is *now rising* are if it has (a) substantially broken through the upper line of the declining price cycle and (b) established a new rising price cycle (a cycle with higher tops and higher bottoms). See Figures 3.14, 3.15, and 3.16 for examples.

FIGURE 3.14 Current rising cycle outside of a declining cycle.

FIGURE 3.15   Current rising cycle outside of a declining cycle.

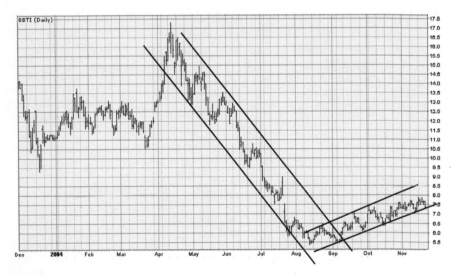

FIGURE 3.16   Current rising cycle outside of a declining cycle.

Downward Moving Stocks   In the context of covered calls, downward moving stocks are those that have had significant price declines in the preceding months and are *continuing to decline*. These stocks should be avoided. They have *not* substantially broken through the upper line of the declining price cycle and established a new rising price cycle (a cycle with

FIGURE 3.17   Downward moving stock.

FIGURE 3.18   Downward moving stock.

higher tops and higher bottoms). See Figures 3.17 and 3.18 for examples of downward moving stocks.

Sideways Moving Stocks   Sideways moving stocks are suitable for covered call investment and are characterized by predominantly stable bottoms and tops; that is, the tops and bottoms of the cycle are getting neither higher nor lower. When a stock is sideways moving, the market is in consolidation. See Figures 3.19 and 3.20 for examples.

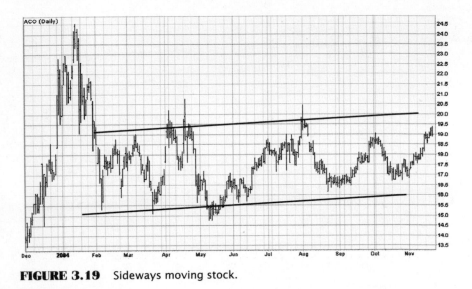

FIGURE 3.19 Sideways moving stock.

FIGURE 3.20 Sideways moving stock.

The Buying Low Rule for Covered Calls

The buying low rule for covered calls exists to ensure that new covered call positions are only entered into in the lower portion of a stock's current price cycle. Investing in stocks that are in the lower portion of the current price cycle increases the likelihood that the stock price will increase after entering into a new position and, therefore, increases the likelihood of being called out at the end of the option month. Being called out at the end of the option month is a primary objective of covered call investing.

The buying low rule for covered calls includes two stipulations:

1. Invest in stocks that are upward moving or sideways moving.
2. Only invest in a stock when it is in the lower 25 percent of the current price cycle. Investing in the lower 25 percent of the cycle makes it more likely that the stock will move up after entering the transaction and, therefore, increases the likelihood of being called out.

See Figures 3.21 and 3.22 for examples.

FIGURE 3.21 Satisfying the buying low rule.

FIGURE 3.22   Satisfying the buying low rule.

In contrast, the stock shown in Figure 3.23 does *not* qualify for investment. The current cycle is horizontal with upward bias, but the stock is trading at about 75 percent of the cycle. The near-term bias is down. This stock does *not* meet the buying low rule.

FIGURE 3.23   Buying low rule not satisfied.

INVESTING IN NON-U.S. MARKETS

Those electing to invest in non-U.S. markets must be aware of the limitations of these markets compared to the U.S. markets. The primary drawbacks of investing in markets outside the United States are the significantly smaller numbers of optionable stocks in foreign markets, the lower option premiums due to lower volatility levels, and the lack of tools such as the CSE Screener to assist in finding and analyzing potential covered call opportunities.

It is highly advisable that investors wanting to commit new funds to the covered call technique do so in the U.S. market. However, if you already own stocks in foreign markets and want to continue holding these stocks, see if they are optionable and then start selling covered calls on them! You are in a win-win situation; you have already assumed the risk of owning the stock and can only benefit from selling the covered call.

If you don't own any existing stocks and would like to start investing in covered calls in a foreign market, the stocks you should focus on are those with the most liquid options markets, those that provide consistent *near month* call expirations, and those that provide superior yields.

A *near month* call is a call that expires in the current month—for example, if we are in March, a near month call would expire at the end of March. It is optimal for covered call writing that a stock always has a near month call.

As the CSE Screener does not extend its services to foreign markets, if you would like to start investing in covered calls in a foreign market, you will need to conduct a reasonable amount of research before doing so. You will need to understand:

- What stocks in the foreign market are optionable.
- What stocks in the foreign market have consistent near month call expirations.
- Which stocks have adequate volatility levels and, therefore, reasonable covered call yields.
- How many shares each option contract relates to in the foreign market.

You must also recognize that it is unlikely that you will be able to find covered call opportunities in foreign markets that meet the U.S. covered call search criteria as previously discussed, because foreign markets are smaller than the U.S. market and provide less variety and opportunity. You may need to relax or even eliminate the fundamental and technical search criteria discussed. Doing without these criteria is further reason why new funds committed to the covered call technique should be committed in the U.S. market.

If you still want to invest in covered calls in a foreign market, to begin with, buy only enough stock to sell one covered option contract and concentrate on stocks with relatively low stock prices—this will minimize your initial capital investment. Sell covered calls on just one or two stocks until you have the confidence to commit more capital to the market.

If you find that the minimum investment in stock to sell one option contract makes you uncomfortable due to its dollar value, or if this amount represents more than 10 percent of the capital you would like to ideally have invested in covered calls (once you are comfortable with the technique), then you should invest in the U.S. market because doing so will allow you to gain acceptable levels of diversification with a smaller capital base (U.S. option contracts generally relate to only 100 shares).

This being said, then, the six rules for entering new covered call positions in foreign markets are:

1. You can establish new positions only on down market days. A down market day is a day when the major market average index for that market is in the red (trading lower than the close of the previous trading day).

2. You must always only sell the near month call when entering a new covered call position.

3. You should assess the universe of optionable stocks for the fundamental and technical data outlined in the U.S. covered call search criteria. Preference should be given to stocks that more fully meet these criteria.

4. You should assess the universe of optionable stocks in the chosen market for both uncalled and called returns and invest in the highest yielding opportunities.

5. Always give priority to maintaining acceptable levels of diversification—never have more than 10 percent of your investment capital in any one stock. Preferably construct a portfolio of between 10 and 20 stocks.

6. Buy the stock first and then immediately sell the call. Do not hesitate. If you buy the stock and wait for a better price for the call, you are no better than a speculator, and you will get burned!

CHAPTER 4

Management Rules

The difference between great success and complete mediocrity in the business of writing covered calls is how well you can profitably manage your way out of a position that is not performing as you would like. It would be fantastic if every time you entered into a transaction, you were called out at the end of the month, got all your money back, and started again. It would even be great if you didn't get called out and were able to sell the same strike price again in the near month and to maintain both a good called and uncalled return. Unfortunately, such is not the reality of this business.

Covered calls require *management*. You must manage positions for consistent monthly income, regardless of market direction, to achieve portfolio growth and compounding using this technique. This chapter highlights the management techniques needed to achieve consistent monthly income from a stock investment, regardless of market direction.

CLOSING POSITIONS ON THE DELTA EFFECT

Occasionally a stock's price may increase significantly after a covered call position has been established. This increase may allow investors to close out the position for an overall transaction profit by buying back the short call and selling the stock. The investor is able to achieve this profit because the stock price generally increases more than the call price on a dollar-to-dollar basis. This is known as the *delta effect*.

The delta of a stock option is the rate of change of the option price with respect to the price of the underlying stock. It is a measure of how much an option's price will increase or decrease for an incremental increase or decrease in the stock price.

Let's look at an example of a call that has a delta of 0.60. This number means that when the stock price changes by an amount, the option price will change by 60 percent of that amount. For example, if the stock price increases by $1.00, then the option will increase in price by $0.60 (60 percent of the stock price's increase). If the stock price increased just $0.50, then the option price would increase by only $0.30 (60 percent of the stock price increase).

The delta of the stock is always 1 or 100 percent; for a $1.00 move in the stock price, the stock moves up, obviously, $1.00 or 100 percent of that move. So, when a new covered call position is entered into and the stock price increases significantly, the profit the investor can make by selling the stock will almost always be larger than the loss realized by buying back the call. Consequently, if the stock price moves up far enough after entering a transaction, investors can close the position immediately with a profit and then reinvest and compound the proceeds.

Let's look at an example. John buys MDR stock at $20.00 and sells the June $20.00 call for $1.00. You should understand that the delta of the stock is always 1 and the delta of the call for the purposes of this example is 0.50. If the stock price jumps up by, for example, $2.00 after entering this position, the option price will only increase by $1.00 (50 percent of $2.00). John's position would look like this:

Profit on stock sale	= $22.00 − $20.00 =	$2.00
Loss on call buyback	= $ 1.00 − $ 2.00 =	−$1.00
Net Profit on transaction close	= $ 2.00 − $ 1.00 =	$1.00, or 5%

In this instance, it would be wise for John to simply close the transaction and then reinvest and compound the proceeds. He would do so by simply buying back the short call and then immediately selling the stock.

New covered call positions should be monitored for an opportunity to close the position on the delta effect. Closing positions on the delta effect occurs regularly when the stock price increases significantly after entering a new position.

THE MID-MONTH RULE

Once you have entered into the covered call position, all you need to do is have patience and wait for the option's expiration at the end of the month. However, you can decide to be a little more proactive during the month and utilize the mid-month rule, which can have the effect of significantly increasing your returns on the position.

The mid-month technique involves buying back the short call for a profit in the first two weeks of the month. The five rules for implementing this technique are:

1. If you have sold a call for a 5 percent uncalled return or more, the mid-month technique may be considered.
2. If within the first two weeks of the month you are able to buy back the call and lock in an uncalled return of 4 percent for the month, then do so.
3. You then put in a good til canceled (GTC) order to sell the same call for more than you bought it back for.
4. If the GTC order executes, wait until the end of the month to see if you will be called out.
5. If the GTC order does not execute, or if the position is uncalled at expiration, move to the secondary call sales rule.

Good til Canceled (GTC): An order to buy or sell a stock or option that remains in effect until it is executed or canceled by the investor who placed it.

Here's an example of utilizing the mid-month rule. John selects a new covered call position on MDR. He purchases the stock for $19.75 and sells the one-month out $20.00 call option for $1.00. This transaction has generated a 5.1 percent uncalled return ($1.00/$19.75).

In assessing the chart, John has identified that the stock is an upward moving stock and is in the lower 25 percent of the rising price cycle. If the stock price falls after entering the position, he may be able to implement the mid-month rule to enhance yield. John calculates that a 4 percent return on this position would equate to about $0.80 (0.04 × $19.75). So for John to make a net 4 percent or $0.80 uncalled return on this position, he would need to buy back the call at a price of $0.20 ($1.00 – $0.80).

John would then attempt to sell the same call again at a value greater than what he bought it back for sometime before the end of the month. The price at which he would resell the call depends on (1) the time left in the option month and (2) the position of the stock in relation to its current price cycle.

The price at which the call should be resold is based on judgment and is a skill investors develop with time and experience. Less active investors should simply put in a GTC order to resell the call for a price higher than they bought it back for. More active investors should wait until the stock reaches 75 percent of the price cycle and then resell the call. This explanation will be become more clear in the following section on secondary call sales rules.

Remember, John would only buy back the call in the first two weeks of the month. If he buys the call back later than this, then there is less than two weeks left until the option expires. Due to accelerating time decay in the last two weeks of an option's life, it is unlikely that the price of the option will increase enough to make it worthwhile for John to sell it again.

By buying back the call, you are locking in a fantastic 4 percent return for the month, but you are leaving a little bit of money on the table, in this example, $0.20 or 1 percent. You are doing this because it is likely that, sometime in the next two or three weeks before the option's expiration, the stock will jump up a little and allow you to resell the call for a greater value than you bought it back for. Practitioners of this technique understand that this is a regular occurrence. Remember, the covered call position was entered into at the bottom 25 percent of a rising or sideways price cycle, and the stock has obviously fallen further to allow the buyback of the call for a profit. It is therefore highly likely that the stock price will then increase back into its regular cycle, thus allowing the resale of the same call for higher premium.

SECONDARY CALL SALES

A *secondary call sale* is any call sale that occurs after you have bought back the original call or the original call has expired. At the end of the first month, you either got called out or you didn't. If you got called out, you now have all your money back in your account and you are ready to start again. Go back to the rules for entering new covered call positions provided in Chapter 3. Enter these positions as quickly as possible. The longer you wait, the more time value is eroding in the next month's option contracts and the lower your covered call yield will be. You need to assess how much cash you have made during the month and try to reinvest it all so your money can start compounding. Remember, *compounding* is the key.

If you didn't get called out and you are investing in the U.S. market, you have a nice 4–8 percent cash return sitting in your brokerage account in one month. A 7 percent return would be a very good return for a mutual fund in a year, and you have made that return in just one month! And if you have several positions, your returns for the month may represent enough cash for you to enter a whole new position and really have your money compounding.

The Rules for Secondary Call Sales

If you were not called out, that means the call has expired worthless. You now have a stock without a call and are ready to sell a call for the next month. The rules for selling secondary calls are significantly different from the rules for entering new covered call transactions. The six rules for secondary call sales are:

1. Secondary calls can only be sold when the markets are in the green (higher than the close of the previous day). For the United States, the markets are in the green when both the Dow Jones Industrial Average and the NASDAQ are trading above the close of the previous day. Foreign markets are in the green when the major market index for that market is trading above the close of the previous day.

2. For the U.S. market, if you can sell a near month call where the uncalled and called returns are both greater than 4 percent, then do so. For foreign markets, if you can sell a near month call where the uncalled and called returns are both greater than 1.5 percent, then do so.

3. If rule 2 isn't applicable, you should use the TSS for income while being sure to adhere to the selling high rule (both discussed in detail in the following section). Move the expiration of the call out to the second to last expiration and sell a call that provides an uncalled return of minimum 10 percent. Do not sell the last expiration of the option series. This must be kept in reserve for defensive techniques.

4. The minimum uncalled return of 10 percent for a TSS for income call sale is based on your purchase price of the stock or the current market value, whichever is higher.

5. The greater the uncalled return generated on the TSS for income call sale, the quicker the call will be bought back as the stock price declines. You may select a lower strike price to allow an easier buyback to the extent the strike price of the call selected plus the call's bid price is greater than the current price of the stock.

6. Once a TSS for income call is sold, it should be bought to close at any time a 5 percent net return can be realized or when the stock reaches 25 percent of the current cycle, whichever occurs first.

Implementing the Secondary Call Sales Rules

While the objective with covered calls is generally to sell a near month call and have the time decay factor working strongly in your favor, this is often not practically achievable. In situations where new covered call positions are entered into and are not called out, it is often not possible to sell a near month call where the uncalled and called returns are both greater than 4 percent (the preceding rule 2). For example, let's assume it's early May and John selects a new covered call position on MDR. He purchases the stock for $19.75 and sells the May $20.00 call for $1.00. If the stock finishes the option month at $18.00, the position will not be called out. John will keep the $1.00 in premium and will be left to reassess a secondary call sale on MDR. It's now June and the near month option chain appears as shown in Table 4.1.

We can see from Table 4.1 that John will not be able to sell the June (near month) $20.00 call for an uncalled and called return of 4 percent or greater (the preceding rule 2) as the premium for this call is just $0.20 or a 1 percent uncalled return. John could sell the June $17.50 call for an uncalled return of 6.1 percent, but the called return would be –5.3 percent [($17.50 – $19.75 + $1.20)/$19.75]. That sale would violate rule 2, which stipulates both the uncalled and called returns must be 4 percent or greater in order to sell a near month call.

In this situation, John must use the TSS for income while being sure to adhere to the selling high rule (the preceding rule 3).

TABLE 4.1   MDR Near Month Option Chain

Strike	Ticker	Bid Price	Ask Price	Delta
June				
7.50	JPMIY	10.60	10.70	1.00
10.00	JPMIF	8.10	8.20	1.00
12.50	JPMIZ	5.60	5.70	1.00
15.00	JPMIG	3.20	3.40	1.00
17.50	JPMIU	1.20	1.35	0.91
20.00	JPMIH	0.20	0.30	0.33
22.50	JPMIV	0.00	0.05	—
25.00	JPMII	0.00	0.05	—
27.50	JPMIW	0.00	0.05	—
30.00	JPMIJ	0.00	0.05	—

THE TETHERED SLINGSHOT FOR INCOME AND THE SELLING HIGH RULE

The tethered slingshot (TSS) for income and the selling high rule are very important techniques for the covered call writer as they allow consistent generation of income in situations where the stock price is trading below an investor's cost in the stock.

The rules for the TSS for income are embedded in the preceding rules for secondary call sales. These rules state that when a call cannot be sold in the near month that provides both an uncalled and called return of 4 percent or greater, the investor must use the TSS for income. The investor should select the second to last expiration and sell a strike price call that results in an uncalled return of minimum 10 percent. Before this call can be sold, the investor *must* ensure that the selling high rule has been satisfied. The selling high rule relates to the *timing* of the TSS for income call sale— it is very important that TSS for income calls are sold at the high point of the price cycle.

> *TSS for Income:* A covered call management technique used to generate income when the stock price has declined after entry.

The Selling High Rule

The *selling high* rule states that secondary call sales using the TSS for income can only be made when a stock is in the upper 75 percent of its current price cycle.

When a secondary call is sold using the TSS for income, the investor's objective must be to generate income and *buy back* the call (buy the call to close) as soon as possible for a positive net return. To achieve a positive net return on a buyback, one or both of the following circumstances must occur: (1) The stock price must decrease in value and/or (2) time value must diminish.

The selling high rule draws on point 1 by assisting the investor to identify when the stock is trading at the high point of its current price cycle. This rule is essentially the opposite of the buying low rule for covered calls, which ensures that you are buying into new positions when the market is down and the stock is in the lower 25 percent of its price cycle. Conversely, the selling high rule ensures that you are selling a secondary call when the market is up and the stock is in the upper 75 percent of its price cycle. This condition greatly increases the chances that the stock will fall and you will be able to buy back the call for a profit.

Remember, too, that decay in time value is also working significantly in the covered call writer's favor. This factor also greatly increases the opportunity for a profitable call buyback.

It is important to make the distinction that our objective is not speculation when using the TSS for income and selling high rule. What we are trying to do is sell in the vicinity of the top of the cycle and buy the call back for a profit at lower stock prices in the near future. If you sell a call and the stock keeps moving up, *you do not take a loss on the call*. Rather, investors should have patience and wait for the stock price to come back to the bottom of the cycle. Stocks cycle up and down—they do not go straight up and they do not go straight down. If the stock doesn't come down to allow a profitable call buyback we can use other management and defensive techniques, primarily exiting on the delta effect (see earlier in this chapter) or the surrogate stock replacement (covered in Chapter 5).

Patience and management are critical factors for success. You must have patience to *wait* for the stock price to meet the selling high rule before selling a TSS for income call. You must also have patience to *wait* for the stock price to cycle down after selling a TSS for income call to allow a profitable buyback. Patience is key.

It is very rare that a call will be sold and the very next day the stock cycles down. It is not possible to pick the absolute top of the market and have the call immediately fall in price—this is an unrealistic expectation. It is much more common that over a period of one to four weeks after selling a TSS for income call, the stock cycles down and allows a profitable buyback. During the period of waiting, *patience* is required. Novice investors often panic when a TSS for income call cannot be immediately bought back for a profit. Such immediacy is against the nature of this technique. Again, when using the TSS for income and the selling high rule, patience is key.

But what if we sell a TSS for income call at what we believe is the top of the price cycle and the stock breaks cycle, shoots straight up, and never trades at a lower price? This scenario is common and simply requires investors to implement one of many management strategies:

- Closing the position on the delta effect (discussed previously).
- Buying back the call profitably at higher stock prices due to the decay in time value.
- Using the surrogate stock replacement to exit the position (discussed in Chapter 5)
- Using the 20¢ rule or TSS for defense (Chapter 5).

Applying the TSS for Income and Selling High Rule

Remember, the selling high rule identifies the *timing* of a TSS for income call sale. It identifies the point on the chart where a TSS for income call can be sold. The selling high rule instructs to only sell a TSS for income call when the stock price is in the upper 75 percent of the current price cycle. Interpretation of the chart is vitally important. The figures in this section show some examples of applying the TSS for income and the selling high rule on various stocks.

Experience indicates that the selling high rule will be satisfied on most stocks approximately once or twice a month over the long-term—particularly when we assess shorter-term cycles (discussed in the next section, "Safely Maximizing TSS for Income Call Sale Opportunities"). Look at Figure 4.1. Assume we bought this stock some time in the past and it is currently trading below our cost. If we were assessing this chart today, it would qualify under the selling high rule. At this point, we would immediately sell the TSS for income call. We do not care if it *appears* that the stock has further to increase before it reaches the absolute top of the cycle—this is speculation. We are not attempting to "pick the top." We just want to sell the TSS for income call in the high region of the price cycle. Picking the absolute top is not reliably achievable and, further, does not contribute to the success of this technique.

FIGURE 4.1 Satisfying the selling high rule.

FIGURE 4.2   The selling high rule is not satisfied.

Once the TSS for income call is sold, the investor then needs to have *patience* and wait for the stock to cycle down. During this period of waiting, the call may be unprofitable to buy back, as the stock price may increase further. The investor must have *patience* and allow the stock to cycle down or time value to erode in order to profitably buy back the call. If the stock shoots straight up we may be able to exit on the delta effect (discussed earlier in this chapter) or will use defensive techniques such as the surrogate stock replacement (discussed in Chapter 5).

We can see from Figure 4.2 that there are always opportunities to continue generating net cash flow using the TSS for income—regardless of the trend of the stock. However, patience is required to wait for the correct point in the price cycle to sell the call. In the preceding example, we would be waiting for the stock to reach 75 percent of the cycle before selling a TSS for income call. As soon as the stock reaches 75 percent of the cycle, we will immediately sell the call.

Safely Maximizing TSS for Income Call Sale Opportunities—Understanding Cycles Within Cycles

When managing fallen positions using the TSS for income, it is important to *maximize call sale opportunities*. Maximizing call sale opportunities means taking advantage of as many movements within the price cycle as possible. In the examples illustrated by Figures 4.1 and 4.2, we assessed the selling high rule based on a 12-month chart. However, depending on the na-

FIGURE 4.3 Maximizing sale call opportunities.

ture of the stock, it is sometimes necessary to assess the selling high rule based on shorter-term cycles. We can see in Figure 4.3, that if assessing the cycles on a 12-month chart, only at approximately nine points would the selling high rule be satisfied.

In order to maximize call sale opportunities when using the TSS for income and selling high rule, investors must be cognizant of shorter-term cycles. We can see from the chart in Figure 4.4 that this stock is cycling upwards over the long-term; however, there are shorter-term *cycles within the long-term cycle—both upward and downward*. Some (not all) of the cycles are highlighted in Figure 4.4 for illustration purposes.

We can see in Figure 4.4 that many more opportunities exist to implement the TSS for income while adhering to the selling high rule when

FIGURE 4.4   Many points on the short-term downward cycle qualify under the selling high rule.

FIGURE 4.5   A stock at the bottom of a longer-term upward cycle.

assessing shorter-term cycles. There are many points on the short-term downward cycle that qualify under the selling high rule. However, it is most important to always understand the longer-term cycle and the position of the stock in relation to that cycle.

We can see in the short-term downward cycle illustrated in Figure 4.5 that the top of this cycle is actually the bottom of the longer-term upward cycle. This is a very common occurrence. In this instance a call should not be sold because, in actuality, the stock is at the bottom of the longer-term upward cycle. Its bias is, therefore, up.

In summary, maximizing call sale opportunities means taking advantage of as many movements within the price cycle as possible. To do this, investors must take advantage of short-term cycles while assessing the selling high rule. However, investors must not ignore the long-term cycle when using the TSS for income and selling high rule. Do not sell a call at the bottom of the long-term cycle. Always view the stock initially over a 12-month time frame to understand the long-term cycle. Shorter-term cycles can then be assessed. The top of a short-term cycle is often the bottom of the long-term cycle.

SELLING CALLS ON EXISTING STOCK HOLDINGS

Investors new to the covered call technique often express concern about being forced to profitably sell their stock in the event of a call out. This concern is particularly common with investors who are considering making their first covered call transactions on existing stock holdings that have significant unrealized capital gains.

If an investor wishes to be successful in the business of covered calls, emotional attachments cannot be held toward any particular stock holding; decisions must be made purely on economic considerations. However, when learning the covered call technique, it is also important that investors are comfortable with their level of financial commitment to the technique, including the commitment to the taxman if significant unrealized capital gains are realized through a call out.

This situation arises if you bought a stock for $15.00 and the stock is now trading at, for example, $30.00. If you were not inclined to continue holding the stock, the rules for selling covered calls on existing stock holdings (detailed later in this section) would instruct you to sell a near month call that will provide a good uncalled and called return. For purposes of illustration, let's assume you sold a $32.50 call. If you were then called out, you would realize a capital gain of $17.50 ($32.50 – $15.00) on the stock. Even though you can simply repurchase the stock after being called out for around the same price as you sold it for and then resell another call, this realization of capital gains liability understandably makes some investors nervous when first starting to use the covered call technique.

One alternative for investors not wishing to risk being called out of a particular stock holding is to *not sell near month calls.* Instead, simply use the TSS for income and selling high rule. This strategy will dramatically decrease (but can never completely eliminate) the risk of being called out. It is the preferred strategy for investors wishing not to be called out of a particular stock position. Investors following this technique should still make themselves familiar with the defensive techniques for preventing a call out (discussed in Chapter 5).

Once experience and comfort are gained with the technique, it is likely that you will realize that the merits of consistent monthly cash flow outweigh the very small chance of a possible realization of a large capital gain on a particular stock when using the TSS for income. However, if this does concern you and if you wish to initiate selling covered calls on your existing portfolio, simply choose stocks in your portfolio that will not result in significant tax liabilities in the event of a call out. It would also be advisable that while familiarizing yourself with the technique, you do not sell calls on stocks that will result in a negative called return. Instead, while learning the technique, choose stocks in your portfolio that are trading close to or slightly above the price you paid for them.

The Rules for Selling Calls on Existing Stock Holdings

The four rules for selling covered calls on existing stock holdings are:

1. New calls may only be sold on up market days. For the U.S. market, an up market day is when the Dow Jones Industrial Average and the NAS-DAQ are in the green (trading higher than the close of the previous day). For foreign markets, an up market day is when the major market average index for that country is in the green (trading higher than the close of the previous day).

2. If the market price of the stock is *higher* than your cost in the stock, both the called and uncalled return calculations should be based on the *current market price* of the stock. If the market price of the stock is *lower* than your cost in the stock, all return calculations should be based on *your cost* in the stock.

3. If you have no desire to keep the stock, your objective should be to sell a *near month* call that will provide a satisfactory uncalled and called return. If you can sell a near month call with a resulting uncalled and called return of minimum 2.0 percent for the U.S. market or minimum 1.0 percent for foreign markets, then do so. This minimum return requirement is highly dependant on the volatility of the individual stock. With experience, you will gain a greater understanding of what is a reasonable uncalled and called return for your particular stock holdings.

4. If you cannot satisfy rule 3 or you do not want to be called out of the stock holding, then use the TSS for income while being sure to adhere to the selling high rule. These rules are detailed in the rules for secondary call sales listed earlier in the chapter.

What to Do When Called Out

If you plan to implement a covered call strategy over existing stock holdings, the situation will arise when you are called out of such holdings and left with excess capital to invest back into the market. If you wish to continue holding the stock you were called out of, you may simply construct a new covered call position on that stock. When doing so, be sure that you satisfy the buying low rule for covered calls. You must not construct a covered call position at the top end of the price cycle, even if it is on a stock that you have just been called out of.

IMPLEMENTING A COVERED CALL STRATEGY USING OTHER STOCK SELECTION METHODS

Many investors choose to implement a covered call strategy on stocks that have been selected by a professional fund manager or broker. For example, a fund manager or broker may suggest a diversified portfolio of stocks as an attractive long-term investment. The investor educated in the covered call technique may then simply choose to invest in these stocks yet add the covered call strategy to enhance yield and reduce risk in the portfolio. The most common strategy to implement in this instance is the TSS for income while adhering to the selling high rule to allow yield enhancement to the portfolio without having stocks called out on a regular basis.

While this is generally a very conservative strategy, investors should understand that the covered call yields realized using this stock selection method would be lower than the yields realized using the stock selection methods outlined in this book. That being said, utilizing the covered call strategy over a diversified portfolio of blue-chip stocks selected by a value- (not growth) orientated broker or professional fund manager is the most conservative and low-risk equity strategy available to investors.

It is important for those choosing to implement a covered call strategy over such a portfolio that after being called out of a particular stock, investors *do not* construct a new covered call position on that particular stock *until* the buying low rule for covered calls has been satisfied.

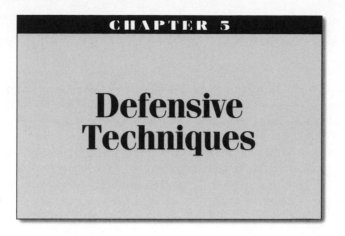

CHAPTER 5

Defensive Techniques

We have established that the difference between great success and complete mediocrity in the business of writing covered calls is *management*. Management primarily involves generating consistent monthly income from a stock investment regardless of the direction or trend of the stock.

With this chapter, we move on to defensive techniques, which are as important as management techniques but used more sparingly. Defensive techniques serve several very important functions, including:

- Identifying if a position is in danger of being unprofitably called out.
- Preventing an unprofitable call out while maintaining positive cash flow.
- Remedying a TSS for income call sale that is not able to be bought back for a profit.
- Reducing the profitable exit price of an underperforming position.
- Generating income on deeply depressed stock positions.

The defensive techniques presented in this chapter cover the entire scope of worst-case scenarios that may be encountered by the covered call investor. These techniques provide a so-called "light at the end of the tunnel" for poorly performing covered call positions and, when properly understood, provide investors with the confidence to implement the mind-set of never selling a stock for a loss.

BASIC DEFENSIVE TECHNIQUES

The 20¢ Rule

You should recall that option contracts are rarely exercised until the last two weeks before expiration because doing so results in a loss of time value to the option buyer. In practically, the vast majority of option contracts are exercised on the third Friday of expiration.

It is very rare that an option contract will be exercised before the last two weeks of the option month, even if it is in the money. As such, defensive measures to avoid an unprofitable call out need only be taken when the option contract is *within its last two weeks before expiration*. If someone does exercise on you early, you are unlucky and it will probably never happen again.

The 20¢ rule provides investors with a method to determine whether an investment is in danger of being called out and if it is, therefore, necessary to implement the tethered slingshot (TSS) for defense to prevent being called out.

The 20¢ rule states that if you have a negative called return when an option contract has two weeks or less to expiration, take the strike price of your call, add the cost of buying back that call (the *ask price*) and subtract the market price of the stock. So:

20¢ rule = Call strike price + Call buyback price (ask) – Stock price

If the 20¢ rule value is equal to $0.20 or less, you are in the danger zone of being called out and you need to take defensive action using the TSS for defense.

The need for the 20¢ rule also arises when an investor has lowered the strike price on a call sale and has a *negative* called return on a position. While this situation arises very rarely when using the covered call techniques presented in this book, it happens quite often when adopting traditional covered call methods, which instruct to sell near month calls with lower strike prices in order to maintain yield. Regardless, awareness of how to avoid an unprofitable call out is very important.

Let's look at an example. Assume an investor buys a stock for $14.75 and sells the June $15.00 call for $0.80. In this example the return calculations would be:

Uncalled return = $0.80/$14.75 = 5.4%
Called return   = ($0.80 + $15.00 – $14.75)/$14.75 = 7.1%

The stock price then falls to $12.50 and the call expires worthless leaving the investor with a return of 5.4 percent for the month. This investor then elects to sell the July $12.50 strike. (Note that this would not be the course of action if correctly following the secondary call sales rules—this is for illustration purposes only. The correct course of action would be to use the TSS for income [sell the second to last expiration of the option chain and a call that allows for a minimum of 10 percent uncalled return while adhering to the selling high rule].)

Let's assume that the stock price now rises and the investor is unable to buy back the near month $12.50 strike call back for a profit. The stock price is now $13.30. As the stock price is now *above* the strike price of the call sold, it may be in the interest of the option buyer to exercise his or her option. The covered call writer may have to sell the stock at a loss. This investor may be in danger of being called out for a loss and needs to use the 20¢ rule for guidance. Thus:

$$20¢ \text{ rule} = \$12.50 + \$0.85 \text{ (trading near intrinsic value)} - \$13.30$$
$$= \$0.05$$

Since the 20¢ rule value is less than $0.20, this position is likely to be called out and defensive action is necessary.

Remember, the 20¢ rule is only used in the last two weeks of the option month and only on positions with negative called return. You must monitor such positions carefully during the last two weeks of the option month to make sure you are not in danger of being called out *unprofitably*. If at any time during the last two weeks of the option month you have sold a call that results in a negative called return and the 20¢ rule equals $0.20 or less, you must immediately take defensive action using the TSS for defense.

Tethered Slingshot for Defense

You should implement the TSS for defense immediately if the 20¢ rule has indicated that you are in danger of being called out and that this call out will be unprofitable.

The functions of the TSS are:

- Preventing an unprofitable call out.
- Generating additional covered call income.
- Allowing the investor to move the strike price of the call back to where the called return is positive.

The eight rules for using this technique are:

1. Implement the TSS for defense if the 20¢ rule indicates that you are in danger of being called out and that this call out will be unprofitable.

2. Immediately buy back the existing call (this results in a temporary loss).

3. Select the same call strike price but move the expiration date out to the second to last expiration.

4. You have now generated additional covered call income, as the price you received for selling the TSS for defense call is always higher than the cost of buying back the near month. You no longer have a temporary loss.

5. Buy back this new call when the net gain is at least equal to the temporary loss generated in rule 2.

6. You now have a stock with no call obligation, did not get called out, and made additional income every step of the way.

7. You should now be patient and wait for an upswing in the stock price that will allow you to sell a near month call for a minimum of 4 percent uncalled and called return for the U.S. market and 1.5 percent for foreign markets that will allow a positive called return.

8. If the stock reaches 75 percent of the price cycle and does not allow for application of rule 7, go back to the rules for secondary call sales given in Chapter 4.

ADVANCED DEFENSIVE TECHNIQUES

The defensive techniques presented in this section are considered advanced because they draw on the use of debit spreads. A *debit spread* involves selling a call option while using another long call option for cover, rather than the stock. The general technique of using debit spreads is discussed in detail in Part II on calendar LEAPS spreads. Here we discuss how to use debit spreads as a specific defensive tool for covered call investors. These advanced defensive techniques are indispensable when using the covered call technique.

Many brokers do not allow the use of debit spreads in a retirement account such as an IRA or 401k. It is important for investors to understand that this is a software-related issue at the particular brokerage house rather than a legal requirement that prevents the use of debit spreads in a retirement account. To keep your business, many brokerage firms will tell you debit spreads are "not allowed in a retirement account." This is a misleading statement. Debit spreads *are* allowed in a retirement account; however, most brokerage houses do not have the software to cater for them. For a list of Compound Stock Earnings recommended brokers, including those that allow debit spreads in a retirement account, go to www.compound stockearnings.com/brokers.

Surrogate Stock Replacement

Surrogate stock replacement (SSR) is an invaluable covered call defensive technique. The function of the SSR is to expedite the profitable close-out of a covered call transaction where the following three conditions apply:

1. An investor has used the TSS for income on the position.
2. The stock has continued to move up after selling the TSS for income call. The investor is therefore unable to buy back the TSS for income call due to this buyback being unprofitable.
3. The investor now has a *profit* in the stock position, but is prevented from closing the entire transaction (buying back the call and selling the stock) because doing so would result in an overall transaction loss. In all instances this is due to the loss on buyback of the TSS for income call exceeding the potential profit from selling the stock.

See, for example, the position shown in Table 5.1. This investor has a $2.00 profit in the stock position; however, the position cannot be closed due to a $4.50 loss on the TSS for income call. Closing the position would result in an overall transaction loss of $2.50.

Given this scenario, if the investor does not implement the SSR, the strategy going forward with this position would be to take one of the following two actions:

TABLE 5.1 Example Position Appropriate for Use of SSR

Position	Entry Price	Current Price	Profit/ Loss
Long GE stock	$35.00	$37.00	$2.00
Short Jan 2007 $30 call	$ 5.00	$ 9.50	−$4.50

1. Wait for the stock price to move down or for time value to erode so the investor can profitably buy back the TSS for income call.

2. Wait for a large increase in the stock price, which, in most cases, will eventually lead to the position becoming profitable due to the delta ratio.

The SSR serves the function of expediting the closeout of a TSS for income call sale that has gone bad. This function is highly valuable to the covered call investor because waiting for the conditions to arise to permit either action (1) or (2) can, in many instances, take several months. During this period of waiting for the position to improve through either a large increase or decrease in the stock price, the capital invested in the position becomes dormant and unproductive. This period of waiting represents an opportunity cost to the investor—the cost of returns that could have been made if that capital were invested in productive positions.

When using the SSR, the objective is to restructure the position through the following three actions:

1. Closing out the existing position by buying back the call and selling the stock. In every case, this creates a temporary loss (the restructure cost).

2. Purchasing a LEAPS or a longer-term call in place of the stock.

3. Selling a near month or two month out call that will provide a positive called return on the entire transaction (including recuperating the restructure cost).

> *LEAPS:* Acronym for long-term equity anticipation securities. They are simply long-term options. They have exactly the same standardized characteristics as a normal option but with a long-term expiration. Contracts with one year or more to expiration and a January 200x expiration are known as LEAPS.

The ten rules for using the SSR technique are:

1. The SSR is to be used on a covered call position where an investor has an open TSS for income call.

2. The investor has a profit in the stock position.

3. The position cannot be closed for a profit, as the loss on buyback of the call is greater than the potential profit from selling the stock. Therefore, if the position is closed out, a net loss for the investor would be created.

4. Use the SSR Worksheet to calculate the net loss in closing the transaction (the SSR Worksheet is part of the Covered Call Toolbox, one month's complementary access to which is available by going to www.compoundstockearnings.com/freemonth). This net loss is the restructure cost.

5. Input various LEAPS contracts into the SSR Worksheet. The SSR usually works better when using the second to last expiration LEAPS, rather than the furthest out LEAPS contract. Start one strike price out of the money and move into the money three or four contracts.

6. Input various near month and two month out call contracts into the SSR Worksheet. Start two strikes out of the money and move into the money two contracts.

7. The SSR should be executed if the SSR Worksheet presents a transaction that has both an uncalled and called return of greater than 2 percent. Preference should be given to the SSR transaction with the highest returns. Preference should also be given to selling the near month call.

8. It is also preferable that the SSR be cash flow positive. Investors with excess capital may still choose to execute the SSR if it is cash flow negative. Optimally, the transaction should generate net cash.

9. If the transactions presented by the SSR Worksheet do not meet the return requirements or cash flow requirements in items (7) and (8), more aggressive investors may choose to enter shorter-term calls into the SSR Worksheet as an alternative to using a LEAPS. Aggressive investors may buy a shorter-term call to construct a SSR if the shorter-term call provides an SSR that meets rules (7) and (8). If buying a shorter term call:

    (a) Preference must be given to the longest-term call that meets rules (7) and (8).

    (b) An investor must not purchase a call when that call's price consists of more than 15 percent time value. This limit ensures that the investor is purchasing primarily intrinsic value (exercisable value) and will not be affected greatly by time decay in the event that the position is not exited quickly.

    (c) When purchasing a shorter-term call, investors must be aware that in the event the stock begins trading down, the call will need to be rolled out.

10. In the event the call that was shorted in the SSR restructure expires worthless (the position was not called out), the position should be managed like a regular LEAPS position (discussed in depth in Chapter 8) with the following exception:

(a) The investor should always give preference to selling a near month call if that call will provide a positive called and uncalled return. Remember, the objective of the SSR is not to manage the position for income, but to exit the unproductive position as soon as possible.

An Example of Implementing SSR   Figure 5.1 shows the entry of a covered call position on OVTI, at a price of $15.13, in the middle of June. The stock then proceeded to fall, and the TSS for income was applied on several occasions to maintain return on the position even though it was depressed. In late October, a TSS for income call was sold in accordance with the selling high rule. The call sold was the January 07 $12.50 at a price of $2.85.

The stock then broke to the top of the declining price cycle and increased strongly over the following month. During this time, the position could not be closed for a profit, as the loss on buyback of the TSS for income call was always in excess of the realizable profit on the stock. As is sometimes the case, the delta ratio on the position was not acting as it should. The position was then as depicted in Table 5.2.

It is clear that this position could not be closed for a profit, as the loss on call buyback was greater than the profit when selling the stock. Without using the SSR restructuring, the strategy going forward on this position would be either to wait for a further increase in the stock price and an

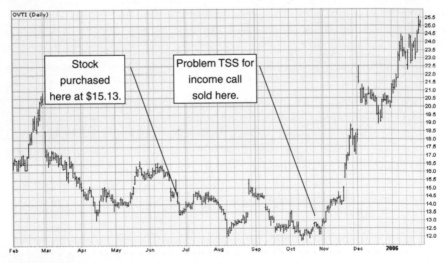

FIGURE 5.1   History of a covered call position.

TABLE 5.2	Data for Position Shown in Figure 5.1	
Current stock price		$21.66
Cost in stock		15.13
Profit on sale		$ 6.53
Call sell price		$ 2.85
Current call price		10.50
Loss on buyback		–$ 7.65
Loss if position closed		–$ 1.12

eventual exit on the delta effect (this would be difficult given that the call is now very deep in the money and the delta is near 1) or to wait for a decline in the stock price to allow a profitable buyback of the TSS for income call. This position (Figure 5.2) is, therefore, an ideal candidate for the SSR technique to be applied according to the following steps.

Step 1: *Assess the restructure cost.* The restructure cost is the temporary loss generated when the unproductive position is closed out or "restructured." It is the same as the loss if the position is closed. In this instance, the restructure cost is –$1.12. See Table 5.3.

FIGURE 5.2 Application of the SSR technique to the covered call position depicted in Figure 5.1.

TABLE 5.3 Assessing Restructure Cost	
Current stock price	$21.66
Cost in stock	15.13
Profit on sale	$ 6.53
Call sell price	$ 2.85
Current call price	10.50
Loss on buyback	–$ 7.65
Restructure cost	–$ 1.12

Step 2: *Assess the option chain for an appropriate SSR.* In this step, we look at the at-the-money and in-the-money LEAPS contracts (second to last expiration is the most likely to provide an acceptable transaction) and match these contracts with a near month (ideally) or a two month out call. This creates a LEAPS transaction with a short-term call sold against it. The objective is to select a transaction that:

- Provides a positive called return—including recuperation of the restructure cost.
- Provides an acceptable uncalled return of greater than 3 percent.
- Is cash positive—meaning that the SSR will free up cash when executed. This cash can then be reinvested into new positions.

To achieve these objectives, investors should use the SSR Worksheet (part of the Covered Call Toolbox, one month's complementary access to which is available by going to www.compoundstockearnings.com/freemonth). The SSR Worksheet allows investors to enter various LEAPS and call combinations to find the optimal SSR for a position. It is very important that the position is constructed to provide a positive called return *including* recuperation of the restructure cost. Otherwise, the call out will be at a loss. The calculation of uncalled and called returns, including recuperation of the restructure cost, is performed by the SSR Worksheet.

Looking at the option chain and entering the appropriate LEAPS and call contracts into the SSR Worksheet as instructed in the SSR rules produces the results as shown in Table 5.4. The SSR restructure that is optimal for this particular transaction is highlighted. After closing out the existing stock and TSS for income call position, the investor should immediately buy the $15.00 January 2007 call for $8.60 and immediately sell the $25.00 January 2006 call for $0.60. This is the transaction that provides the best

TABLE 5.4 Potential SSR Combinations

	Long Call Candidate			Sell Call Jan-06 $22.50			Sell Call Jan-06 $25.00			Sell Call Jan-06 $27.50		
Exp	Strike	Ask Price	Cash Free Up	Bid Price	Uncalled Return	Called Return	Bid Price	Uncalled Return	Called Return	Bid Price	Uncalled Return	Called Return
2007	$12.50	$10.40	5.0%	1.30	12.5%	-2.1%	0.60	5.8%	15.2%	0.20	1.9%	35.4%
2007	15.00	8.60	16.9	1.30	15.1	-10.7	0.60	7.0	10.2	0.20	2.3	34.7
2007	17.50	7.00	27.5	1.30	18.6	-26.0	0.60	-8.6	-0.3	0.20	2.9	29.7
2007	20.00	5.60	36.7	1.30	23.2	-52.1	0.60	-10.7	-20.0	0.20	3.6	17.5

uncalled and called return and also frees up a high percentage of cash from the position.

Shorting the $22.50 strike is not acceptable as doing so leads to negative called returns. Shorting the $27.50 strike is not optimal because it would require a very large movement in the stock price to be called out. Additionally, the uncalled return is very low (which is what the investor is likely to receive at January expiration given the very out-of-the-money $27.50 strike).

In regard to the long call selected, the optimal selection is to long the January 07 $15.00 strike rather than the $12.50 strike as this frees up more cash and provides a higher uncalled return when matched with the January 06 $25.00 strike.

Step 3: *Execute the SSR.* In this instance, the investor should close the existing position, generating a restructure cost of –$1.12. The investor should then long the January 2007 $15.00 at $8.60 and short the January 2006 (one month to expiration at time of execution) $25.00 at $0.60.

Executing this transaction will free 16.9 percent of the capital from the position.

Note: The SSR Worksheet is designed to carry forward the restructure cost when calculating the called return. The called return presented by the SSR Worksheet includes recuperation of the restructure cost. This function is very important to the success of the SSR. If the called return and restructure cost are not correctly accounted for, the position will be called out at a loss.

If uncalled, the return on this position will be 7.0 percent (see Table 5.4), and if called the return will be 10.2 percent (see Table 5.4). The investor is now back into productive management of this position and has a very high likelihood of exiting the entire position in one month's time through a call out. Remember, the cycle is now up, and that is why we are unable to buy back the TSS for income call profitably.

If the stock price continues up and does not reach the strike of the short call, the investor will keep the premium of the short call at expiration and also benefit from capital appreciation of the LEAPS. This situation often results in the investor being able to sell the LEAPS for an overall transaction profit immediately following worthless expiration of the short call. Exiting the position profitably does not specifically require a call out. This is a very important characteristic of the SSR technique.

Step 4: *Close the SSR and complete the transaction.* In this particular instance, the $25.00 January 2006 call expired worthless and the $15.00 January 2007 LEAPS was sold on the Monday following the third Friday. The transaction was closed for an overall profit (Figure 5.3).

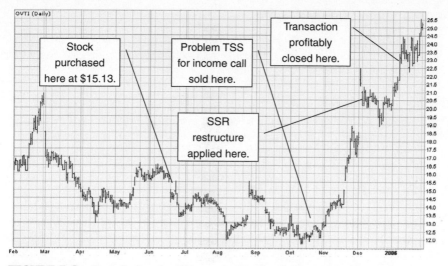

FIGURE 5.3 Completing the SSR transaction for the covered call position depicted in Figure 5.1.

The profit on the transaction was as follows:

Profit from TSS for income call sales and buybacks prior to SSR	$1.80
Loss on restructure	–$1.12
Profit from SSR $25.00 January 2006 call at expiration	$0.60
Profit from sale of LEAPS on Monday following January 2006 expiration	$1.17
Total OVTI transaction profit at closeout	$2.45
Profit on original $15.13 investment	16.2%

What if the SSR is uncalled and the LEAPS cannot be sold for an overall transaction profit? If the position is uncalled at January expiration and the transaction still cannot be closed for an overall profit, the investor should just resell the February 2006 $25.00 call provided that doing so results in a satisfactory uncalled return of 3 percent or more. If not, the position should be managed to exit like a regular LEAPS transaction. The process of managing a LEAPS transaction is discussed in Chapter 8.

Cardiopulmonary Resuscitation

Cardiopulmonary resuscitation (CPR) is an advanced covered call defensive technique that is used to literally resuscitate a fallen stock. The CPR has two typical applications:

1. To dramatically expedite the closing of a new covered call position where the stock price has suffered an immediate decline after entering the transaction. The CPR provides this ability as, in many cases, it allows the investor to lower the strike price of the short call in the near month, yet continue to maintain a positive called return.

2. To generate income and reduce the cost basis in a deeply depressed position. The CPR can effectively be applied where an underperforming stock is now in an upward cycle but the cycle's depth is too shallow to effectively use the TSS for income.

The Structure of a CPR   For any given stock position, the construction of a CPR is accomplished as follows:

1. An investor holds a long position of 100 shares of stock.
2. The investor buys one near month (or two month out) call.
3. The investor sells two near month (or two month out) calls with a higher strike price than the call selected in step 2.

In the preceding example, the investor owns 100 shares of stock, yet has sold two calls against the position. The stock holding covers one of these calls and the second call is covered by the purchase of the long call.

The CPR always follows this structure: The investor will always purchase the number of call options that relates to his or her stock holding and will always sell *two times* the number of call options that relates to his or her stock holding. For example, (1) an investor holds a long position of 300 shares of stock; (2) the investor buys three near month (or two month out) calls; and (3) the investor sells six near month (or two month out) calls with a higher strike price than the call selected in (2).

This structure of selling two times the number of calls than the investor purchases predominantly finances the purchase of the long call. This is an important structural aspect of the technique and limits the downside of the strategy in the event of an unfavorable stock price at expiration (discussed later in this section).

Let's look at the construction of a typical CPR on the stock FMD. The objective of this example is to illustrate the structure of the CPR. The rules for selecting expirations and strikes, timing, and pay-off scenarios are discussed later in this section.

Let's assume it's early January and John owns 100 shares of FMD at a cost of $32.50. A typical CPR construction as previously described would appear as follows:

1. John owns 100 shares of FMD at a cost of $32.50.
2. John buys one $25.00 January 06 call at $4.00.
3. John then sells two $30.00 January 06 calls at $1.50.

Understanding the Net Debit of a CPR Using the prices in the preceding example, John has outlaid $4.00 to purchase the $25.00 call, yet has received $3.00 by the sale of *two* $30.00 calls. The net cash cost of this CPR to John is $1.00 [$4.00 – (2 × $1.50)]. This $1.00 net cost when constructing a CPR is known as the *net debit*. The net debit should always be expressed on a per share basis:

Net debit = Price of long call – (2 × Price of short call)

It should now be clear that when an investor places a CPR, he or she is, in effect, purchasing a near-term call to take advantage of a rising stock price. This call, however, is being predominantly financed through the sale of two calls at a higher strike price. This financing limits the downside in case the stock price does not increase. If the stock price goes down significantly, the loss to the investor will be the $1.00 per share net debit rather than the $4.00 per share cost of buying the short-term call on its own.

The net debit of the CPR is the *maximum* loss to the investor. However, the cost of this limited downside to the investor is that the investor's upside is now *capped* at the strike price of the short call ($30.00 in this case). In the event that the stock price increases above the strike price of the short call, the investor will be called out of the position (both the stock position and the long option position) at the strike price of the short call.

In summary, the CPR provides very small downside to the investor. This downside is equal to the net debit. However, this small downside comes at a cost: The investor's upside is capped at the strike price of the short call.

Understanding the Payoff from a CPR Now that the structure of the CPR is understood, let's examine the payoff from the strategy. The rules for selecting expirations and strikes and timing are discussed later in this section. Continuing with the preceding example of John owning 100 shares of FMD at a cost of $32.50, a CPR would be constructed as follows:

1. John owns 100 shares of FMD at a cost of $32.50.
2. John buys one $25.00 January 06 call at $4.00 (near month).
3. John then sells two $30.00 January 06 calls at $1.50 (near month).

We now use the CPR Worksheet (part of the Covered Call Toolbox, one month's complementary access to which is available by going to www .compoundstockearnings.com/freemonth) to understand the payoff from the strategy at expiration of the long and short call options.

Table 5.5 shows the profit to the investor at various stock prices at expiration. A CPR is an *expiration-based strategy* meaning that once a CPR is constructed, it is generally held until expiration of the contracts. The highlighted line in the table shows the payoff of the strategy at various stock prices at expiration, represented as a percentage of the $32.50 investment in the stock.

CPR Is Unprofitable at Expiration   We can see from Table 5.5 that if the stock price finishes at $25.00 or below on the third Friday of January 2006, the CPR will lose the investor 3.1 percent of his or her $32.50 investment in the stock (a loss of $1.00). This loss is equal to the net debit and is computed as follows:

Long $25.00 strike call:
- Cost is $4.00
- Expired worthless
- Loss of $4.00

Short 2 × $30.00 strike call:
- Premium received is $3.00 ($1.50 × 2)
- Expired worthless
- Profit of $3.00

CPR return:
- Loss of $4.00 on long call
- Profit of $3.00 on short calls
- Net loss of $1.00

This $1.00 loss represents 3.1 percent of the $32.50 investment in the stock. Regardless of how low the stock price goes, the investor's maximum loss for this CPR is capped at the net debit of $1.00 or 3.1 percent.

The maximum loss of all CPRs is equal to the net debit of the transaction.

TABLE 5.5 Profit at Various Stock Prices at Expiration

					Stock Price at Expiration					
	$24.00	$25.00	$26.00	$27.00	$28.00	$29.00	$30.00	$31.00	$32.00
Long $25 and Short $30									
Will I get called out?	No	No	No	No	No	No	Yes	Yes	Yes
Profit (loss) if called based on cost							$ 1.50	$ 1.50	$ 1.50
How much did I get all up when called?							$34.00	$34.00	$34.00
Current market price to repurchase							$30.00	$31.00	$32.00
Cash return or called return %	−3.1%	−3.1%	0.0%	3.1%	6.2%	9.2%	4.6%	4.6%	4.6%

91

CPR Is Profitable at Expiration but Not Called Out   We can also see from Table 5.5 that this strategy becomes profitable at stock prices of $27.00 or greater at expiration. If the stock finishes the option month at $27.00, the profit from the CPR will be $1.00 or 3.1 percent of the $32.50 investment in the stock. This profit is computed as follows:

Long $25.00 strike call:
- Cost is $4.00
- Sell for intrinsic value of $2.00 on third Friday
- Loss of $2.00

Short 2 × $30.00 strike call:
- Premium received is $3.00 ($1.50 × 2)
- Expired worthless
- Profit of $3.00

CPR return:
- Loss of $2.00 on long call
- Profit of $3.00 on short calls
- Net profit of $1.00

This $1.00 profit represents 3.1 percent of the $32.50 investment in the stock. In order to realize this profit, the investor must take the following steps on the third Friday of expiration:

1. Buy back one of the short $30.00 calls. This buyback can normally be executed for $0.05, as the call will expire worthless at the end of the trading day. This buyback frees the long $25.00 call for sale, as it is no longer needed to cover one of the short calls.
2. Sell the long $25.00 call. The sale price will be around the intrinsic value of $2.00.
3. Allow the second call to expire worthless at the end of the trading day.

These three steps must be executed on the third Friday of expiration in all CPRs when (a) the long call is in the money and (b) the short call is out of the money (the CPR will not be called out). Following these steps allows the investor to salvage the intrinsic value in the long call before that call expires worthless or the broker automatically exercises it.

CPR Is Called Out at Expiration   In the event that the stock price finishes above the strike price of the short call, the short calls will be exercised and the position will be called out. This situation will generally occur only on the third Friday of expiration. Using the preceding FMD example, if the stock price is above $30.00 on the third Friday of January, the position will be called out. John will be required to deliver 200 shares of FMD stock at a price of $30.00. The following transactions will automatically occur in his account as a result of the call out:

- John's holding of 100 shares of FMD will be sold at the short call exercise price of $30.00. John's cost in FMD stock is $32.50, so he has sold the stock for a loss of $2.50 per share.
- John will keep the $3.00 premium received for the short calls.
- John has an obligation to deliver an additional 100 shares of FMD stock at $30.00 as he has sold two $30.00 calls. His broker will thus automatically exercise John's $25.00 strike call and he will buy 100 shares at this price. The broker will then automatically sell this stock at the short strike price of $30.00 to deliver John's obligations from the $30.00 short call. John has, therefore, purchased 100 FMD shares at $25.00 and immediately sold these at the short strike price of $30.00. He has made $5.00 profit per share on these 100 shares.
- John will then lose the $4.00 premium he paid for the long call option, as this call has now been exercised.
- Adding these figures, John's overall profit on call out is $1.50 or 4.6 percent of his $32.50 investment in the stock. This profit is computed as follows:

  (a) Loss of $2.50 per share on the stock sale plus

  (b) Profit of $3.00 per share from short call premium plus

  (c) Profit of $5.00 per share from buying the stock at $25.00 and selling at $30.00 plus

  (d) Loss of $4.00 per share from the exercised long option equals

  (c) Overall transaction return of $1.50 per share or 4.6 percent of the $32.50 investment in the stock.

We now understand that this CPR will be called out for a return of 4.6 percent if the stock price is above $30.00 at expiration. Importantly, regardless of how high the stock price is at expiration, John's called return is capped at 4.6 percent. He will receive the same called return regardless of how high above $30.00 the stock price is at expiration because his upside in the transaction has been capped by the sale of the $30.00 call option.

Understanding the CPR Worksheet Now that we understand the basic structure of the CPR, let's look at entering this particular transaction into the CPR Worksheet. The CPR Worksheet is part of the Covered Call Toolbox (one month's complementary access to which is available by going to www.compoundstockearnings.com/freemonth). The CPR Worksheet allows investors to quickly and accurately perform the following three tasks automatically:

1. Assess various strike prices and expirations to find the optimal CPR for a given position.
2. Calculate the net debit of the transaction.
3. Understand the profit and loss of the CPR at various stock prices at expiration.

We continue with the preceding example of assessing a CPR on FMD stock, which an investor owns at a cost of $32.50. The first step in assessing a CPR on this position is to enter the position details into the CPR Worksheet as indicated by the highlighted cells thereon.

CPR Worksheet Inputs   The inputs for our example as shown in Table 5.6 are:

- The stock code is FMD.
- The purchase price is the investor's cost of 32.50.
- The net premium to date is $0.00. For simplicity, we have assumed the investor has not made any income from call sales and buybacks. Importantly this figure is *net premium*. Net premium is cumulative call premium from closed positions only. When assessing a CPR you must not include the premium from an open call position. If an investor wishes to construct a CPR, the stock must not have an open call position. Any open call positions will first need to be closed. The profit or

TABLE 5.6   CPR Worksheet Inputs

Inputs

Stock	FMD			
Purchase price	$32.50			
Net premium to date	$ 0.00	0.0%		
P&L analysis—start price	$24.00			
P&L analysis—$ increment	$ 1.00			
CPR potential strikes	$25.00	$30.00		$35.00
Bid or ask	Ask	Bid	Ask	Bid
Option price	$ 4.00	$1.50	$1.65	$ 0.30
Net debit CPR with $25 and $30	$ 1.00	3.6%		
Net debit CPR with $30 and $35	$ 1.05	3.2%		

loss on closure should be included in total net premium to date on the position.

- The P&L analysis—start price is $24.00.
- The P&L analysis—$ increment is $1.00.
- The CPR potential strikes are $25.00, $30.00, and $35.00. The potential strikes were selected arbitrarily from the option chain. In general, the strikes that most often construct effective CPRs are in the range of two strikes in the money to two strikes out of the money. This is explained in more detail later in this chapter.
- The option prices entered are the relevant bid and the ask prices for the near month or near month + 1 contract. The CPR should always be constructed with the near month call if this call provides the desired return outcome. If it does not, the CPR can be constructed with near month + 1 contracts. This, again, is discussed in more detail later in this chapter.

Using the inputs provided, the CPR Worksheet then calculates the net debit for the two possible CPRs on this position.

Understanding the CPR Worksheet Outputs   Once the details of a particular position and the potential CPR strikes and market prices have been entered, the CPR Worksheet will produce the profit and loss from the particular CPR at various stock prices at expiration.

Table 5.7 shows the profit and loss scenarios for two different CPRs that have been generated by the CPR worksheet:

1. Long $25.00 and short $30.00
2. Long $30.00 and short $35.00

The investor then needs to assess both potential CPRs to select the best construction for the position. We achieve this by looking in Table 5.7 and comparing the rows "Cash Return or Called Return %" for each CPR. We can see that the $25.00 and $30.00 CPR becomes profitable with stock prices at expiration above $27.00 and that a profitable call out of 4.6 percent will occur at stock prices at expiration (one or two months away) of $30.00 and above (remember, the cost in the stock is $32.50). The maximum loss on this CPR is the net debit, which is 3.1 percent.

Alternatively, if the $30.00 and $35.00 strike CPR is selected, the CPR will become profitable at stock prices at expiration of $32.00 and above, and a positive called return of 19.8 percent will result with stock prices greater than $35.00 at expiration. We can see that this CPR needs a greater increase in the stock price in order to become profitable and provides more upside to the investor due to the higher strike price. Again, the maximum loss of this CPR is the net debit, which is 3.2 percent.

TABLE 5.7 Stock Breakeven Analysis

					Stock Price at Expiration						
	$25.00	$26.00	$27.00	$28.00	$29.00	$30.00	$31.00	$32.00	$33.00	$34.00	$35.00
Long $25 and Short $30											
Will I get called out?	No	No	No	No	No	Yes	Yes	Yes	Yes	Yes	Yes
Profit (loss) if called based on adj. cost						$ 1.50	$ 1.50	$ 1.50	$ 1.50	$ 1.50	$ 1.50
Do I need to rebuy stock?	No	No	No	No	No	No	No	No	No	No	No
How much did I get all up when called?						$34.00	$34.00	$34.00	$34.00	$34.00	$34.00
Current market price to repurchase						$30.00	$31.00	$32.00	$33.00	$34.00	$35.00
Reduction in cost/cash return						$ 1.50	$ 1.50	$ 1.50	$ 1.50	$ 1.50	$ 1.50
Cash return or called return $	–$ 1.00	$ 0.00	$ 1.00	$ 2.00	$ 3.00	$ 1.50	$ 1.50	$ 1.50	$ 1.50	$ 1.50	$ 1.50
Cash return or called return $	–$ 1.00	$ 0.00	$ 1.00	$ 2.00	$ 3.00	$ 1.50	$ 1.50	$ 1.50	$ 1.50	$ 1.50	$ 1.50
Cash return or called return %	–3.1%	0.0%	3.1%	6.2%	9.2%	4.6%	4.6%	4.6%	4.6%	4.6%	4.6%
Adjusted cost	$33.50	$32.50	$31.50	$30.50	$29.50	$28.50	$29.50	$30.50	$31.50	$32.50	$33.50
Profit or loss if immediately sell stock	–$ 8.50	–$ 6.50	–$ 4.50	–$ 2.50	–$ 0.50	$ 1.50	$ 1.50	$ 1.50	$ 1.50	$ 1.50	$ 1.50
Long $30 and Short $35											
Will I get called out?	No	No	No	No	No	No	No	No	No	No	Yes
Profit (loss) if called based on adj. cost											$ 6.45
Do I need to rebuy stock?	No	No	No	No	No	No	No	No	No	No	No
How much did I get all up when called?											$38.95
Current market price to repurchase											$35.00
Reduction in cost/cash return											$ 6.45
Cash return or called return $	–$ 1.05	–$ 1.05	–$ 1.05	–$ 1.05	–$ 1.05	–$ 1.05	–$ 0.05	$ 0.95	$ 1.95	$ 2.95	$ 6.45
Cash return or called return $	–$ 1.05	–$ 1.05	–$ 1.05	–$ 1.05	–$ 1.05	–$ 1.05	–$ 0.05	$ 0.95	$ 1.95	$ 2.95	$ 6.45
Cash return or called return %	–3.2%	–3.2%	–3.2%	–3.2%	–3.2%	–3.2%	–0.2%	2.9%	6.0%	9.1%	19.8%
Adjusted cost	$33.55	$33.55	$33.55	$33.55	$33.55	$33.55	$32.55	$31.55	$30.55	$29.55	$28.55
Profit or loss if immediately sell stock	–$ 8.55	–$ 7.55	–$ 6.55	–$ 5.55	–$ 4.55	–$ 3.55	–$ 1.55	$ 0.45	$ 2.45	$ 4.45	$ 6.45

For this particular position, at this moment in time, the CPR should be constructed using the $25.00 and $30.00 strike. While both positions will provide a positive called return, the $25.00 and $30.00 strike CPR:

- Becomes profitable at stock prices above $27.00 versus $32.00 for the higher strike CPR. (See the "Cash Return or Called Return %" row in Table 5.7.)
- Will allow the investor to exit the position through a call out at a price of $30.00 versus an exit price of $32.00 for the higher strike CPR. *Note:* A call out will occur for the $30.00 and $35.00 CPR at a price of $35.00; however, the position will be able to be profitably closed at a stock price at expiration of $32.00 or greater because the CPR, at a stock price of $32.00 at expiration, generates uncalled return of $0.95. This uncalled return lowers the investor's cost in the stock to $31.55 ($32.50 – $0.95). The investor can then sell the stock at the current market price of $32.00 to realize a net return of $0.45 ($32.00 – $31.55) or 2.9 percent.
- Provides much lower likelihood of losing the net debit of the transaction as this occurs at stock price of $25.00 and below versus $30.00 and below for the higher strike CPR.

To summarize, the $25.00 and $30.00 CPR is superior as it will provide higher levels of profit at lower stock prices; will allow the investor to exit the entire position at a significantly lower stock price at expiration; and provides less likelihood of the investor realizing a loss equal to the net debit.

In all instances where both potential CPRs provide a positive called return, the CPR that provides the lowest profitable exit price should be used. The objective of a CPR that has a positive called return is to exit the position profitably at the lowest possible stock price at expiration. We discuss later in this chapter the objectives of a CPR that does not provide a profitable called return.

Applying the CPR Technique   The CPR has two typical applications:

1. To dramatically expedite the closing of a new covered call position where the stock price has suffered a decline after entering the transaction.
2. To generate income and reduce the cost basis in a depressed position where the cycle of the stock is now increasing but this cycle is too shallow to effectively use the TSS for income.

Using the CPR to Expedite the Close of a New Covered Call Position
Using the CPR to expedite the close of a new covered call position is its

most significant function. When the stock price falls after entering a new covered call position, correct use of the CPR allows an investor, in most instances, to lower the strike price of the near month call yet maintain a positive called return. This stance greatly increases the likelihood that the position will be called out for a profit. Take the following simplified example for illustration of this function:

- Stock is purchased in January at $34.00 and the January $35.00 strike call is sold for $1.50.
- Stock price falls sharply to $30.00 and the call can now be bought to close for $0.80, leaving a profit of $0.70, or 2.0 percent.
- Immediately apply CPR with January expirations at strikes of $25.00 and $30.00.
- Yield enhancement in the form of uncalled return will occur at stock prices greater than $27.00 at expiration.
- Profitable call out will now occur at a stock price of $30.00 rather than the original call sale strike of $35.00, resulting in a 15 percent reduction in the profitable call out price. This reduction is very significant.

We can see, then, that the CPR was used as a defensive measure on a new covered call position immediately following a large decline in the stock price. The CPR had the effect of enhancing uncalled return at stock prices higher than $27.00 and, more important, lowering the profitable call out price from a $35.00 strike to $30.00. This defensive outcome is regularly achievable using the CPR technique on newly established covered call positions that fall.

The following example illustrates the complete process of using the CPR to expedite the close of a covered call position on a fallen stock.

Step 1: *Enter a new covered call position.* In mid-December (Figure 5.4), a new covered call position was identified and executed as follows:

- BTO 500 FMD @ $33.33
- STO 5 FMD $35.00 Jan 06 calls @ $1.35

The stock met the fundamental requirements for investment, was an upward moving stock, and was in the bottom 25 percent of the rising price cycle. A few days after entering the position, the stock fell 16 percent to $28.00. This is an ideal time to assess a potential CPR to expedite the close of this fallen position (Figure 5.5).

Step 2: *Assess the potential CPR and execute if acceptable.* We now hold a covered call position on FMD, which, in all likelihood, will not be called out at the end of the month due to the call being sold at a strike of

FIGURE 5.4   Entering a covered call on FMD.

$35.00 and the current stock price being around $28.00. However, we do have a profit in the call due to the fall in the stock. This profit is significantly to our advantage when we construct the CPR. Without the profit in the buy-back of the call, the CPR may not be able to be structured with a positive called return.

We then enter the details of the position and the option contracts we may use into the CPR Worksheet as shown in Table 5.8.

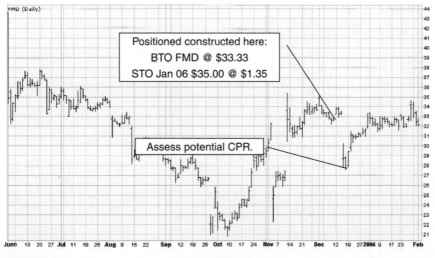

FIGURE 5.5   When to assess the need for CPR.

TABLE 5.8   CPR Worksheet Inputs Pertaining to Figure 5.5

Inputs

Stock	FMD			
Purchase price	$33.33			
Net premium to date	$ 0.95	2.9%		
P&L analysis—start price	$25.00			
P&L analysis—$ increment	$ 1.00			
CPR potential strikes	$25.00	$30.00		$35.00
Bid or ask	Ask	Bid	Ask	Bid
Option price	$ 4.00	$1.40	$1.45	$ 0.30
Net debit CPR with $25 and $30	$ 1.20	3.6%		
Net debit CPR with $30 and $35	$ 0.85	2.6%		

In this instance, the option expiration selected is January. January is the same month as the original call sold when entering the position. It is our preference to use the January expiration; however, February can be used in the event that a CPR cannot be favorably constructed with January expirations. Favorable construction in this regard is a CPR with a positive called return.

You will also notice that net premium to date has been entered into the CPR Worksheet as $0.95. If we wish to construct this CPR, we will need to buy to close the open January 06 $35 call, which we originally sold for $1.35. The ask price for this contract when assessing the CPR was $0.40. Buying back the call at this price will realize net premium of $0.95. The net premium we receive when buying back the call is critical to the CPR construction having adequate called return.

The CPR Worksheet produces the output as shown in Table 5.9. We can see that both CPRs will provide a positive called return. From previous discussion, we know that when assessing two CPRs that both have positive called returns, the CPR with the lowest strike prices should always be selected. The reasons for this choice have been explained previously and are not repeated here. As such, we will immediately apply the CPR with $25.00 and $30.00 strikes to this stock. The process is as follows:

- Buy back five January 06 $35.00 calls at $0.40 for a gain of $0.95, or 2.9 percent.
- BTO 5 Jan 06 $25.00 calls at $4.00.
- STO 10 Jan 06 $30.00 calls at $1.40.
- The net debit is $1.20, or 3.6 percent.

We have now executed the CPR (see Figure 5.6).

TABLE 5.9 Stock Breakeven Analysis Pertaining to Figure 5.5

	Stock Price at Expiration										
	$25.00	$26.00	$27.00	$28.00	$29.00	$30.00	$31.00	$32.00	$33.00	$34.00	$35.00
Long $25 and Short $30											
Will I get called out?	No	No	No	No	No	Yes	Yes	Yes	Yes	Yes	Yes
Profit (loss) if called based on adj. cost						$ 1.42	$ 1.42	$ 1.42	$ 1.42	$ 1.42	$ 1.42
Do I need to rebuy stock?	No	No	No	No	No	No	No	No	No	No	No
How much did I get all up when called?						$33.80	$33.80	$33.80	$33.80	$33.80	$33.80
Current market price to repurchase						$30.00	$31.00	$32.00	$33.00	$34.00	$35.00
Called return						$ 1.42	$ 1.42	$ 1.42	$ 1.42	$ 1.42	$ 1.42
Uncalled return $	–$ 0.25	$ 0.75	$ 1.75	$ 2.75	$ 3.75						
Uncalled or called return $	–$ 0.25	$ 0.75	$ 1.75	$ 2.75	$ 3.75	$ 1.42	$ 1.42	$ 1.42	$ 1.42	$ 1.42	$ 1.42
Uncalled or called return %	–0.8%	2.3%	5.3%	8.3%	11.3%	4.3%	4.3%	4.3%	4.3%	4.3%	4.3%
Adjusted cost	$33.53	$32.58	$31.58	$30.58	$29.58	$28.58	$29.58	$30.58	$31.58	$32.58	$33.58
Profit or loss if immediately sell stock	–$ 8.53	–$ 6.58	–$ 4.58	–$ 2.58	–$ 0.58	$ 1.42	$ 1.42	$ 1.42	$ 1.42	$ 1.42	$ 1.42
Long $30 and Short $35											
Will I get called out?	No	No	No	No	No	No	No	No	No	No	Yes
Profit (loss) if called based on adj. cost											$ 6.77
Do I need to rebuy stock?	No	No	No	No	No	No	No	No	No	No	No
How much did I get all up when called?											$39.15
Current market price to repurchase											$35.00
Called return											$ 6.77
Uncalled return $	$ 0.10	$ 0.10	$ 0.10	$ 0.10	$ 0.10	$ 0.10	$ 1.10	$ 2.10	$ 3.10	$ 4.10	
Uncalled or called return $	$ 0.10	$ 0.10	$ 0.10	$ 0.10	$ 0.10	$ 0.10	$ 1.10	$ 2.10	$ 3.10	$ 4.10	$ 6.77
Uncalled or called return %	0.3%	0.3%	0.3%	0.3%	0.3%	0.3%	3.3%	6.3%	9.3%	12.3%	20.3%
Adjusted cost	$33.23	$33.23	$33.23	$33.23	$33.23	$33.23	$32.23	$31.23	$30.23	$29.23	$28.23
Profit or loss if immediately sell stock	–$ 8.23	–$ 7.23	–$ 6.23	–$ 5.23	–$ 4.23	–$ 3.23	–$ 1.23	$ 0.77	$ 2.77	$ 4.77	$ 6.77

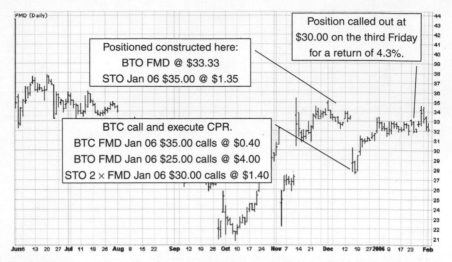

FIGURE 5.6   Using CPR to profitably close out of an underperforming covered call position.

Step 3: *Wait for expiration Friday of the calls.* Our profit and loss on the position at January expiration is shown in Table 5.10.

It is very important to understand that the returns presented by the CPR Worksheet include the net premium to date. Therefore, all cash returns and called returns in the Worksheet include the $0.95 already made in net premium.

For example, this position will be called out at stock prices above $30.00. The return on call out will be a total transaction return of 4.3 percent. The called return is not 4.3 percent plus the 2.9 percent already realized in net premium. Additionally, at a stock price at expiration of $27.00, the cash return will be 5.3 percent. This is the total transaction cash return and includes the net premium to date of 2.9 percent. All returns presented by the CPR Worksheet are *overall* transaction returns and include any net premium to date.

If the stock finishes the option month above $30.00, we will be called out for an overall transaction return of 4.3 percent. Originally, our profitable call out strike was $35.00 so we have drastically lowered the profitable exit price of this position. This is the most important aspect of the CPR technique. The technique is designed to profitably expedite the close out of an underperforming covered call position through lowering of the strike price while maintaining a positive transaction called return.

If the stock finishes the option month between $25.00 and $30.00, the position will not be called out, yet the investor will be left with a cash return

TABLE 5.10 Stock Breakeven Analysis

Inputs

Stock	FMD	
Purchase price	$33.33	
Net premium to date	$ 0.95	2.9%
P&L analysis—start price	$25.50	
P&L analysis—$ increment	$ 1.00	

CPR potential strikes	$25.00	$30.00		$35.00
Bid or ask	Ask	Bid	Ask	Bid
Option price	$ 4.00	$1.40	$1.45	$ 0.30

Net debit CPR with $25 and $30	$ .20	3.6%
Net debit CPR with $30 and $35	$ 0.85	2.6%

Stock Price at Expiration

	$25.50	$26.00	$26.50	$27.00	$27.50	$28.00	$28.50	$29.00	$29.50	$30.00	$30.50
Long $25 and Short $30											
Will I get called out?	No	No	No	No	No	No	No	No	No	Yes	Yes
Profit (loss) if called based on adj. cost										$ 1.42	$ 1.42
Do I need to rebuy stock?	No	No	No	No	No	No	No	No	No	No	No
How much did I get all up when called?										$33.80	$33.80
Current market price to repurchase										$30.00	$30.50
Called return										$ 1.42	$ 1.42
Uncalled return $	$ 0.25	$ 0.75	$ 1.25	$ 1.75	$ 2.25	$ 2.75	$ 3.25	$ 3.75	$ 4.25		
Uncalled or called return $	$ 0.25	$ 0.75	$ 1.25	$ 1.75	$ 2.25	$ 2.75	$ 3.25	$ 3.75	$ 4.25	$ 1.42	$ 1.42
Uncalled or called return %	0.3%	2.3%	3.8%	5.3%	6.8%	8.3%	9.8%	11.3%	12.8%	4.3%	4.3%
Adjusted cost	$33.08	$32.58	$32.08	$31.58	$31.08	$30.58	$30.08	$29.58	$29.08	$28.58	$28.08
Profit or loss if immediately sell stock	–$ 7.58	–$ 6.58	–$ 5.58	–$ 4.58	–$ 3.58	–$ 2.58	–$ 1.58	–$ 0.58	$ 0.42	$ 1.42	$ 1.42

from the CPR. To realize this return, on the third Friday, the investor will need to buy back 5 of the 10 short $30.00 calls and then sell all 5 long $25.00 calls. This process will allow the investor to realize the intrinsic value in the long option before it expires or is exercised automatically by the broker. This process is discussed in detail in the earlier section, "CPR Is Profitable at Expiration but Not Called Out."

If the stock finishes the option month below $25.00, we will lose the net debit of the transaction or 3.6 percent. This loss will be compensated for by the 2.9 percent profit realized from net premium to date. As such, the maximum negative net cash return for the month will be just 0.8 percent. As you can see, there is very small downside to the correct application of the CPR technique. See Table 5.11.

What if the CPR Worksheet does not produce a CPR with a positive called return? If the CPR Worksheet does not produce a transaction with a positive called return using near month or near month + 1 expirations or, in assessing the cycle of the stock, the higher strike price CPR seems to require an unrealistically large movement in the stock price to become profitable, we will simply *wait* for a further increase in the stock price, which will improve the profitability of the potential CPRs.

If at any time an investor is waiting for an improvement in a CPR return before executing the CPR and a call can be sold that meets the secondary call sale rules such as a TSS for income, then these rules should be immediately followed.

Using the CPR Where the Called Return Is Negative   Another useful function of the CPR technique is to generate income and reduce the cost basis on a deeply depressed position. The CPR can effectively be applied where a stock is now in an upward cycle but the cycle's depth is too shallow to effectively use the TSS for income. A cycle with such characteristics is often evident in a stock that has suffered one of the following fates:

- A quick and sharp price decline that is normally the result of a negative news or earnings announcement causing the stock to consolidate in a gradual upward moving or sideways moving cycle.
- A long and protracted decline over a period of months and the stock is now upward moving or sideways moving.

In most instances where the CPR is applied on a deeply depressed stock, an effective CPR cannot be constructed with a positive called return. The investor will, therefore, construct a CPR with a profitable *range* of stock prices at expiration. If the stock price is below this range at expiration, the investor will lose the net debit. If the stock breaks cycle, begins a more aggressive upward cycle, and is above the profitable range, this action can result in the CPR being unprofitable.

TABLE 5.11   Stock Breakeven Analysis

						Stock Price at Expiration					
	$24.00	$24.50	$25.00	$25.50	$26.00	$26.50	$27.00	$27.50	$28.00	$28.50	$29.00
Long $25 and Short $30											
Will I get called out?	No	No	No	No	No	No	No	No	No	No	No
Profit (loss) if called based on adj. cost											
Do I need to rebuy stock?	No	No	No	No	No	No	No	No	No	No	No
How much did I get all up when called?											
Current market price to repurchase											
Called return											
Uncalled return $	–$ 0.25	–$ 0.25	–$ 0.25	$ 0.25	$ 0.75	$ 1.25	$ 1.75	$ 2.25	$ 2.75	$ 3.25	$ 3.75
Uncalled or called return $	–$ 0.25	–$ 0.25	–$ 0.25	$ 0.25	$ 0.75	$ 1.25	$ 1.75	$ 2.25	$ 2.75	$ 3.25	$ 3.75
Uncalled or called return %	–0.8%	–0.8%	–0.8%	0.8%	2.3%	3.8%	5.3%	6.8%	8.3%	9.8%	11.3%
Adjusted cost	$33.58	$33.58	$33.58	$33.08	$32.58	$32.08	$31.58	$31.08	$30.58	$30.08	$29.58
Profit or loss if immediately sell stock	–$ 9.58	–$ 9.08	–$ 8.58	–$ 7.58	–$ 6.58	–$ 5.58	–$ 4.58	–$ 3.58	–$ 2.58	–$ 1.58	–$ 0.58

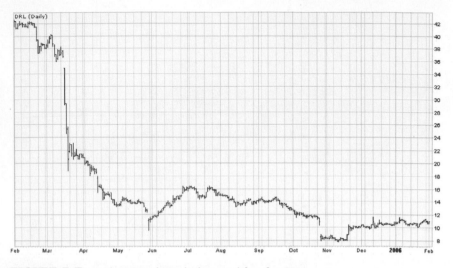

FIGURE 5.7   A depressed stock that qualifies for CPR.

Let's look at an example of implementing the CPR on a deeply depressed stock. Let's assume we own 500 shares of DRL at a cost of $20.00.

Step 1: *Assess the cycle of the stock you wish to CPR.* When a stock is trading deeply below an investor's cost, it is unlikely that a CPR can be constructed using near month or near month + 1 expirations that has a positive called return. If a CPR has a negative called return, it can only be constructed when (1) the stock is in a current upward cycle and (2) the distance between the upper and lower lines of the price cycle is $1.50 or less. If the cycle of the stock does not comply with both (1) and (2), then it is more advantageous for the investor to use the TSS for income on the position.

We can see from Figure 5.7 that DRL is currently stabilizing from severe price declines in the preceding months. DRL qualifies for CPR as it is both an up cycling stock (the bottoms and tops of the current cycle are getting higher) and the current cycle has less than $1.50 of price depth. We can, therefore, assume that the CPR technique can be used on this stock at this point in time rather than the TSS for income.

Step 2: *Input the position data into the CPR Worksheet.* For the purpose of this example, the January 06 expirations were used. At the time of writing, the January contract had 40 days to expiration. See Table 5.12. Note that in this instance, the net premium to date is set at $0.00.

When assessing a CPR that will not result in a positive called return, the net premium should *always* be set to $0.00 regardless of the income earned on the position in the past. We use $0.00 because we are attempting to generate additional income on the position and need to understand the

TABLE 5.12   CPR Worksheet Inputs

Inputs

Stock	FMD				
Purchase price	$20.00				
Net premium to date	$ 0.00	0.0%			
P&L analysis—start price	$ 9.50				
P&L analysis—$ increment	$ 0.50				
CPR potential strikes	$10.00		$12.50		$15.00
Bid or ask	Ask	Bid		Ask	Bid
Option price	$ 2.00	$0.55		$0.60	$ 0.10
Net debit CPR with $10 and $12.50	$ 0.90	4.5%			
Net debit CPR with $12.50 and $15	$ 0.40	2.0%			

profitability of the CPR as an independent strategy. We are not looking to the CPR as a tool to lower the exit price of the stock, as we would if the called return were positive.

Step 3: *Assess the CPR Worksheet outputs.* The CPR worksheet provides the profit and loss of the two potential CPRs. See Table 5.13. The stock price at time of writing was $11.60. The optimal CPR for this position is the $10.00 and $12.50 CPR. This CPR will provide an enhancement to return at stock prices between $11.00 and $14.00 at expiration. This result compares to the $12.50 and $15.00 CPR that does not become profitable until the stock price reaches $13.00—a required increase of 12.1 percent in a month.

If the stock finishes the option month above $12.50 but less than $14.00, the investor will be called out. This call out will be at a loss, but will still result in the investor earning an uncalled return on the position.

We see from Table 5.14 that if the investor is called out, the loss on call out will be $5.90. This loss on call out is calculated as the total capital received on call out ($14.10) minus the cost in the stock ($20.00).

In situations where the investor is called out in a CPR and that call out will be unprofitable, the investor will need to rebuy the stock on the Monday following expiration as the position is yet to be closed for an overall transaction profit. The difference between the total capital received on call out and the current market price to repurchase is the called return in a CPR where the call out is unprofitable versus the investor's overall cost.

Let's look at an example using Table 5.14 and assuming a stock price at expiration of $13.00. In this scenario, the investor will be called out on the third Friday. Total capital received will be $14.10. If the stock price at expiration is $13.00, the investor will be able to repurchase the stock on the

TABLE 5.13 Stock Breakeven Analysis

						Stock Price at Expiration						
	$ 9.50	$10.00	$10.50	$11.00	$11.50	$12.00	$12.50	$13.00	$13.50	$14.00	$14.50	$15.00
Long $10 and Short $12.50												
Will I get called out?	No	No	No	No	No	No	Yes	Yes	Yes	Yes	Yes	Yes
Profit (loss) if called based on adj. cost							-$ 5.90	-$ 5.90	-$ 5.90	-$ 5.90	-$ 5.90	-$ 5.90
Do I need to rebuy stock?	No	No	No	No	No	No	Yes	Yes	Yes	Yes	Yes	Yes
How much did I get all up when called?							$14.10	$14.10	$14.10	$14.10	$14.10	$14.10
Current market price to repurchase							$12.50	$13.00	$13.50	$14.00	$14.50	$15.00
Called return							$ 1.60	$ 1.10	$ 0.60	$ 0.10	-$ 0.40	-$ 0.90
Uncalled return $	-$ 0.90	-$ 0.90	-$ 0.40	$ 0.10	$ 0.60	$ 1.10						
Uncalled or called return $	-$ 0.90	-$ 0.90	-$ 0.40	$ 0.10	$ 0.60	$ 1.10	$ 1.60	$ 1.10	$ 0.60	$ 0.10	-$ 0.40	-$ 0.90
Uncalled or called return %	-4.5%	-4.5%	-2.0%	0.5%	3.0%	5.5%	8.0%	5.5%	3.0%	0.5%	-2.0%	-4.5%
Adjusted cost	$20.90	$20.90	$20.40	$19.90	$19.40	$18.90	$18.40	$18.90	$19.40	$19.90	$20.40	$20.90
Profit or loss if immediately sell stock	-$11.40	-$10.90	-$ 9.90	-$ 8.90	-$ 7.90	-$ 6.90	-$ 5.90	-$ 5.90	-$ 5.90	-$ 5.90	-$ 5.90	-$ 5.90

Long $12.50 and Short $15

Will I get called out?	No	No	No	No	No	No	No	No	No	No	No	Yes
Profit (loss) if called based on adj. cost												–$ 2.90
Do I need to rebuy stock?	No	No	No	No	No	No	No	No	No	No	No	Yes
How much did I get all up when called?												$17.10
Current market price to repurchase												$15.00
Called return												$ 2.10
Uncalled return $	–$ 0.40	–$ 0.40	–$ 0.40	–$ 0.40	–$ 0.40	–$ 0.40	–$ 0.40	$ 0.10	$ 0.60	$ 1.10	$ 1.60	
Uncalled or called return $	–$ 0.40	–$ 0.40	–$ 0.40	–$ 0.40	–$ 0.40	–$ 0.40	–$ 0.40	$ 0.10	$ 0.60	$ 1.10	$ 1.60	$ 2.10
Uncalled or called return %	–2.0%	–2.0%	–2.0%	–2.0%	–2.0%	–2.0%	–2.0%	0.5%	3.0%	5.5%	8.0%	10.5%
Adjusted cost	$20.40	$20.40	$20.40	$20.40	$20.40	$20.40	$20.40	$19.90	$19.40	$18.90	$18.40	$17.90
Profit or loss if immediately sell stock	–$10.90	–$10.40	–$ 9.90	–$ 9.40	–$ 8.90	–$ 8.40	–$ 7.90	–$ 6.90	–$ 5.90	–$ 4.90	–$ 3.90	–$ 2.90

TABLE 5.14 Stock Breakeven Analysis

				Stock Price at Expiration					
	$12.00	$12.50	$13.00	$13.50	$14.00	$14.50	$15.00	$15.50	$16.00
Long $10 and Short $12.50									
Will I get called out?	No	Yes	Yes	Yes	Yes	Yes	Yes	Yes	Yes
Profit (loss) if called based on adj. cost		–$ 5.90	–$ 5.90	–$ 5.90	–$ 5.90	–$ 5.90	–$ 5.90	–$ 5.90	–$ 5.90
Do I need to rebuy stock?	No	Yes	Yes	Yes	Yes	Yes	Yes	Yes	Yes
How much did I get all up when called?		$14.10	$14.10	$14.10	$14.10	$14.10	$14.10	$14.10	$14.10
Current market price to repurchase		$12.50	$13.00	$13.50	$14.00	$14.50	$15.00	$15.50	$16.00
Called return		$ 1.60	$ 1.10	$ 0.60	$ 0.10	–$ 0.40	–$ 0.90	–$ 1.40	–$ 1.90
Uncalled return $	$ 1.10								
Uncalled or called return $	$ 1.10	$ 1.60	$ 1.10	$ 0.60	$ 0.10	–$ 0.40	–$ 0.90	–$ 1.40	–$ 1.90
Uncalled or called return %	5.5%	8.0%	5.5%	3.0%	0.5%	–2.0%	–4.5%	–7.0%	–9.5%
Adjusted cost	$18.90	$18.40	$18.90	$19.40	$19.90	$20.40	$20.90	$21.40	$21.90
Profit or loss if immediately sell stock	–$ 6.90	–$ 5.90	–$ 5.90	–$ 5.90	–$ 5.90	–$ 5.90	–$ 5.90	–$ 5.90	–$ 5.90

Monday following the third Friday for around the $13.00. This $13.00 amount is *less than* the $14.10 total capital received on call out. In this instance, the investor will repurchase the stock for $13.00, yet the investor has just been called out for a total of $14.10, which is a $1.10 difference.

The investor has generated a return of $14.10 − $13.00 = $1.10, or 5.5 percent. This $1.10 return is, in effect, uncalled return, or "free net cash return"; it is the same as the uncalled return received on a profitable call buyback or call expiration. It can be used to invest in other positions or to reduce the cost basis or amortize the investment in the stock.

If the stock finishes the option month between $10.00 and $12.50, the position will not be called out. The investor will need to take action to realize the uncalled return or minimize the loss of the CPR. See Table 5.15.

As previously outlined, when the long call of the CPR finishes in the money and the short call finishes out of the money, the investor must take action on the third Friday of expiration to realize the intrinsic value in the contract before it expires or is automatically exercised by the broker. This process is discussed in detail in the preceding material and will involve the investor taking the following steps on the third Friday of expiration:

1. Buy back half the short calls at around to $0.05 (they will expire worthless at the end of the day).
2. Sell the entire holding of long calls. This price realized will be around intrinsic value.
3. Allow the other half of the short calls to expire worthless at the end of the trading day.

Following this process when there is intrinsic value in the long call yet the short calls are out of the money ensures that the uncalled return will be realized or the loss on the CPR will be minimized.

We can see from Table 5.15 that any stock price at expiration greater than $10.00 and less than $12.50 will require this action. Importantly, at a stock price of $10.50 at expiration, this action will still need to be taken. The result will be a loss on the CPR of 2.0 percent, rather than a loss of the entire net debit of 4.5 percent.

If the stock finishes the option month below $10.00, then both calls will expire worthless leaving the investor with a loss equal to the net debit of 4.5 percent. Regardless of how low the stock price goes, this is the maximum loss of the CPR.

If the stock finishes the option month above $14.00, the investor will be called out for a loss and will not be able to repurchase the stock for less than the $14.10 received at call out. See Table 5.16. In this instance, the investor will need to repurchase the stock at the higher market price and add

TABLE 5.15 Stock Breakeven Analysis

	Stock Price at Expiration								
	$10.00	**$10.50**	**$11.00**	**$11.50**	**$12.00**	**$12.50**	**$13.00**	**$13.50**	**$14.00**
Long $10 and Short $12.50									
Will I get called out?	No	No	No	No	No	Yes	Yes	Yes	Yes
Profit (loss) if called based on adj. cost						–$ 5.90	–$ 5.90	–$ 5.90	–$ 5.90
Do I need to rebuy stock?	No	No	No	No	No	Yes	Yes	Yes	Yes
How much did I get all up when called?						$14.10	$14.10	$14.10	$14.10
Current market price to repurchase						$12.50	$13.00	$13.50	$14.00
Called return						$ 1.60	$ 1.10	$ 0.60	$ 0.10
Uncalled return $	–$ 0.90	–$ 0.40	$ 0.10	$ 0.60	$ 1.10				
Uncalled or called return $	–$ 0.90	–$ 0.40	$ 0.10	$ 0.60	$ 1.10	$ 1.60	$ 1.10	$ 0.60	$ 0.10
Uncalled or called return %	–4.5%	–2.0%	0.5%	3.0%	5.5%	8.0%	5.5%	3.0%	0.5%
Adjusted cost	$20.90	$20.40	$19.90	$19.40	$18.90	$18.40	$18.90	$19.40	$19.90
Profit or loss if immediately sell stock	–$10.90	–$ 9.90	–$ 8.90	–$ 7.90	–$ 6.90	–$ 5.90	–$ 5.90	–$ 5.90	–$ 5.90

TABLE 5.16 Stock Breakeven Analysis

	Stock Price at Expiration								
	$13.00	**$13.50**	**$14.00**	**$14.50**	**$15.00**	**$15.50**	**$16.00**	**$16.50**	**$17.00**
Long $10 and Short $12.50									
Will I get called out?	Yes	Yes	Yes	Yes	Yes	Yes	Yes	Yes	Yes
Profit (loss) if called based on adj. cost	–$ 5.90	–$ 5.90	–$ 5.90	–$ 5.90	–$ 5.90	–$ 5.90	–$ 5.90	–$ 5.90	–$ 5.90
Do I need to rebuy stock?	Yes	Yes	Yes	Yes	Yes	Yes	Yes	Yes	Yes
How much did I get all up when called?	$14.10	$14.10	$14.10	$14.10	$14.10	$14.10	$14.10	$14.10	$14.10
Current market price to repurchase	$13.00	$13.50	$14.00	$14.50	$15.00	$15.50	$16.00	$16.50	$17.00
Called return	$ 1.10	$ 0.60	$ 0.10	–$ 0.40	–$ 0.90	–$ 1.40	–$ 1.90	–$ 2.40	–$ 2.90
Uncalled return $									
Uncalled or called return $	$ 1.10	$ 0.60	$ 0.10	–$ 0.40	–$ 0.90	–$ 1.40	–$ 1.90	–$ 2.40	–$ 2.90
Uncalled or called return %	5.5%	3.0%	0.5%	–2.0%	–4.5%	–7.0%	–9.5%	–12.0%	–14.5%
Adjusted cost	$18.90	$19.40	$19.90	$20.40	$20.90	$21.40	$21.90	$22.40	$22.90
Profit or loss if immediately sell stock	–$ 5.90	–$ 5.90	–$ 5.90	–$ 5.90	–$ 5.90	–$ 5.90	–$ 5.90	–$ 5.90	–$ 5.90

this expense to the overall cost of the position. Importantly, CPRs are constructed with near month or near month + 1 expirations and on stocks with
very little depth in the cycle. Extremely dramatic stock price movements are
unlikely. In the preceding example, DRL's stock price at execution of the
CPR was $11.60. The CPR becomes unprofitable at stock price of $14.00
and higher and thus would require an increase of 20.7 percent [($14.00 −
$11.60)/$11.60)] in one month for the CPR to become profitable. This is a
very dramatic and highly improbable increase given the cycle of the stock.

More importantly, an increase in the stock price of this magnitude (20+
percent) in such a short period (one month) would normally indicate that
some fundamental changes have occurred that have increased the market's
forecast for the company's future earnings. It is therefore likely that the
stock price will continue to increase, and the position will no longer be
underperforming.

PART II

Calendar LEAPS Spreads

CALENDAR LEAPS SPREAD PROCESS FLOWCHART

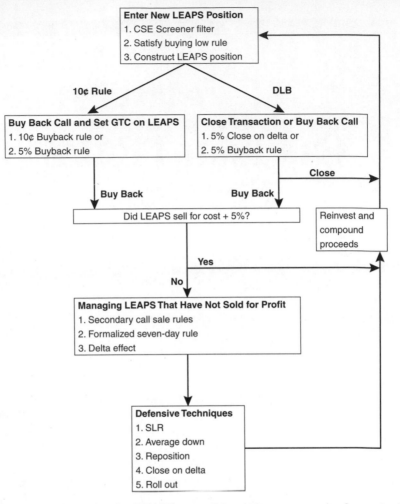

Enter New LEAPS Position
1. CSE Screener filter
2. Satisfy buying low rule
3. Construct LEAPS position

10¢ Rule

DLB

Buy Back Call and Set GTC on LEAPS
1. 10¢ Buyback rule or
2. 5% Buyback rule

Close Transaction or Buy Back Call
1. 5% Close on delta or
2. 5% Buyback rule

Close

Buy Back

Buy Back

Did LEAPS sell for cost + 5%?

Reinvest and compound proceeds

Yes

No

Managing LEAPS That Have Not Sold for Profit
1. Secondary call sale rules
2. Formalized seven-day rule
3. Delta effect

Defensive Techniques
1. SLR
2. Average down
3. Reposition
4. Close on delta
5. Roll out

Each step in the calendar LEAPS spread investing process is shown in the flowchart above—from entering new positions, to managing positions for income, to LEAPS defensive techniques. As with covered calls, investors who are accomplished with our LEAPS method understand that there is a specific technique to address every situation that may occur in the markets. However, when contrasted to covered calls, there are significantly more management and defensive techniques in LEAPS investing. Further, the addition of leverage to the strategy makes LEAPS much more responsive to management when compared to traditional covered calls. Part II of this book will elaborate on, expand on, and provide an example of each step presented in the calendar LEAPS spread process flowchart. You may wish to revisit this flowchart at the beginning of each new topic so you can gain an understanding of where a particular rule or technique is applied in the overall investment process.

CHAPTER 6

An Introduction to Calendar LEAPS Spreads

As noted in Chapter 5, LEAPS stands for long-term equity anticipation security. Despite this complicated name, LEAPS are just long-term options. They are exactly the same as normal options, but allow investors to establish positions with expirations of up to three years.

The use of calendar LEAPS spreads is a technique similar to, yet more sophisticated than, traditional covered calls. The mind-set for using the technique remains the same as for using covered calls (see Chapter 2). However, it is a technique to be used only by investors who have developed a consistent track record of success with the covered call technique. The LEAPS technique requires a greater time commitment than covered calls, but provides the potential for higher returns because the compounding effect is magnified many times over. It is, therefore, ideally suited to those who aspire to eventually make a full-time career out of the markets or those who have more time to commit to their investments.

Calendar LEAPS spreads are most easily performed in the U.S. market. If you wish to use them from outside the United States, you will have to sacrifice by adapting to working for reasonable lengths of time at unusual hours. However, the potential returns from this technique for experienced investors certainly justify such a sacrifice.

In our experience, portfolio growth is much more quickly achieved using the LEAPS technique when compared to traditional covered calls.

ADVANTAGES OF THE LEAPS TECHNIQUE

In a calendar LEAPS spread, we buy a LEAPS for cover rather than buying a stock. The advantages of this technique over writing covered calls are numerous and include the following:

- Investors are able to use higher-priced stocks (many of which are the bluest of blue chip). Investors would not normally be able to use these higher-priced stocks with the covered call technique because the uncalled and called returns would not be high enough.
- Investors are able to utilize the leverage offered by options, as they can control stock using LEAPS with a much lower capital outlay and at much lower prices compared to investing in the stock. Thus the ability to completely amortize (reduce) the cost of a position is dramatically increased when using the calendar LEAPS technique because, rather than paying, for example, $30.00 for a stock, an investor will purchase a LEAPS contract for $10.00 or less (when following the rules outlined in this book). When the same calls are sold against this much cheaper LEAPS, the cost is amortized to zero many times faster.
- Investors are able to much more directly take advantage of upward movements in the stock price. Where they would normally have to wait for the end of the month to be called out, calendar LEAPS spreads allow investors to close out the transaction immediately if the stock price increases, thus allowing much greater compounding of the asset base.
- Investors are able to be much more proactive in the management process when the position is not performing well. This ability assists in maintaining high returns regardless of the direction of the market.
- Because of leverage, investors are effectively able to have the benefits of investing on margin without the detractions of margin (margin calls, etc).

The most significant advantage of LEAPS over covered calls is that they enable experienced investors to close out a transaction potentially many times per month. This capability allows much higher returns and far superior compounding of an investor's asset base.

Growth Through Cash Flow

Correct application of the LEAPS technique provides portfolio growth through cash flow rather than speculative appreciation. When using covered calls, our objective is a cash return of around 4 percent per month, which equates to 48 percent cash return per year (uncompounded) or nearly 100 percent over two years (uncompounded). When using the LEAPS technique, our return objectives are much higher; we aim to achieve consistent monthly cash returns in the high single digits to low teens.

Being Prepared for Extreme Fluctuations in Position Market Value

As previously stated, the calendar LEAPS spreads technique is an advanced covered call technique. Only investors who have developed a consistent track record of success with the covered call technique should use LEAPS. Having such a track record is necessary because of the extreme fluctuation in position market value while managing calendar LEAPS spread positions for cash flow until a profitable exit is realized. Investors must understand that LEAPS are leveraged instruments and their market value fluctuates significantly on a daily basis.

Take the two positions shown in Table 6.1 as an example of leverage. Investors A and B both create a position in JPM at the same time. Investor A purchases the stock at $30.00, while investor B purchases a JPM LEAPS for $6.00. Remember, these two purchases are made at the same time—the JPM stock price is $30.00. The stock then declines 10 percent. Investor A has suffered a 10 percent market value decline in the value of his position. However, investor B, who purchased a JPM LEAPS, has suffered a 35 percent market value decline in the value of his position. This is a significant market value decline and is the result of leverage.

Experienced investors who are familiar with the covered call technique understand the mind-set required to never sell a position for a loss and, instead, to continue to generate and compound cash flow from a fallen position. Those experienced with the correct application of the covered call technique understand that stock prices of good companies go up and down and that cash flow can be consistently generated regardless of market

TABLE 6.1 An Example of Leverage

Investor	Asset Purchased	Asset Price	Stock Declines	Asset Price	Asset Decline
A	JPM Stock	$30.00	10%	$27.00	10%
B	JPM LEAPS	$ 6.00	10%	$ 3.90	35%

direction. For those unaccustomed to the technique, "never selling a position for a loss" is merely a catch phrase, and many investors find this temporary market value loss too large a psychological hurdle. Experienced LEAPS investors understand that correct management of a position leads to the complete amortization of the position, in most instances, in less than one year. Investors using the LEAPS technique must understand and accept market value fluctuations. They must remain focused on the primary objective: *consistently generating and compounding cash flow*.

USING LEAPS FOR COVER

A *covered call* is defined as selling a call when holding the underlying stock or another covering option on the same stock. In Chapter 2, "An Introduction to Covered Calls," we explained selling a covered call and being covered by the stock. This section explains how to be covered by owning a long-term option (LEAPS).

The rules for constructing and managing LEAPS positions are discussed in subsequent chapters, but, for now, let's gain an understanding of how to be covered by a LEAPS instead of a stock. Here is an example.

Citigroup stock is currently trading at $46.00. Let's assume we purchase a Citigroup January 2007 $40.00 LEAPS for $8.00 (remember, this is just a normal option with a very long expiration). We then go ahead and sell a December 2004 $47.50 call for $1.40. Our position is as follows.

| Long | Jan 2007 $40.00 Call at $8.00 |
| Short | Dec 2004 $47.50 Call at $1.40 |

There are two separate return calculations that you must compute and be aware of for every LEAPS transaction: the uncalled return and the called return.

The *uncalled return* is also known as the "percentage return," "downside protection," or "yield" and is simply the premium you received on the call sale divided by the cost of the LEAPS. So in our example we purchased a LEAPS for $8.00 and sold a call for $1.40. The uncalled return in this instance is $1.40/$8.00 = 17.50 percent, which is a very large return and is the result of leverage working in our favor.

The *called return* is the return the investor realizes in the event that the short call is exercised or called out. The formula for calculating the called return is:

Called return = Strike call – Strike LEAPS – LEAPS price + Call price

To calculate the called return, you must understand what happens in the event of a call out. Using our example:

- If we are called out, we have the obligation to deliver Citigroup stock at a price of $47.50. As we own the LEAPS, we have the right to buy Citigroup stock at a price of $40.00.
- In the event of a call out, our broker will automatically exercise the LEAPS on our behalf. We will thus automatically buy the stock at a price of $40.00 and sell the stock at a price of $47.50. We have recovered $7.50 of our capital investment on the stock sale.
- As with covered calls, we get to keep the $1.40 that we sold the call for.

Our total return of capital would, therefore, be:

$$\begin{aligned} \text{Return of capital} &= \text{Strike call} - \text{Strike LEAPS} + \text{Call price} \\ &= \$47.50 - \$40.00 + \$1.40 \\ &= \$8.90 \end{aligned}$$

Remember, we invested $8.00 in this transaction, so the called return would be $8.90 - $8.00 = $0.90 or 11.3 percent ($0.90/$8.00)

Again, the formula for calculating the called return is:

Called return = Strike call − Strike LEAPS − LEAPS price + Call price

In this instance, then:

$$\begin{aligned} \text{Called return} &= \$47.50 - \$40.00 - \$8.00 + \$1.40 \\ &= \$0.90, \text{ or } 11.3\% \ (\$0.90/\$8.00) \end{aligned}$$

So we now know how we can substitute the stock with a LEAPS and still sell a covered call.

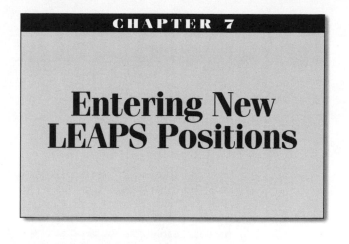

CHAPTER 7

Entering New
LEAPS Positions

SOME BASICS

Markets to Invest In

Unlike traditional covered calls, LEAPS investors are restricted to the U.S. market. Only the U.S. option market has adequate size and liquidity to effectively implement a calendar LEAPS strategy.

If you wish to utilize these techniques from outside the U.S., you will have to adapt to working for reasonable lengths of time at unusual hours. This is a sacrifice; however, the potential returns from this technique for experienced investors certainly justify such a sacrifice. You will also need to be cognizant of foreign exchange risk (see Appendix B).

The Importance of Diversification

Our objective with LEAPS is to construct a well-diversified portfolio of 15 to 20 positions. One significant advantage of LEAPS over conventional covered calls is that you are able to invest in the bluest of blue-chip stocks—including those that are generally excluded to covered call investors due to their high stock prices and subsequent low yields.

You must construct a portfolio with a broad representation of industries. You should also construct your portfolio using *only* large capitalization stocks (those with a market capitalization greater than US$5 billion) from the Dow Jones Industrial Average, the S&P 500, and the NASDAQ. These are the bluest of blue-chip companies available for public investment anywhere in the world. Apart from rare instances (Enron, WorldCom,

123

TABLE 7.1   Industries Suitable for LEAPS Investing

Sector	Example of Industry
Financial	Banks, insurance companies, investment services
Health care	Biotechnology and drugs, health care facilities, major drugs
Consumer noncyclical	Beverages, food, household products
Consumer cyclical	Apparel, footwear, autos
Basic materials	Chemical manufacturing, paper products, plastic and rubber
Technology	Computer equipment, semiconductors, software
Transportation	Air, railroads, trucking
Capital goods	Aerospace and defense, construction services and machinery
Utilities	Electrical, natural gas, water
Energy	Coal, oil and gas, services and equipment
Services	Advertising, broadcasting and cable, retail

etc.) it is very uncommon for these companies go out of business—and that is the only time we ever lose money on a properly constructed position.

Your portfolio should include companies from the industries listed in Table 7.1. As you can see, there are eleven individual sectors. You should try to include about two stocks from each of these sectors in the construction of your LEAPS portfolio.

The importance of diversification cannot be stressed enough. Investors must spread risk between various stocks in different industries. Given the low price of LEAPS contracts (the contracts that investors will purchase following the rules in this book are usually priced between $4.00 and $10.00), a portfolio of 15 LEAPS positions can be constructed with as little as $6,000.

THE RULES FOR ENTERING NEW LEAPS POSITIONS

A new calendar LEAPS position involves buying a LEAPS and selling a call. The six rules for entering into new LEAPS positions are:

1. You can only establish new positions on down market days. A down market day is any time when the Dow and the NASDAQ are in the red (trading lower than the close of the previous day).

2. Use the CSE Screener to filter all stocks in the market for the fundamental criteria (see the following section) for LEAPS investments.

3. You must follow the rules for correctly constructing a LEAPS position (discussed later in this chapter). These rules are imbedded in the CSE Screener.

4. Ensure that the stock adheres to the buying low rule for LEAPS (discussed later in this chapter).

5. Always give priority to maintaining acceptable levels of diversification between stocks and industries—even if a stock you are already invested in presents an excellent opportunity.

6. Buy the LEAPS first and then immediately sell the call. Do not hesitate. If you buy the LEAPS and wait for a better price for the call, you are no better than a speculator, and you will get burned!

USING THE CSE SCREENER TO FILTER LEAPS INVESTMENTS

The first step in the LEAPS process investment flowchart (Figure A.2 on page 190) is to use the CSE Screener to identify a potential LEAPS investment. The CSE Screener is a proprietary covered call and LEAPS search and filter tool designed, developed, and maintained by Compound Stock Earnings. The CSE Screener allows investors to quickly and easily search the stock market for the highest returning covered call or LEAPS positions that meet specific fundamental, technical, and construction requirements. The tool is tailored to accommodate the criteria and rules established in this book for selecting LEAPS positions.

Anyone who purchases *Covered Calls and LEAPS—A Wealth Option* is entitled to one month's complimentary access to the Covered Call Toolbox (which includes the CSE Screener) by going to www.compoundstockearn ings.com/freemonth. Thus readers can actually use the tools while learning about them in this book.

Selection Parameters

The eight parameters you should use to filter LEAPS positions are:

1. Uncalled return of minimum 10 percent.
2. Called return of greater than 0 percent
3. Price-earnings ratio (PE) of 70 or less.
4. Market capitalization of US$5 billion or more.

5. Stock price between $25.00 and $100.00.

6. Average broker recommendation of 2.5 or less.

7. An aggregate of the brokers recommending the stock as "Strong Buy" and "Buy" greater than the number of brokers recommending the stock as "Hold."

8. A consensus earnings per share (EPS) estimate for "Next Fiscal Year" forecast to be greater than the consensus EPS estimate for "This Fiscal Year."

Rationale Behind CSE Screener LEAPS Filters

The fundamental filters for LEAPS and covered calls are slightly different. The LEAPS technique provides the opportunity to exit positions much faster than traditional covered calls, and the companies in which we invest are inherently lower risk due to their larger size, established positions in the market place, very high levels of broker coverage, and increased visibility of earnings. As such, it is necessary to alter the selection criteria for LEAPS investments.

Uncalled and Called Returns   The uncalled return filter of 10 percent or greater ensures we are entering a transaction with adequate return to correctly manage the position. The uncalled return is vitally important as it affects our ability to buy back the call for a profit under a scenario of a small stock price decline after entering the transaction. This scenario is discussed in Chapter 8.

The called return filter of 0 percent or greater simply ensures we are entering a transaction that will provide a positive return if called out. While our objective when entering a LEAPS position is *not* to be called out, and the calls sold are not near month, which all but eliminates the chance of a call out, a position should never be constructed where a loss will be realized on call out. When assessing two positions with different called returns, investors should not view the position with a higher called return more favorably. The only consideration is if the position has a *positive* called return.

PE Ratio   The PE ratio filter of 70 or less reflects the fact that with LEAPS investing, we are dealing with the bluest of blue-chip companies. We thus allow a higher PE ratio than with traditional covered calls. Unlike covered calls, LEAPS allow investment in much higher priced stocks due to the leverage offered by buying the LEAPS rather than the stock itself.

Market Capitalization   The market capitalization filter of $5 billion or greater ensures that we are investing in a company of significant size, with substantial earnings. A company is generally considered blue chip when it has a market capitalization of $5 billion or greater. LEAPS investors should construct positions on qualifying companies from the Dow Jones Industrial Average, the S&P 500, and the NASDAQ. These are the bluest of blue-chip companies available for public investment anywhere in the world.

Stock Price   We also now only select stocks that are priced between $25.00 and $100.00. We do not invest in stocks under $25.00 as lower priced stocks limit leverage in the LEAPS position and also the application of the formalized seven-day rule, which is discussed in Chapter 8. Stocks with prices over $100.00 are also excluded because they are inherently more risky for this technique due to limiting the application of the formalized seven-day rule.

Broker Recommendations   An average broker recommendation of 2.5 or less ensures that the stock is rated at least an average of "buy" by the analysts who cover it. This statement does not imply that we value or follow the opinions of brokers. However, the brokerage community will be in the markets promoting the stock and the masses will be providing buying support for the stock. More importantly, the stock is not likely to go out of business in the short term.

The aggregate of the brokers recommending the stock as Strong Buy and Buy must be greater than the number of brokers recommending the stock as Hold. This criterion simply ensures that more brokers are positive on the stock than are neutral.

Earnings per Share   A forecast consensus EPS estimate for "Next Fiscal Year" greater than the consensus EPS estimate for "This Fiscal Year" simply ensures that the brokers covering the stock believe that the company's earnings will grow next fiscal year and helps prevent investors from buying stocks that are going into a period of contracting earnings.

Readers familiar with the traditional covered call technique will notice that with LEAPS investing, we drop the 75 percent of the 52-week trading range. This omission reflects the more short-term nature of LEAPS investments compared to covered calls. It is not necessary to hold a LEAPS investment to wait for a call out at the end of the month. A LEAPS position can be quickly and profitably closed out with a very small increase in the underlying stock price.

Directions for Using the CSE Screener

To access the covered call search tools, you need to establish a username and password from www.compoundstockearnings.com/freemonth. Then do the following:

1. Go to www.compoundstockearnings.com/cctoolbox.
2. Enter your username and password.
3. Click Log On.
4. Click CSE Screener—LEAPS.

The CSE Screener will search the entire market to find all the stocks that meet the stipulated fundamental and technical criteria. It then looks at the option chains on these stocks and correctly constructs LEAPS positions using the position construction rules outlined later in this chapter.

Correct construction is absolutely critical. Without correct construction, it is highly unlikely that the investor will be able to exit the position quickly and profitably with a small increase in the stock price. Additionally, management for cash flow will be very difficult if the entry position is incorrectly constructed.

The CSE Screener then presents a list of potential positions to the investor. All positions meet the fundamental requirements listed previously (PE ratio, market capitalization, broker rating, etc.) and are *correctly constructed* to expedite a profitable close out and assist management for cash flow.

Figure 7.1 is a typical screenshot of the CSE Screener for LEAPS transactions. Each position presented by the screener meets both the fundamental and construction criteria outlined in this book.

Remember, The CSE Screener only filters for fundamental criteria and correctly constructs the position. You must ensure that companies meet the technical criteria (upward or sideways moving stock and adherence to the buying low rule discussed in the next section) before entering the position.

The fundamental and construction criteria for selecting LEAPS positions have remained substantially the same for many years. However, from time to time, the criteria have been modified to adapt to the current conditions of the market. When such a change is needed, the authors adapt the default criteria of the CSE Screener to keep investors in step with the current conditions of the markets. Therefore, it is highly recommended that investors simply use the default criteria of the CSE Screener when searching for new positions.

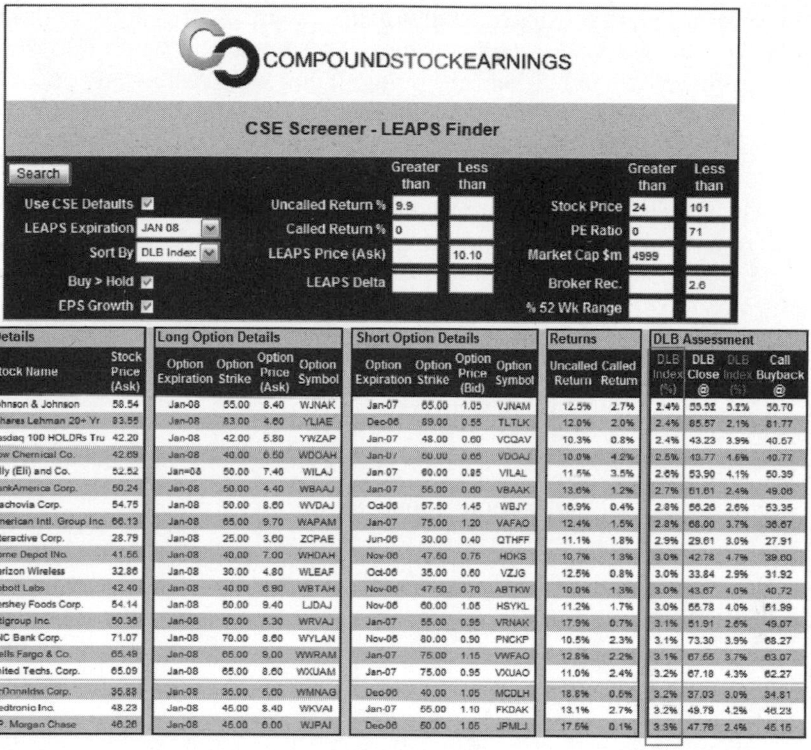

COMPOUNDSTOCKEARNINGS

CSE Screener - LEAPS Finder

	Search		Greater than	Less than		Greater than	Less than
Use CSE Defaults ☑		Uncalled Return %	9.9		Stock Price	24	101
LEAPS Expiration	JAN 08	Called Return %	0		PE Ratio	0	71
Sort By	DLB Index	LEAPS Price (Ask)		10.10	Market Cap $m	4999	
Buy > Hold ☑		LEAPS Delta			Broker Rec.		2.6
EPS Growth ☑					% 52 Wk Range		

Stock Details			Long Option Details				Short Option Details				Returns		DLB Assessment			
Stock Code	Stock Name	Stock Price (Ask)	Option Expiration	Option Strike	Option Price (Ask)	Option Symbol	Option Expiration	Option Strike	Option Price (Bid)	Option Symbol	Uncalled Return	Called Return	DLB Index (%)	DLB Close @	DLB Index (%)	Call Buyback @
JNJ	Johnson & Johnson	58.54	Jan-08	55.00	8.40	WJNAK	Jan-07	65.00	1.05	VJNAM	12.5%	2.7%	2.4%	53.35	3.3%	56.70
TLT	iShares Lehman 20+ Yr	83.55	Jan-08	83.00	4.60	YLIAE	Dec-06	89.00	0.55	TLTLK	12.0%	2.0%	2.4%	85.57	2.1%	81.77
QQQQ	Nasdaq 100 HOLDRs Tru	42.20	Jan-08	42.00	5.80	YWZAP	Jan-07	48.00	0.60	VCQAV	10.3%	0.8%	2.4%	43.23	3.9%	40.57
DOW	Dow Chemical Co.	42.68	Jan-08	40.00	6.50	WDOAH	Jan-07	50.00	0.65	VDOAJ	10.0%	4.2%	2.5%	43.77	1.6%	40.77
LLY	Lilly (Eli) and Co.	52.52	Jan-08	50.00	7.40	WILAJ	Jan-07	60.00	0.85	VILAL	11.5%	3.5%	2.6%	53.90	4.1%	50.39
BAC	BankAmerica Corp.	50.24	Jan-08	50.00	4.40	WBAAJ	Jan-07	55.00	0.60	VBAAK	13.6%	1.2%	2.7%	51.61	2.4%	49.06
WB	Wachovia Corp.	54.75	Jan-08	50.00	6.60	WVDAJ	Oct-06	57.50	1.45	WBJY	16.9%	0.4%	2.8%	56.26	2.6%	53.35
AIG	American Intl. Group Inc.	66.13	Jan-08	65.00	9.70	WAPAM	Jan-07	75.00	1.20	VAFAQ	12.4%	1.5%	2.8%	68.00	3.7%	36.67
IACI	Interactive Corp.	28.79	Jan-08	25.00	3.60	ZCPAE	Jun-06	30.00	0.40	QTHFF	11.1%	1.8%	2.9%	29.61	3.0%	27.91
HD	Home Depot INo.	41.55	Jan-08	40.00	7.00	WHDAH	Nov-06	47.50	0.75	HDKS	10.7%	1.9%	3.0%	42.78	4.7%	39.60
VZ	Verizon Wireless	32.86	Jan-08	30.00	4.80	WLEAF	Oct-06	35.00	0.60	VZJG	12.5%	0.8%	3.0%	33.84	2.9%	31.92
ABT	Abbott Labs	42.40	Jan-08	40.00	6.90	WBTAH	Nov-06	47.50	0.70	ABTKW	10.0%	1.3%	3.0%	43.67	4.0%	40.72
HSY	Hershey Foods Corp.	54.14	Jan-08	50.00	9.40	LJDAJ	Nov-06	60.00	1.05	HSYKL	11.2%	1.7%	3.0%	55.78	4.0%	51.99
C	Citigroup Inc.	50.36	Jan-08	50.00	5.30	WRVAJ	Jan-07	55.00	0.95	VRNAK	17.9%	0.7%	3.1%	51.91	2.6%	49.07
PNC	PNC Bank Corp.	71.07	Jan-08	70.00	8.60	WYLAN	Nov-06	80.00	0.90	PNCKP	10.5%	2.3%	3.1%	73.30	3.9%	68.27
WFC	Wells Fargo & Co.	65.49	Jan-08	65.00	9.00	WWRAM	Jan-07	75.00	1.15	VWFAO	12.8%	2.2%	3.1%	67.55	3.7%	63.07
UTX	United Techs. Corp.	65.09	Jan-08	65.00	8.60	WXUAM	Jan-07	75.00	0.95	VXUAO	11.0%	2.4%	3.2%	67.18	4.3%	62.27
MCD	McDonalds Corp.	35.83	Jan-08	35.00	5.00	WMNAG	Dec-06	40.00	1.05	MCDLH	16.8%	0.6%	3.2%	37.03	3.0%	34.81
MDT	Medtronic Inc.	48.23	Jan-08	45.00	8.40	WKVAI	Jan-07	55.00	1.10	FKDAK	13.1%	2.7%	3.2%	49.79	4.2%	46.23
JPM	J.P. Morgan Chase	46.20	Jan-08	45.00	6.00	WJPAI	Dec-06	50.00	1.05	JPMLJ	17.5%	0.1%	3.3%	47.76	2.4%	45.16

FIGURE 7.1 Sample screenshot of the CSE Screener for LEAPS transactions.

USING PRICE CHARTS WITH THE LEAPS TECHNIQUE

Simply because the CSE Screener has presented a position does not automatically qualify it as an acceptable investment. Revisit the "Rules for Entering New LEAPS Positions" listed earlier. At this point we just want to emphasize the rule that relates to price charts:

- Ensure that the stock adheres to the buying low rule for LEAPS.

Before entering a new LEAPS position, investors *must* assess the stock's chart. Correct assessment of the price chart is absolutely critical to optimizing returns when using the LEAPS technique. Investors who get caught up in hype and buy when markets are going up or who panic and sell when markets are going down are categorically the losing investors in the markets. You must buy low and sell high: You must buy when markets are falling and sell when markets are rising. If you were selling any product as a business venture, you would be attempting to buy the product low and to sell it high. Financial markets are no different. The importance of this rule cannot be stressed enough.

The detailed information provided in the "Using Price Charts" section in Chapter 3 also applies to entering a LEAPS position. Review the material therein about identifying and assessing price cycles and how to look at a price chart. And remember: If you do not understand a chart, *do not* invest in the stock.

THE BUYING LOW RULE FOR LEAPS

The second step in the LEAPS investment process flowchart (Figure A.2 on page 190) is to satisfy the buying low rule. The buying low rule defines the point in the stock's price cycle at which an investor can enter into new positions. It attempts to ensure that investors are buying when prices are low. The three components of the rule are:

1. Investment in new LEAPS positions can only be made when a stock's overall or current cycle is increasing or horizontal.

2. Investment in new LEAPS positions can only be made when a stock is in the lower 25 percent of its overall or current price cycle.

3. A stock's current price cycle must have at minimum $1.50 of price between the upper and lower lines for a position to be eligible for investment. This third rule ensures that there is enough potential upward movement in the stock price to exit the position.

By ensuring that you enter into new positions on stocks whose general or current cycle is either increasing or horizontal and the stock is trading in the lower end of the cycle, the buying low rule provides you with greater probability that the stock price will increase and allow you to close out the transaction.

Implementing the Buying Low Rule

Figures 7.2 through 7.14 provide examples of implementing the buying low rule. Study each of these carefully. Turnover of capital (meaning the quick and profitable exit of positions) is critical to your success as a LEAPS investor. Correct assessment of the price chart expedites the profitable exit of LEAPS positions. Incorrect assessment of the price chart leads to increasing the number of positions that require management for income.

Bottom 25 Percent of an Overall Rising or Horizontal Cycle

We can see in Figure 7.2 that the overall trend for HON is rising because the significant bottoms and tops on the chart are getting *higher*. We can also see that there is around $5.00 of price depth in the cycle (~$38.50 – ~$33.50). HON is also reaching the bottom 25 percent of the overall rising cycle (indicated by the stock's movement below the bold line drawn on the chart). This is the safest and most profitable chart position for a new LEAPS investment. Given the position on the chart, it would be ideal to construct a LEAPS position on HON now.

Investing at or below the bottom 25 percent of an overall rising or horizontal cycle is ideal for LEAPS positions.

Let's look at another example in Figure 7.3. To assist us in identifying when the stock is trading in the lower 25 percent of its price cycle, we draw in a 50 percent line directly in the middle of the upper and lower lines (should be parallel). We can see from the chart in Figure 7.3 that the overall trend for PG is horizontal with slight upward bias, because the significant bottoms and tops on the chart are generally stable with slight upward bias. We can also see that there is around $7.00 of price depth in the cycle (~$58.00 – ~$51.00). Again, this is the safest and most profitable chart position for a new LEAPS investment. Given the position on the chart, it would be ideal to construct a LEAPS position on PG now.

Only invest in new positions when the stock is trading at or below 25% of the generally rising price cycle.

FIGURE 7.2   Identifying the bottom 25 percent of an overall rising cycle.

Only invest in new positions when the stock is trading at or below 25% of a generally horizontal price cycle.

FIGURE 7.3   Identifying the bottom 25 percent of a horizontal cycle.

Only invest in new positions when the stock is trading at or below 25% of a current rising or horizontal price cycle.

FIGURE 7.4   Identifying the bottom 25 percent of a current rising cycle.

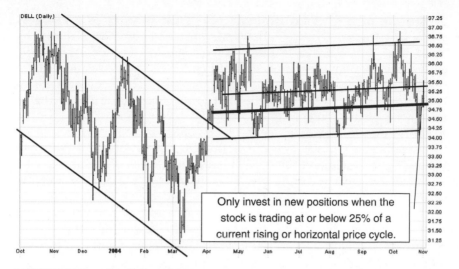

FIGURE 7.5 Identifying the bottom 25 percent of a current cycle that is horizontal with a slight upward bias.

Investing at or below the bottom 25 percent of an overall rising or horizontal cycle is ideal for LEAPS positions.

Bottom 25 Percent of a Current Rising Cycle   When the stock drops into the lower 25 percent of the price channel (below the bolded line), it qualifies under the buying low rule. We can see that Figure 7.4 differs significantly from the preceding examples. In contrast, this stock is not in an overall rising cycle, but the current cycle is rising. This chart is also optimal for constructing new LEAPS positions.

Investing at or below the bottom 25 percent of a current rising cycle is ideal for LEAPS positions.

We can see that Figure 7.5 also differs significantly from the preceding examples. In this case, the current cycle is horizontal with slight upward bias. Again, this chart is optimal for constructing new LEAPs positions.

When Constructing a Position at the Bottom 25 Percent of a Current Rising or Horizontal Cycle Is a Poor Choice

There are two distinct occasions when the bottom 25 percent of a current rising or horizontal cycle is, in fact, a very poor place to construct a position. The following examples apply to chart interpretation for both covered call and LEAPS positions.

1. Bottom of a Current Rising Cycle That Is Part of a Longer-Term Downward Cycle Perhaps the most common chart misinterpretation made by novice investors is not recognizing that a current rising cycle is part of a longer-term downward cycle. This is the result of an investor ignoring the longer-term cycle of the stock. This shortsightedness leads investors to construct positions in a short-term upward cycle that is merely the continuation of a longer-term downward cycle.

Study Figure 7.6. We can see that while BSX is in a current rising cycle, the overall cycle is down. Now compare Figure 7.6 to Figure 7.7. Notice in Figure 7.7 that the top of the declining price cycle has been substantially broken by the current rising cycle. This differs from Figure 7.6 where the current rising cycle was still trading *within* the declining price cycle.

Do not invest in a stock where the current rising cycle has not substantially broken through the top of the overall declining price cycle. This occurrence is critically important to prevent misinterpretation of the current cycle of the stock.

Let's look at another example. Study Figure 7.8. Again, we can see that the current rising cycle is actually a part of the long-term declining cycle. LEAPS positions should not be constructed at the bottom of such a cycle.

2. Current Cycles That Are Close to the Yearly High Another common chart misinterpretation by novice investors is investing at the bottom of current cycles that are very close the yearly high for the stock. This

FIGURE 7.6 A rising current cycle that is part of a long-term downward cycle.

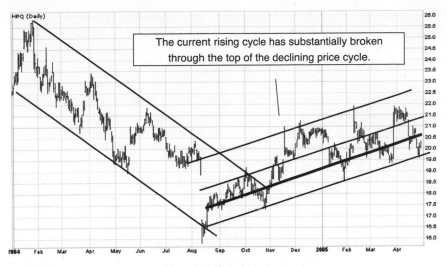

FIGURE 7.7 Evidence that the overall cycle is increasing.

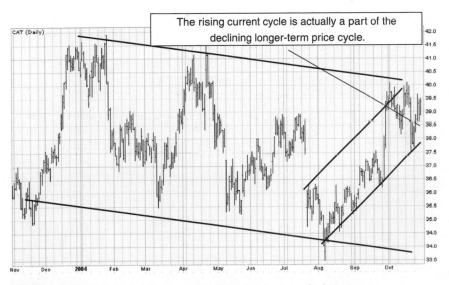

FIGURE 7.8 Another rising current cycle that is part of a long-term declining cycle.

point, in many instances, is a "greed trap," where investors see a stock continually rising over a yearly time frame and they are entering into new positions very near to the yearly high for a stock. While this strategy is fine if the stock continues its strength, eventually it *will* turn around. Investors who consistently enter new positions near the yearly high will accumulate a portfolio of underperforming positions that require management for income. When a stock breaks cycle after making a yearly high, it may be months or even years before the stock price ever trades higher than this major yearly high. Very few stocks can consistently make yearly highs month after month. All stocks eventually cycle down.

Remember, our objective when using the buying low rule is to buy when markets are falling and to enter a position at the lower point of the market. We do not want to be caught up in the hype of the losing investors who consistently buy stocks at the high end of the market. At this point, it is important to think about what the term "buying low" actually means. "Buying low" means entering into a position at an inexpensive price relative to the market. *Relativity* is the key word. We want to enter into new positions at a relatively inexpensive price compared to what other investors have recently paid for the stock. Relativity is the key.

See, for example, Figures 7.9 and 7.10. Figure 7.9 shows entering a new position in the lower 25 percent of an overall rising cycle. Figure 7.10 highlights the entry point from Figure 7.9, the point where we are comfortable constructing a new LEAPS position if we were assessing this chart today. This point is the lower 25 percent of the overall rising cycle. Notice that many investors have recently paid prices significantly higher than our entry price. Relatively speaking, our entry price is *inexpensive*.

Similarly, Figure 7.11, on Dell, shows entering a new position under the buying low rule at the bottom of a current horizontal cycle. Notice in Figure 7.12 that the vast majority of investors have recently paid prices significantly higher than our entry price. Again, relatively speaking, our entry price is *inexpensive*.

Now that we more fully understand the concept of buying low, let's address the common mistake of investing at the bottom of a current rising cycle that is very close to the yearly high for a stock. Take Figure 7.13 as an example. It is clear that this stock is both in an overall upward cycle and within the bottom 25 percent of this cycle. Why then, is this a very poor place to construct a new LEAPS position? See Figure 7.14 for the answer.

We can see very clearly from Figure 7.14 that while the stock is generally rising over a yearly time frame and is at the bottom of a current rising cycle, we are paying almost the yearly high for the stock. Very few investors

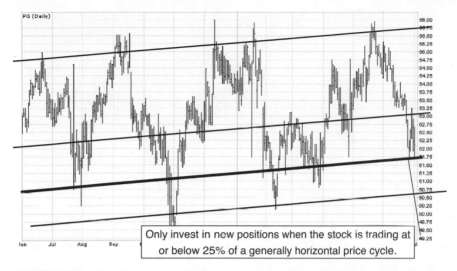

Only invest in new positions when the stock is trading at or below 25% of a generally horizontal price cycle.

FIGURE 7.9 Entering a new position in the lower 25 percent of an overall rising cycle.

Many investors have paid higher prices for the stock compared to our entry price.

FIGURE 7.10 Relative entry price.

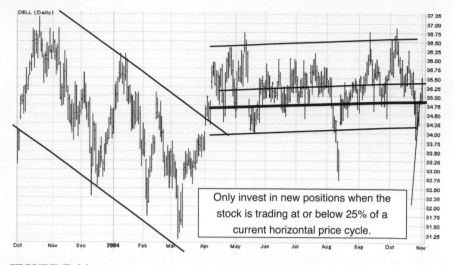

FIGURE 7.11   Entering a new position at the bottom of a current horizontal cycle.

have recently purchased the stock at higher prices. We are, in actuality, buying high, rather than low. We are getting caught up in the hype and exuberance of a strongly appreciating stock price.

   This is a very poor place to construct a LEAPS position. Sure, the stock may continue its strong run upwards and we may quickly exit the position. However, in the event that the stock does turn around and makes a signifi-

FIGURE 7.12   Relative entry price.

FIGURE 7.13 A stock in an upward cycle and within the bottom 25 percent of the cycle.

cant change in trend, it is very unlikely that there will be higher prices for the stock for months, if not years. As such, we will be forced into a protracted period of management for income on this position (management for income is discussed in depth in Chapter 8). While there are numerous management rules and techniques that allow the continued generation of income from a position regardless of market direction, having to rely on

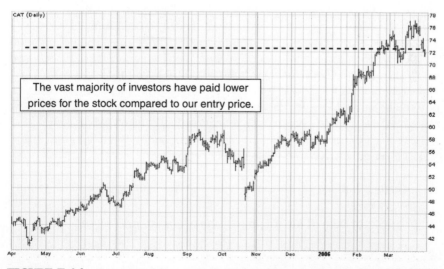

The vast majority of investors have paid lower prices for the stock compared to our entry price.

FIGURE 7.14 A current rising cycle that is actually very close to the yearly high.

management for cash flow is *not* the optimal outcome. The optimal outcome for LEAPS investors is to quickly enter and exit LEAPS transactions. The regular reinvestment of capital plus cash returns allows for fast and dramatic compounding of the asset base.

Whenever entering a new position, investors should ask themselves: "Am I paying a relatively cheap or expensive price? Have many investors recently purchased the stock at a higher price than my entry price?" As we have just seen, the answers will reveal the suitability of entering the position.

Identifying a Change in the Cycle and the First Buy Point

We now understand that new LEAPS positions can only be constructed at the bottom 25 percent of an overall or currently rising or horizontal cycle. Therefore, two very important skills are needed:

1. Knowing how to identify a change in cycle.
2. Knowing how to identify the first buy point of a new price cycle.

How to Identify a Change in Cycle   This topic applies equally to covered call and LEAPS techniques. However, it is discussed in this section rather than in Part I, Covered Calls, since it is an advanced charting technique. Investors using both techniques can use this to understand a change in cycle from declining to rising and to, consequently, identify the first buy point of a new rising cycle. In *each and every* change in cycle from declining to rising, two chart events occur. These events do not necessarily occur in the same order for each individual change in cycle and they do not *guarantee* a change in cycle; however, both events do occur *each and every time* a cycle actually changes direction. Therefore, investors should be watching cycles for these events—and when they unfold, they warn of a potential change in cycle. Because we are talking about entering into new positions, we are assessing a change from a declining to a rising cycle.

The two chart events that occur in *each and every* change of trend from a declining to a rising cycle are:

1. A higher bottom or bottoms, which may occur within the declining price cycle.
2. A break through of the top line of the declining price cycle.

Without these two events occurring, a change of cycle direction *cannot* take place. Therefore, watching for and identifying these events as they

FIGURE 7.15 Identifying a change in cycle.

occur is an excellent early warning to watch for a change of cycle direction. See the examples in Figures 7.15 and 7.16.

Now that we know that when following a declining cycle, higher bottoms and a break to the top of the declining cycle provide a red flag that the cycle may, in fact, be about the change, we need to know how to identify the first buy point of a new, rising cycle.

FIGURE 7.16 Another example of identifying a change in cycle.

How to Identify the First Buy Point of a New Price Cycle   The most difficult part of the buying low rule for LEAPS is identifying the first buy point of a new price cycle. The first buy point of a new price cycle is literally the first point in a new cycle at which the buying low rule is satisfied. This definition does not mean that new positions can *only* be constructed at the first buy point; however, the first buy point provides confirmation of a new rising cycle.

The first buy point of a new cycle is always preceded by a minimum of two tops and a minimum of one bottom. The second top must be higher than the first; otherwise the cycle is declining and is ineligible for investment.

Study Figure 7.17. We can see that the first buy point of a new cycle is always preceeded by a mimimum of two tops (the second top being higher than the first) and a minimum of one bottom. The first buy point can then easily be estimated by first connecting the higher tops, identifiying the first bottom of the cycle, and then extrapolating a bottom parallel line from this bottom. Remember, when attempting to identify the first buy point, the second bottom of the cycle is yet to form—the bottom line must be estimated by drawing a parallel line from the first bottom.

Remember, this technique is only a tool for identifying the first buy point of a new cycle. It is not necessary to only enter new positions at the first buy point. It is completely reasonsable to enter into new positions after the current rising cycle is well established (after it has made several higher bottoms and tops).

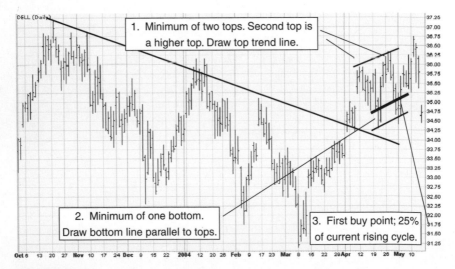

FIGURE 7.17   Identifying the first buy point of a new price cycle.

CONSTRUCTING A LEAPS POSITION

Now that we understand how to use the CSE Screener to identify a potential LEAPS position and how to qualify a stock using the buying low rule, we are ready to discuss position construction. The CSE Screener only presents positions that follow the correct construction rules as outlined in this section, which is a significant advantage to investors, as position construction has already been performed. However, it is essential that investors understand the fundamental rules and reasoning behind the construction of a position. So let's look at the rules for constructing a LEAPS position.

Selecting a LEAPS

- You must select a LEAPS that is *one strike price in the money*. The reason for this requirement relates to the delta ratio, which is discussed later in this chapter.
- You may not select a LEAPS that costs more than $10.00; the less it costs, the better. Low cost is necessary to generate leverage. Also, the higher the cost of your LEAPS, the more difficult the position will be to manage in a market downturn.
- The LEAPS selected must have at minimum 12 months to expiration, with the longest-term LEAPS available always given preference.

Selecting the Call

- You must sell a call as soon as you buy a LEAPS. If you wait to get a higher price for the call, you are no better than a speculator and you will get burned!
- You must select a call that results in a positive called return. To make this selection, take the LEAPS strike price and add the cost of the LEAPS and you will arrive at an approximate strike price for the call.
- The call expiration that you select must not be equal to the expiration of the LEAPS. The shortest-term call that meets the requirements for a correct construction should be selected to allow management depth (discussed later).
- The call selected must combine with the LEAPS selected to have a delta ratio (see next section) of 1.90 or more.

Let's look at an example of constructing a calendar LEAPS Spread on JP Morgan (JPM). For the purpose of this example, assume that the fundamental and buying low rule requirements have been met and that the CSE Screener is not being used. Remember, the CSE Screener will not present a position for investment unless it meets the construction rules. However, it is essential that investors understand these rules and the logic behind them.

Refer back to Table 1.7 (on page 12), which shows an option chain for JPM. (Option chains on U.S. stock are available as part of the Compound Stock Earnings Covered Call Toolbox.) An option chain is just a list of all available option contracts on a particular stock and the prices the contracts are trading in the market.

To construct a LEAPS Position on JPM according to the rules, we need to select a LEAPS that is (1) one strike price in the money; (2) not more than $10.00 in value; and (3) the longest-term LEAPS available in the option chain.

The first step is to go out to the longest-term LEAPS available. From the option chain shown as Table 1.7, the longest-term LEAPS available is the January 2007. We then need to find the January 2007 LEAPS that is one strike price in the money. As JPM is trading at $39.38, the $35.00 strike is one strike price in the money. We need to invest in a LEAPS that costs no more than $10.00. We can buy the January 2007 $35.00 for $7.30. (If the January 2007 $35.00 were more than $10.00, we would simply disregard this position and identify a new stock for investment. However, it is not necessary to do so in this instance, as we have met the selection criteria.) We will try to construct a spread using the January 2007 $35.00 for $7.30.

We now need to select a call to sell against this LEAPS. From the rules we know that we must select a call that (1) results in a positive called return and (2) a minimum uncalled return of 10 percent; (3) whose expiration is not equal to the expiration of the LEAPS selected (the shortest-term call that allows a correct construction should be selected); and (4) has a delta ratio of 1.90 at a minimum.

Next we need to select the call strike price. Remember, our goal is to ensure that we create a position with a positive called return and an uncalled return of minimum 10 percent. We estimate the correct call strike price that will provide a positive called return by adding the LEAPS strike price of $35.00 to the cost of the LEAPS. So we add $35.00 to $7.30 for a total of $42.30. We should thus attempt to sell a $42.50 call for a minimum uncalled return of 10 percent. The cost of the LEAPS is $7.30, so we need to sell a call for $0.73 or more (10 percent or more). We look at the option chain (Table 1.7) for a $42.50 strike call that we can sell for $0.73 or more.

We see that the shortest-term $42.50 strike call that we can sell for $0.73 or more is the March 2005. This call would meet the rules previously outlined because (1) it results in a positive called return; (2) it is the nearest month that allows for a minimum 10 percent uncalled return (the January 2005 $42.50 is trading at $0.60 and will not provide a 10 percent return); and (3) the call expiration that we selected is not equal to the expiration of the LEAPS selected.

Finally, we need to assess the delta ratio. The rationale and importance of the delta ratio is discussed in the following section, but for now you only need to know how to calculate it per the following equation:

$$\text{Delta ratio} = \text{LEAPS delta/Call delta}$$

So for our example:

$$\text{Delta ratio} = 0.61/0.26$$
$$= 2.34$$

Now have met all criteria for entering into a new position, which is as follows:

Buy LEAPS	Jan 07 $35.00 for $7.30 delta of 0.61
Sell call	Mar 05 $42.50 for $0.90 delta of 0.26
Uncalled return	$0.90/$7.30 = 12.3%
Called return	$42.50 − $35.00 − $7.30 + $0.90
	= $1.10 or 15.1%

The Delta Ratio

As noted earlier in the book, the delta of a stock option is the rate of change of the option price with respect to the price of the underlying stock. It is a measure of how much an option's price will increase or decrease for an incremental increase or decrease in the stock price.

Let's look at an example of a call that has a delta of 0.60. This number means that when the stock price changes by an amount, the option price will change by 60 percent of that amount. For example, if the stock price increases by $1.00, then the option will increase in price by $0.60 (60 percent of the stock price's increase). If the stock price increased just $0.50, then the option price would increase by only $0.30 (60 percent of the stock price increase).

The delta ratio is a measure of the interaction between the LEAPS delta and the call delta and is represented by the following formula:

$$\text{Delta ratio} = \text{LEAPS delta/Call delta}$$

A position with a delta ratio of 1.90 or more ensures that, when the stock price rises, the LEAPS price increases much faster than the cost of buying back the call. This high delta ratio will assist greatly in the closing of a transaction when the stock price continues to rise after entering a new position. The delta ratio also assists in closing positions on the delta effect when performing a secondary call sale. (Secondary call sales are discussed in Chapter 8.)

Completing the Construction

Remember, the CSE Screener will only present positions that meet the preceding construction rules. Consequently, we needn't go through the construction process on each position. We only need to do the following three things:

1. Use the CSE Screener to identify positions that meet the fundamental criteria and can be correctly constructed.
2. Ensure that the position is on a stock with an overall or current upward or horizontal cycle.
3. Ensure the position meets the buying low rule.

Assuming that the portfolio diversification rules are also met, we can then enter the position.

CHAPTER 8

Management Rules

A fter entering new LEAPS positions, you need to know the rules for managing these positions in the event that the stock price initially increases or decreases. You also need to know how to manage a position for cash flow until you completely amortize the cost of the LEAPS in the event the stock price never increases to a point where you can exit the transaction (refer to Figure A.2 on page 190). Correct management is the difference between great success and complete mediocrity in the business of both covered calls and LEAPS.

THE 10¢ AND 5% BUYBACK RULES

With an established position in the LEAPS and the call, there are two possibilities:

1. The stock price *increases* and triggers the 10¢ buyback rule.
2. The stock price *decreases* and triggers the 5% buyback rule.

These rules are intended to expedite the closing of the transaction so you can get your capital back and reinvest it to compound your assets.

You must understand that your objective with LEAPS spreads is not the same as with covered calls. With LEAPS spreads your objective is always to exit the entire spread as soon as possible for a 5 percent profit on the whole transaction. Unlike covered calls, it is not necessary to hold the position until the expiration of the short call. The position can be very quickly closed for a profit if the stock price increases by a small amount after entering the transaction.

The 10¢ Buyback Rule

The objective of the 10¢ buyback rule is to allow the buyback of the call if the stock price moves up after entering the position and then to sell the LEAPS for a profit if the stock price continues to move up. Application of this rule facilitates the timely close of the transaction by preventing the call price from increasing as the LEAPS price is increasing. Remember, the LEAPS position is constructed at the bottom 25 percent of a rising or horizontal cycle where the bias for the stock is to move up after entering the transaction.

The 10¢ buyback rule instructs investors to do two things:

1. Buy back the call at market if the *bid* price of the LEAPS moves to 10¢ above your cost in the LEAPS.

2. Then add the cost of the call buyback to your cost in the LEAPS, add 5 percent to that total, and put in a good til canceled (GTC) order to sell the LEAPS at this price.

For example, if your cost in a LEAPS is $7.30, you would buy back the call if the market *bid* price of the LEAPS reaches $7.40. This is a very important point: We are referring to the market *bid* price of the LEAPS, not the ask price or the last price.

When you buy back a call under the 10¢ buyback rule, it usually involves a loss on buyback of $0.20 to $0.40. Let's assume the call buyback creates a loss of $0.30. Continuing with our example, you would calculate your GTC sell order for the LEAPS as follows:

$$
\begin{aligned}
\text{GTC sell order} &= (\text{LEAPS cost} + \text{Loss on buyback}) \times 1.05 \\
&= (\$7.30 + \$0.30) \times 1.05 \\
&= \$7.98
\end{aligned}
$$

So you would set your GTC order at $8.00. If this stock moves up a little further, this order will execute, you will have your money back in your account plus your 5 percent return, and you will be ready to reinvest your money and compound your assets. If the order does not execute, you will have the option of selling another call. This option is discussed in the later section on secondary call sales.

The 5% Buyback Rule

The 10¢ buyback rule applies in the event the stock price initially increases after entering the transaction. Conversely, the 5% buyback rule allows you to take advantage of a downward movement in the stock price after establishing a new position by taking the following two steps:

1. Buy back the call for a net uncalled return of 5 percent if market prices decline.
2. Then add 5 percent to the cost of the LEAPS and place a GTC order to sell the LEAPS at this price.

Let's continue with the preceding example in which you have a LEAPS that cost $7.30 and a call you sold for $0.90. If there were a drop in the stock price, you would buy back the call at a price of $0.55 to leave a net return of $0.35, or a 4.8 percent gain ($0.35/$7.30). You would then put in a GTC to sell the LEAPS at a price of $7.70 ($7.30 x 1.05) for an additional gain of 5.5 percent. If this stock went back up and this order executed, a total net gain of 10.3 percent would result.

Based on the example given here, if the 10¢ buyback rule were triggered, you would attempt to sell the LEAPS for $8.00 for a total transaction gain of 5 percent. However, if the 5% buyback rule were triggered, you would sell the LEAPS for $7.70 for a total transaction gain of 10 percent. Thus you can see that it is often more advantageous for the stock price to drop after initially entering a transaction! This advantage is another unique aspect of the LEAPS technique. It is the reason why we do not attempt to pick the bottom of the market. Entering a position at or around 25 percent of the cycle often leads to the stock initially falling before it cycles back up. An initial fall is a significant advantage in a LEAPS position as it can result in double the return and a lower exit price.

If you buy back the call for a profit and your order to sell the LEAPS at cost plus 5 percent does not execute, then what? Well, you have locked in a great 5 percent return over just a few days and you then assess the possibility of selling another call. This activity is discussed in detail in the later section on secondary call sales rules.

THE DELTA LOW BRIDGE

The delta low bridge (DLB) is an alternative technique to the 10¢ rule LEAPS technique. The primary difference between the two techniques is:

- DLB investors do not buy back the short call under the 10¢ rule if the stock price rises after entering a transaction.

Instead, if the stock price rises after entering the transaction, DLB investors exit the entire transaction on the delta effect. Exiting the transaction on the delta effect involves buying back the call and immediately selling the LEAPS when a 5 percent net return can be realized. This technique thus provides DLB investors with greater downside protection because they are not exposed to a downturn in the market after buying back the call and waiting for the stock price to increase and the LEAPS to sell.

If the stock price declines after entering the transaction, as with 10¢ rule transactions, DLB investors will also buy back the initial call for a profit of 5 percent and then sell the LEAPS for cost plus 5 percent.

Closing a Transaction Using the Delta Effect

As previously discussed (in Chapter 7), the delta of a stock option is the rate of change of the option price with respect to the price of the underlying stock. It is a measure of how much an option's price will increase or decrease for an incremental increase or decrease in the stock price.

Recall from the position construction rules that LEAPS transactions must be established with a minimum delta ratio of 1.90. In a correctly constructed LEAPS position, the LEAPS delta is always significantly higher than the call delta. As such the value of the LEAPS increases much faster than the buyback cost of the call. This is a critical factor for DLB investors who rely on the LEAPS increasing in value much faster than the buyback cost of the call in order to exit the transaction.

Closing a transaction on the delta effect means waiting for a point where the buyback cost of the call is exceeded by the profit available when selling the LEAPS. Take the following position as an example:

- BTO GE $35.00 Jan 2007 LEAPS @ $5.00; delta of 0.60
- STO GE $40.00 Dec 2005 Call @ $0.50; delta of 0.30

Closing this position on the delta effect when the stock price increases would involve immediately buying back the call and selling the LEAPS when a 5 percent net return could be realized. For example, suppose the stock price increases after entering this transaction and the current market prices of the LEAPS and call are as follows:

- GE $35.00 Jan 2007 LEAPS @ $5.00; current bid price $5.60
- GE $40.00 Dec 2005 Call @ $0.50; current ask price $0.80

This position could be closed on the delta effect to realize a $0.60 profit on the LEAPS and a $0.30 loss on the call. The overall profit would therefore be $0.30, or 6.0 percent ($0.30/$5.00) of the invested value of the LEAPS.

Such a situation is common for the LEAPS investor using the DLB technique. The call is never bought back for a loss under the 10¢ rule; rather, the delta effect is relied on to provide a profitable exit.

The DLB Rules

The process of investing with the DLB technique is similar to that for normal LEAPS transactions. Investors still go through the regular LEAPS investment process previously outlined in Chapter 7, including:

- Using The CSE Screener to meet fundamental and construction requirements.
- Ensuring the stock is in an overall or current rising or horizontal cycle.
- Ensuring the stock meets the buying low rule.

Once these actions have been accomplished, DLB investors must perform one additional activity to ensure a realistic position is being entered into:

- Assessing the stock chart for the upward price move required to exit the DLB transaction.

As DLB transactions require exit on the delta effect, they generally need a larger movement in the stock price to close the transaction for cost plus 5 percent than is required for 10¢ rule transactions.

When assessing a particular position as a DLB, it is important to look at the "DLB Close @" column of the CSE Screener. This column tells the investor at what stock price a particular LEAPS construction will close on the delta effect for a 5 percent return. This is a very valuable component of the tool and allows a realistic position to be entered into. The "DLB Close @" column is highlighted in Figure 8.1.

The position shown on HD in Figure 8.1 would close out on the delta effect for a 5 percent return when the stock price increases to $42.78, which is a 2.4 percent increase from the current stock price of $41.55. Remember, all LEAPS positions are constructed at the lower 25 percent of an overall or

COMPOUNDSTOCKEARNINGS

CSE Screener - LEAPS Finder

	Greater than	Less than		Greater than	Less than
Search					
Use CSE Defaults ☑	Uncalled Return % 9.9		Stock Price	24	101
LEAPS Expiration JAN 08	Called Return % 0		PE Ratio	0	71
Sort By DLB Index	LEAPS Price (Ask)	10.10	Market Cap $m	4999	
Buy > Hold ☑	LEAPS Delta		Broker Rec.		2.0
EPS Growth ☑			% 52 Wk Range		

Stock Details			Long Option Details				Short Option Details				Returns		DLB Assessment			
Stock Code	Stock Name	Stock Price (Ask)	Option Expiration	Option Strike	Option Price (Ask)	Option Symbol	Option Expiration	Option Strike	Option Price (Bid)	Option Symbol	Uncalled Return	Called Return	DLB Index (%)	DLB Close @	DLB Index (%)	Call Buyback @
JNJ	Johnson & Johnson	58.54	Jan-08	55.00	8.40	WJNAK	Jan-07	65.00	1.05	VJNAM	12.5%	2.7%	2.4%	59.92	3.2%	56.70
TLT	iShares Lehman 20+ Yr	83.55	Jan-08	83.00	4.60	YLIAE	Dec-06	89.00	0.55	TLTLK	12.0%	2.0%	2.4%	85.57	2.1%	81.77
QQQQ	Nasdaq 100 HOLDRs Tru	42.20	Jan-08	42.00	5.80	YWZAP	Jan-07	48.00	0.60	VCOAV	10.3%	0.8%	2.4%	43.23	3.9%	40.57
DOW	Dow Chemical Co.	42.69	Jan-08	40.00	6.60	WDOAH	Jan-07	50.00	0.65	VDOAJ	10.0%	4.2%	2.5%	43.77	4.5%	40.77
LLY	Lilly (Eli) and Co.	52.52	Jan-08	50.00	7.40	WILAJ	Jan-07	60.00	0.85	VILAL	11.5%	3.5%	2.6%	53.90	4.1%	50.39
BAC	BankAmerica Corp.	50.24	Jan-08	50.00	4.40	WBAAJ	Jan-07	55.00	0.60	VBAAK	13.6%	1.2%	2.7%	51.61	2.4%	49.06
WB	Wachovia Corp.	54.75	Jan-08	50.00	8.60	WVDAJ	Oct-06	57.50	1.45	WBJY	16.9%	0.4%	2.8%	56.28	2.6%	53.35
AIG	American Intl. Group Inc.	66.13	Jan-08	65.00	9.70	WAPAM	Jan-07	75.00	1.20	VAFAO	12.4%	1.5%	2.8%	68.00	3.7%	36.67
IACI	Interactive Corp.	28.79	Jan-08	25.00	3.60	ZCPAE	Jun-06	30.00	0.40	QTHFF	11.1%	1.8%	2.9%	29.61	3.0%	27.91
HD	Home Depot INc.	41.55	Jan-08	40.00	7.00	WHDAH	Nov-06	47.50	0.75	HDKS	10.7%	1.3%	3.0%	42.78	4.7%	39.60
VZ	Verizon Wireless	32.86	Jan-08	30.00	4.80	WLEAF	Oct-06	35.00	0.60	VZJG	12.5%	0.8%	3.0%	33.84	2.9%	31.92
ABT	Abbott Labs	42.40	Jan-08	40.00	6.90	WBTAH	Nov-06	47.50	0.70	ABTKW	10.0%	1.3%	3.0%	43.67	4.0%	40.72
HSY	Hershey Foods Corp.	54.14	Jan-08	50.00	9.40	LJDAJ	Nov-06	60.00	1.05	HSYKL	11.2%	1.7%	3.0%	55.78	4.0%	51.99
C	Citigroup Inc.	50.36	Jan-08	50.00	6.30	WRVAJ	Nov-06	55.00	0.95	VRNAK	17.9%	0.7%	3.1%	51.91	2.6%	49.07
PNC	PNC Bank Corp.	71.07	Jan-08	70.00	8.60	WYLAN	Nov-06	80.00	0.90	PNCKP	10.5%	2.3%	3.1%	73.30	3.9%	68.27
WFC	Wells Fargo & Co	66.49	Jan-08	66.00	9.00	WWRAM	Jan-07	75.00	1.15	VWFAO	12.8%	2.2%	3.1%	67.55	3.7%	63.07
UTX	United Techs. Corp.	65.09	Jan-08	65.00	8.60	WXUAM	Jan-07	75.00	0.95	VXUAO	11.0%	2.4%	3.2%	67.18	4.3%	62.27
MCD	McDonalds Corp.	35.88	Jan-08	35.00	5.50	WMNAG	Dec-06	40.00	1.05	MCDLH	18.6%	0.5%	3.2%	37.03	3.0%	34.81
MDT	Medtronic Inc.	48.23	Jan-08	45.00	8.40	WKVAI	Jan-07	55.00	1.10	FKDAK	13.1%	2.7%	3.2%	49.79	4.2%	46.23
JPM	J.P. Morgan Chase	46.26	Jan-08	45.00	6.00	WJPAI	Dec-06	50.00	1.05	JPMLJ	17.5%	0.1%	3.3%	47.78	2.4%	45.15

FIGURE 8.1 The "DLB Close @" column tells the investor at what stock price a particular LEAPS construction will close on the delta effect for a 5 percent return.

current rising or horizontal cycle, so the bias is the for the stock price to increase in the short term. However, investors must ensure that a particular DLB position will close out on the delta effect by the time the stock reaches 75 percent of the cycle. The assessment of the stock price at which the position will close is critical to the timely exit of the position. Let's assess the HD price chart shown as Figure 8.2 and make a judgment on this particular position.

We can see from the "DLB Close @" column in Figure 8.1 that this particular position will close out on the delta effect for a 5 percent return when the stock price reaches $42.78. This point is well before the stock reaches 75 percent of the current rising cycle; actually, the position will close out before the stock reaches 50 percent of the cycle. As such, this position meets the requirements and is an acceptable investment. If the stock price needs to increase more than 75 percent of the current cycle, the position is

This DLB position will close out at $42.78, a price that is actually below 50% of the cycle. This is an acceptable DLB position.

FIGURE 8.2 Price chart showing an acceptable DLB position.

not optimal, and we would simply select and qualify another position. As an alternative, we may choose to enter this position as a 10¢ rule transaction, which does not depend on the delta effect to exit.

Understanding the DLB Index

Another very important function of the CSE Screener is the ability to filter the market for LEAPS investments that have a high DLB index. The DLB index is a calculation for any given LEAPS position of the percentage the stock price must rise in order for the position to exit on the delta effect with a 5 percent return. For example, a position with a DLB index of 3.5 percent will close out on the delta effect for a 5 percent return when the underlying stock price increases by 3.5 percent. A position with a DLB index of 2.0 percent will close out on the delta effect for a 5 percent return when the underlying stock price increases by 2.0 percent.

Obviously, the most desirable DLB transactions are those that close out with the *smallest* increase in the underlying stock price. The CSE Screener can be used to effectively identify the best DLB positions (those with the lowest DLB index). See Figure 8.3. The default search criteria of the CSE Screener automatically ranks the positions in relation to their DLB index. The positions with the lowest DLB index are presented at the top of the results table. Investors choosing to use the DLB technique can simply start at the top of the list to identify positions with the lowest DLB index, qualify positions under the buying low rule, and then, finally, ensure that the required stock price increase is within 75 percent of the cycle.

COMPOUNDSTOCKEARNINGS

CSE Screener - LEAPS Finder

		Greater than	Less than			Greater than	Less than
[Search]							
Use CSE Defaults ☑	Uncalled Return %	9.9		Stock Price		24	101
LEAPS Expiration JAN 08 ▼	Called Return %	0		PE Ratio		0	71
Sort By DLB Index ▼	LEAPS Price (Ask)		10.10	Market Cap $m		4999	
Buy > Hold ☑	LEAPS Delta			Broker Rec.			2.6
EPS Growth ☑	% 52 Wk Range						

Stock Details			Long Option Details				Short Option Details				Returns		DLB Assessment			
Stock Code	Stock Name	Stock Price (Ask)	Option Expiration	Option Strike	Option Price (Ask)	Option Symbol	Option Expiration	Option Strike	Option Price (Bid)	Option Symbol	Uncalled Return	Called Return	DLB Index (%)	DLB Close @	DLB Index (%)	Call Buyback @
JNJ	Johnson & Johnson	58.54	Jan-08	55.00	8.40	WJNAK	Jan-07	65.00	1.05	VJNAM	12.5%	2.7%	2.4%	59.92	3.2%	56.70
TLT	iShares Lehman 20+ Yr	83.55	Jan-08	83.00	4.80	YLIAE	Dec-06	89.00	0.55	TLTLK	12.0%	2.0%	2.4%	85.57	2.1%	81.77
QQQQ	Nasdaq 100 HOLDRs Tru.	42.20	Jan-08	42.00	5.80	YWZAP	Jan-07	48.00	0.60	VCQAV	10.3%	0.8%	2.4%	43.23	3.9%	40.57
DOW	Dow Chemical Co.	42.68	Jan-08	40.00	6.50	WDOAH	Jan-07	50.00	0.60	VDOAJ	10.0%	4.2%	2.8%	43.77	4.5%	40.77
LLY	Lilly (Eli) and Co.	52.52	Jan-08	50.00	7.40	WILAJ	Jan-07	60.00	0.95	VILAL	11.5%	3.5%	2.6%	53.90	4.1%	50.39
BAC	BankAmerica Corp.	50.24	Jan-08	50.00	4.40	WBAAJ	Jan-07	55.00	0.50	VBAAK	13.6%	1.2%	2.7%	51.61	2.4%	49.06
WB	Wachovia Corp.	54.75	Jan-08	50.00	8.60	WVDAJ	Oct-06	57.50	1.45	WBJY	16.9%	0.4%	2.8%	56.26	2.6%	53.35
AIG	American Intl. Group Inc.	66.13	Jan-08	65.00	9.70	WAPAM	Jan-07	75.00	1.20	VAFAO	12.4%	1.5%	2.8%	68.00	3.7%	36.67
IACI	Interactive Corp.	28.79	Jan-08	25.00	3.60	ZCPAE	Jun-06	30.00	0.40	QTHFF	11.1%	1.8%	2.9%	29.61	3.0%	27.91
HD	Home Depot INc.	41.55	Jan-08	40.00	7.00	WHDAH	Nov-06	47.50	0.75	HDKS	10.7%	1.3%	3.0%	42.78	4.7%	39.60
VZ	Verizon Wireless	32.86	Jan-08	30.00	4.80	WLEAF	Oct-06	35.00	0.60	VZJG	12.5%	0.8%	3.0%	33.84	2.9%	31.92
ABT	Abbott Labs	42.40	Jan-08	40.00	6.90	WBTAH	Nov-06	47.50	0.70	ABTKW	10.0%	1.3%	3.0%	43.67	4.0%	40.72
HSY	Hershey Foods Corp.	54.14	Jan-08	50.00	9.40	LJDAJ	Nov-06	60.00	1.05	HSYKL	11.2%	1.7%	3.0%	55.78	4.0%	51.99
C	Citigroup Inc.	50.36	Jan-08	50.00	5.30	WRVAJ	Jan-07	55.00	0.95	VRNAK	17.9%	0.7%	3.1%	51.91	2.6%	49.07
PNC	PNC Bank Corp.	71.07	Jan-08	70.00	8.60	WYLAN	Nov-06	80.00	0.90	PNCKP	10.5%	2.3%	3.1%	73.30	3.9%	68.27
WFC	Wells Fargo & Co.	65.49	Jan-08	65.00	9.00	WWRAM	Jan-07	75.00	1.15	VWFAO	12.8%	2.2%	3.1%	67.55	3.7%	63.07
UTX	United Techs. Corp.	65.09	Jan-08	65.00	8.60	WXUAM	Jan-07	75.00	0.95	VXUAO	11.0%	2.4%	3.2%	67.18	4.3%	62.27
MCD	McDonalds Corp.	35.88	Jan-08	35.00	5.00	WMNAG	Dec-06	40.00	1.05	MCDLH	18.8%	0.5%	3.2%	37.03	3.0%	34.81
MDT	Medtronic Inc.	48.23	Jan-08	45.00	8.40	WKVAI	Jan-07	55.00	1.10	FKDAK	13.1%	2.7%	3.2%	49.79	4.2%	46.23
JPM	J P Morgan Chase	46.26	Jan-08	45.00	6.00	WJPAI	Dec-06	50.00	1.05	JPMLJ	17.5%	0.1%	3.3%	47.76	2.4%	45.15

FIGURE 8.3 CSE Screener ranks positions by DLB index.

SECONDARY CALL SALES: MANAGING LEAPS THAT HAVE NOT SOLD FOR A PROFIT

Remember, the objective is to consistently generate and compound cash flow regardless of the direction of the market. This section explains how we accomplish this objective through secondary call sales. A secondary call sale is any call sale that occurs after you have bought back the original call you sold when constructing a position. You need to use the secondary call sale rules on positions where the stock price has not increased enough to sell your LEAPS for cost plus 5 percent after buying back the short call.

LEAPS Secondary Call Sales Rules

The objective when selling a secondary call on a LEAPS is to buy back that call as soon as possible for at least a 5 percent net return. The methods and timing of secondary call sales are discussed in depth later in this section, but for now you must gain an understanding of the rules for selecting strike prices and expirations for secondary call sales—this function is not performed buy the CSE Screener.

The underlying function of the rules for selecting strike prices and expirations on a secondary call sale is to ensure, if possible, that you sell a secondary call that is both (1) the same strike price as the original call selected when constructing the position and (2) the shortest expiration possible that allows the minimum required return. The eleven rules are:

1. A secondary call can only be sold when the markets are in the green (trading higher than the close of the previous day). The markets are in the green any time when both the Dow Jones Industrial Average and the NASDAQ are trading above the close of the previous day.

2. A secondary call can only be sold after implementing either the 10¢ or 5% buyback rule.

3. A secondary call cannot be sold if the market bid price of the LEAPS is within 10 percent of your GTC sale price.

4. A secondary call can only be sold when the formalized seven-day rule has been satisfied (discussed in depth later in this section).

5. A secondary call sale should generate a minimum 10 percent uncalled return.

6. The aim is to buy back the call for a net uncalled return of 5 percent.

7. It is preferable to select the same call strike price as the strike price used when the position was established. Simply move the expiration date out in order to maintain a minimum 10 percent uncalled return using the same strike price. This move ensures that the delta ratio remains intact. A call may be sold up to but not exceeding the expiration date of the LEAPS.

8. Preference should always be given to a shorter-term call if this call provides the minimum uncalled return requirement of 10 percent (time value erodes more quickly in the investor's favor).

9. If a minimum 10 percent uncalled return with the same strike price cannot be maintained, drop the strike price one increment toward in the money. Preference should always be given to a shorter-term call if this provides the minimum uncalled return requirement of 10 percent.

10. Continue to drop the strike price to generate yield up to the point that the call strike price is equal to the LEAPS strike price. Do not sell a call with a strike price lower than the strike of the LEAPS.

11. In the event that a 10 percent uncalled return cannot be generated without violating rule 10, the LEAPS should be repositioned (discussed in Chapter 9).

Example of Selecting a Strike and Expiration for a Secondary Call Sale   Let's assume some time ago you entered into the following position on JP Morgan (JPM):

- BTO Jan 2007 $45.00 @ $6.50
- STO Jan 2006 $50.00 @ $1.50

After entering the position, the stock price declined and the call was bought back for $1.20 for an uncalled return of 4.6 percent. Subsequently, the stock price broke cycle and began cycling down. You are thus unable to sell the LEAPS for cost plus 5 percent and are now assessing a secondary call sale.

When selecting a call from the option chain, the LEAPS secondary call sales rules stipulate that:

- The bid price of the LEAPS must not be within 10 percent of the GTC sale price of the LEAPS.
- The call selected must generate a minimum 10 percent uncalled return.
- It is preferable to select the same call strike price as the strike price used when the position was established. If this call will not generate the uncalled return requirement, move the expiration date out to a maximum of the expiration of the LEAPS contract. Preference is always given to the shorter-term contract that provides the minimum uncalled return of 10 percent.
- If a minimum 10 percent uncalled return with the same strike price cannot be maintained, drop the strike price one increment toward in the money. Preference is always to sell the shortest-term call that provides the minimum uncalled return requirement of 10 percent.

Assume that the market is in the green and that the formalized seven-day rule (FSDR) has been met. (The FSDR governs the point in the price cycle where a secondary call can be sold and is covered in detail in the next section). Let's assess the option chain for JPM (Table 8.1) to find a call that meets the preceding requirements.

Because the stock price has declined since entering the position, the LEAPS originally purchased for $6.50 is now trading for $2.70 to $2.90. The original call sold was the January 2006 $50.00 at $1.50. This call is now trading for $0.60 to $0.70.

The first preference is to sell the original call sold when entering the transaction, if this call will provide a minimum 10 percent uncalled return on the position, or a minimum $0.65. We can see from the option chain that this call can only be sold for $0.60, which is less than the required minimum uncalled return of $0.65. You need to increase yield on the call sale. The preference is to maintain the same strike price, yet move the expiration of

TABLE 8.1 JP Morgan Option Chain Example

Strike	Ticker	Bid Price	Ask Price	Delta	Strike	Ticker	Bid Price	Ask Price	Delta
September					**Mar-05**				
27.50	JPMIY	11.80	12.00	1.00	27.50	JPMCY	11.90	12.10	0.98
30.00	JPMIF	9.30	9.50	1.00	30.00	JPMCF	9.50	9.70	0.97
32.50	JPMIZ	6.80	7.00	1.00	32.50	JPMCZ	7.20	7.40	0.92
35.00	JPMIG	4.40	4.50	1.00	35.00	JPMCG	5.20	5.30	0.81
37.50	JPMIU	1.95	2.05	0.91	37.50	JPMCU	3.30	3.50	0.63
40.00	JPMIH	0.30	0.35	0.33	40.00	JPMCH	1.90	2.05	0.44
42.50	JPMIV	0.00	0.05	—	42.50	JPMCV	0.90	1.05	0.26
45.00	JPMII	0.00	0.05	—	45.00	JPMCI	0.35	0.45	0.14
47.50	JPMIW	0.00	0.05	—	47.50	JPMCW	0.10	0.20	0.06
50.00	JPMIJ	0.00	0.05	—	50.00	JPMCJ	0.00	0.10	—
October					**Jan-06**				
27.50	JPMJY	11.90	12.00	1.00	20.00	WJPAD	19.30	19.50	0.95
30.00	JPMJF	9.40	9.50	1.00	25.00	WJPAE	14.40	14.60	0.94
32.50	JPMJZ	6.90	7.00	1.00	30.00	WJPAF	10.10	10.20	0.87
35.00	JPMJG	4.40	4.60	0.97	35.00	WJPAG	6.30	6.50	0.68
37.50	JPMJU	2.20	2.25	0.79	37.50	WJPAU	4.80	4.90	0.56
40.00	JPMJH	0.55	0.65	0.39	40.00	WJPAH	3.40	3.60	0.44
42.50	JPMJV	0.05	0.10	0.10	42.50	WJPAV	2.40	2.55	0.33
45.00	JPMJI	0.00	0.05	—	45.00	WJPAI	1.55	1.70	0.23
47.50	JPMJW	0.00	0.05	—	47.50	WJPAW	1.00	1.10	0.16
50.00	JPMJJ	0.00	0.05	—	50.00	WJPAJ	0.60	0.70	0.11
December					**Jan-07**				
30.00	JPMLF	9.40	9.60	0.99	25.00	VJPAE	14.40	14.90	0.88
32.50	JPMLZ	7.00	7.20	0.97	30.00	VJPAF	10.60	10.80	0.78
35.00	JPMLG	4.80	4.90	0.89	35.00	VJPAG	7.20	7.30	0.61
37.50	JPMLU	2.80	2.95	0.69	40.00	VJPAH	4.60	4.80	0.43
40.00	JPMLH	1.30	1.40	0.42	45.00	VJPAI	2.70	2.90	0.27
42.50	JPMLV	0.50	0.55	0.20	50.00	VJPAJ	1.50	1.60	0.16
45.00	JPMLI	0.10	0.15	0.07					
47.50	JPMLW	0.00	0.10	—					
Jan-05									
25.00	JPMAE	14.30	14.50	0.99					
30.00	JPMAF	9.40	9.60	0.98					
32.50	JPMAZ	7.10	7.30	0.95					
35.00	JPMAG	4.90	5.10	0.85					
37.50	JPMAU	3.00	3.20	0.66					
40.00	JPMAH	1.55	1.65	0.43					
42.50	JPMAV	0.60	0.70	0.23					
45.00	JPMAI	0.15	0.25	0.10					
47.50	JPMAW	0.05	0.10	0.04					
50.00	JPMAJ	0.00	0.05	—					

the call out to generate yield. In this instance, the only option is to move to the January 2007 expiration. We know that you must attempt to sell a call with the same strike price as the original call sold, if this call provides the minimum uncalled return of 10 percent. In this instance the January 2007 $50.00 is selling for $1.50, well in excess of your minimum uncalled return requirement of $0.65. This is the call you would sell.

In the event that the January 2007 $50.00 did not provide an uncalled return of minimum 10 percent, you would drop the strike price one increment and sell the shortest-term call that provides an uncalled return of 10 percent or greater. This process can be continued up to, but not exceeding, the strike price of the LEAPS. If, in order to generate an uncalled return of minimum 10 percent, you need to sell a call with a strike less than the strike of the LEAPS, the LEAPS needs to be repositioned. Repositioning of a LEAPS is discussed in detail in Chapter 9.

The Formalized Seven-Day Rule

Now that we have covered how to select the strike price and expiration for a secondary call sale, in this section we discuss an equally important aspect of secondary call sales: timing. Timing relates to where on the price chart a secondary call sale is executed. Timing is critical to the ability of an investor to continually generate cash flow from a position, regardless of market direction.

Readers familiar with covered calls will realize that the FSDR is essentially the selling high rule for covered calls applied to the LEAPS technique. While the concept remains the same, the one very significant advantage of applying this technique to a LEAPS position compared to a traditional stock position is *leverage*. When applying the FSDR on LEAPS, buyback returns can be realized with *much smaller* movements in the underlying stock price, because the profitable buyback amount is so much smaller due to a smaller dollar investment in the LEAPS contract versus the stock. For example, a 5 percent net return on a $5.00 LEAPS is just $0.25, whereas a 5 percent net return on a $30.00 stock is $1.50. Much smaller movements in the underlying stock price allow for profitable call sales and buybacks. It follows, then, that very small cycles of the stock price can and should be utilized to sell and profitably buy back a call when managing a LEAPS position. The need to pay close attention to stock price cycles is part of the reason why LEAPS require a much greater time commitment to management than do covered calls. However, the greater time commitment is compensated for by much higher returns when used by experienced investors.

To achieve a profitable buyback on a call using the FSDR technique we need one or both of the following to occur: (1) The stock price must drop sometime in the future or (2) time value must diminish.

The FSDR concentrates on point 1 by identifying when a stock is in the high region of its price cycle. This rule is essentially the opposite of the buying low rule that ensures you are buying into new positions when the market is down and a stock is in the lower 25 percent of its cycle. Conversely, the FSDR ensures that you are selling a secondary call when the market is up and the stock is in the upper 75 percent of its current cycle. This condition greatly increases the chances that the stock will fall and you will be able to buy back the call for a profit.

It is important to make the distinction that our objective is not speculation. What we are trying to do is simply buy low and sell high or sell high and buy low, as the case may be. If you sell a call and the stock keeps moving up, you may be able to close the position on the delta effect (previously discussed) or implement other defensive strategies such as the surrogate LEAPS replacement technique (see Chapter 9).

The FSDR encompasses two components:

1. Secondary call sales can only be made when a stock is in the upper 75 percent of its current price cycle.
2. A rising price cycle must have a minimum of $1.50 of price between the upper and lower lines of its price cycle.

By ensuring that you sell secondary calls at the high end of the price cycle, it is more likely that the stock will decline and you will be able to buy the call back for a profit. Remember, the decay in time value is also working significantly in the covered call writer's favor. This factor also greatly increases the opportunity for a profitable call buyback.

It is important to make the distinction that our objective is not speculation when using the FSDR. What we are trying to do is sell in the vicinity of the top of the cycle and buy the call back for a profit at lower stock prices in the near future. If you sell a call and the stock keeps moving up, *you do not take a loss on the call*. Rather, investors should have patience and wait for the stock price to come back to the bottom of the cycle. Stocks cycle up and down—they do not go straight up and they do not go straight down. If the stock doesn't come down to allow a profitable call buyback we can use other management and defensive techniques (see Chapter 9).

Patience and management are critical factors for success. You must have patience to *wait* for the stock price to meet the FSDR before selling the secondary call. You must also have patience to *wait* for the stock price to cycle down after selling the call to allow a profitable buyback. Patience is key.

It is very rare that a call will be sold and the very next day the stock cycles down. It is not possible to pick the absolute top of the market and have the call immediately fall in price—this is an unrealistic expectation. It is much more common that over a period of one to four weeks after selling a secondary call, the stock cycles down and allows a profitable buyback. During the period of waiting, *patience* is required. Novice investors often panic when an FSDR call cannot be immediately bought back for a profit. Such immediacy is against the nature of this technique. Again, when using the FSDR, patience is key.

But what if we sell an FSDR call at what we believe is the top of the price cycle and the stock breaks cycle, shoots straight up, and never trades at a lower price? This scenario is common and simply requires investors to implement one of many management strategies:

- Closing the position on the delta effect.
- Buying back the call profitably at higher stock prices due to the decay in time value.
- Using the surrogate LEAPS replacement to exit the position (discussed in Chapter 9).

Applying the FSDR   Remember, the FSDR identifies the timing of a secondary call sale. It identifies the point on the chart where a secondary call can be sold. The FSDR instructs to only sell a secondary call when the stock price is in the upper 75 percent of the price cycle (Figure 8.4). This section illustrates the practical application of this technique. Interpretation of the chart is vitally important.

FIGURE 8.4   The FSDR instructs to only sell a secondary call when the stock price is in the upper 75 percent of the price cycle.

Readers should revisit "Using Price Charts," discussed in Chapter 3. The FSDR is essentially the selling high rule for covered calls when applied to LEAPS. The commentary and examples provided for the selling high rule apply equally to the FSDR.

Identifying the First Sell Point of a New Price Cycle   This topic applies equally to covered call and LEAPS techniques. However, it is discussed in this section rather than in Part I, Covered Calls, since it is an advanced technique for optimizing the management of positions. This level of optimization is not critical to the success of the covered call strategy, yet it will most definitely increase returns of that strategy. When using the LEAPS technique, however, we are leveraged, and aggressive management of underperforming positions is critical to the success of the strategy.

The most difficult task regarding the FSDR is identifying the first sell point of a new price cycle. While it is not critical to enter new positions at the first buy point, identifying the first sell point of a new cycle is much more important. The reason for its importance is that when assessing an FSDR, the investor is already in a management situation on the particular position and needs to maximize call sales to maximize the cash flow from that position. Consistently missing the first sell point of a new cycle means an investor is consistently missing an opportunity to generate cash flow, reduce cost base in the position, and compound the asset base.

When assessing the first buy point, we do so from the perspective of entering into new positions after the current cycle has changed from declining to increasing. In identifying the first sell point, many of the principals of identifying a change in cycle remain the same as those for identifying the first buy point, so now is a good time to revisit the section "Identifying the First Buy Point" in Chapter 7. In using the FSDR, however, we are discussing management of positions in *any* cycle and how to identify the first sell point of a new cycle, whether it is increasing or declining.

When managing a position for income where the current cycle is declining, we should be watching for higher bottoms and a break to the top of the declining cycle to indicate a potential change of cycle direction, as shown in Figure 8.5. When managing a position for income where the current cycle is rising, we should be watching for lower tops and a break to the bottom of the declining cycle to indicate a potential change of cycle direction, as shown in Figure 8.6.

Once we have spotted a potential change in cycle, whether increasing or declining, we can identify the first sell point of a new cycle as follows:

- The first sell point of a new cycle is always preceded by a minimum of two bottoms and one top.

FIGURE 8.5   Break through top of a declining cycle.

See Figure 8.7 for an example of identifying the first sell point of a new rising cycle. As previously noted, the first sell point of a new cycle is always preceeded by a mimimum of two bottoms and a minimum of one top. So we first connect the two bottoms, then identifiy the first top of the cycle, and then extrapolate a top parallel line from this top. Remember, when attempting to identify the first sell point, the second top of the cycle is yet to

FIGURE 8.6   Break through bottom of a rising cycle.

FIGURE 8.7   Identifying the first sell point of a new rising cycle.

form—the top line must be estimated by drawing a parallel line from the first top.

An example of identifying the first sell point of a new declining cycle is shown in Figure 8.8. Since the first sell point of a new cycle is always preceeded by a mimimum of two bottoms and a minimum of one top we first connect the two bottoms, then identifiy the first top of the cycle, and then

FIGURE 8.8   Identifying the first sell point of a new declining cycle.

extrapolate a top parallel line from this top. Remember, when attempting to identify the first sell point, the second top of the cycle is yet to form—the top line must be estimated by drawing a parallel line from the first top.

Exception to FSDR—Declining Cycles   The FSDR is applicable to stocks regardless of whether the stock price is rising, falling, or going sideways. The rules for applying the FSDR remain substantially the same regardless of the direction of the cycle. However, one very important exception to the FSDR exists for falling stocks, and it is known as the *25% buyback rule*.

When implementing the FSDR on a declining cycle, investors should *not* aim for a net buyback return of 5 percent. Instead, for larger buyback returns, investors should only buy back the call when the stock reaches the bottom 25 percent of the cycle. The 25% buyback rule leverages off the fact that the current cycle is *declining*. As such, it is wise to take full advantage of this declining stock price in order to enhance returns.

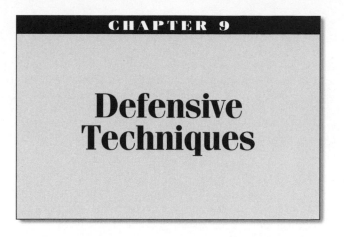

CHAPTER 9

Defensive Techniques

In the preceding chapters we discuss in detail the process of entering new LEAPS positions, the buyback and close out rules, and managing unproductive positions for consistent cash flow regardless of market direction. Now we present the defensive techniques available to LEAPS investors (refer to Figure A.2).

The flexibility of LEAPS allows investors a significant array of defensive techniques. These techniques can be used to effectively manage any poorly performing LEAPS position to an eventual profitable exit. They vary in nature and are used for the following purposes:

- To prevent an unprofitable callout.
- To reduce capital in an underperforming position.
- To reduce the average LEAPS cost in an underperforming position.
- To allow continued call sales on a LEAPS that has fallen significantly.
- To prevent high levels of time decay in a LEAPS.

When learning the defensive techniques, it is important to remember the three primary objectives of LEAPS investing:

1. Closing the transaction as quickly as possible for a profit.

2. Generating consistent income on underperforming positions.

3. Reinvesting and compounding these proceeds.

The defensive techniques exist to *quicken* the realization of these objectives and allow faster compounding of the asset base.

SURROGATE LEAPS REPLACEMENT

The surrogate LEAPS replacement (SLR) is a highly valuable defensive technique that is very regularly applied by LEAPS investors. The SLR is used when an investor sells a call under the FSDR and the stock price continues to move up, preventing a profitable call buyback. It allows investors to reduce capital in the position and realize profits on a LEAPS by taking advantage of a rising stock price—without unprofitably buying back the short call.

The SLR is very effective when the stock price has not moved up enough to exit the entire position on the delta effect or the position has a poor delta ratio due to incorrect construction. Thus, it is to be used when the following three conditions exist:

1. An investor has sold a secondary call and the stock price has moved up, not allowing that call to be bought back for a profit.
2. The investor can sell the LEAPS for a 5 percent or better profit but is prevented from closing the transaction as doing so would result in an overall negative return due to the buyback cost of the call.
3. The stock is in the upper 75 percent of its current cycle.

Take the position shown in Table 9.1 as an example. We can see that this investor has a LEAPS with a cost of $5.00 and has sold a call for $1.00. Since selling the call, the underlying stock price has increased. As such, the call has not been able to be bought back for a profit and is now trading at $3.00. As the stock price has increased, so has the value of the investor's LEAPS. The investor now has a $1.50 profit in the LEAPS but is prevented from realizing this profit because of the larger loss on the call. *The loss on the call is preventing the transaction from being closed out; even through the investor has a large profit in the LEAPS.* This is an ideal situation in which to use the SLR.

TABLE 9.1 Sample Position Suitable for SLR

Contract	Entry Price	Current Price	Profit (Loss)
LEAPS	$5.00	$6.50	$1.50
Call	$1.00	$3.00	($2.00)

The SLR Rules

There are two basic rules for using the SLR:

1. If the stock price is in the upper 75 percent of the cycle and you are able to sell the original LEAPS for a return of 5 percent or more, then the SLR can be considered.

2. Select the same expiration date; however, move the strike price up one or two increments (preferably not equal to the strike price of the call). Buy this LEAPS and then immediately sell the LEAPS you own.

Once you have taken action based on these rules, there are two distinct scenarios:

1. Stock price continues up. In this scenario you should take advantage of the rising stock price. If you are able to sell the SLR LEAPS for a 5 percent profit, then do so. After selling this LEAPS, you must immediately buy another LEAPS. Simply move the strike price up one increment. You have now performed a second SLR. Continue to take 5 percent profits and SLR the LEAPS to the extent that the strike price of your LEAPS is not higher than the strike price of the call. You can SLR up to the point that the LEAPS and the call have an identical strike price.

2. Stock price declines. In this scenario you should buy back the problematic call, but only when you can exit the call at approximately the cost you sold it for. Once you have bought back the call, go back to the FSDR.

Following the rules for this technique achieves several important objectives:

- Investors can take advantage of the high point of the price cycle and realize a profit on the LEAPS.
- Investors can continually reduce the capital invested in the position by selecting a higher strike price LEAPS. Excess capital can then be reinvested into new positions.
- If the stock price rises, investors can profit from continued strength in the stock by selling LEAPS for 5 percent profits.
- If the stock price declines, investors can exit a problematic call.
- After buying back the call, investors have the potential to exit the entire position on the next high point of the price cycle.

Applying the SLR

Here is a detailed example of implementing the SLR in five steps.

Step 1: *Enter new position.* Figure 9.1 shows the entry into a new position at the bottom of a current horizontal cycle. The stock then broke cycle, allowing the call to be bought back to lock in a 5 percent uncalled return.

Step 2: *Sell a call at top of cycle, which then becomes problematic.* After buying back the initial call, our interpretation of the chart as shown in Figure 9.2 is that the stock was in a current declining cycle. A secondary call was sold at the top of this declining cycle. The stock immediately broke to the top of the declining cycle. The call could not be bought back for a profit.

Step 3: *LEAPS becomes profitable, so perform an SLR.* The stock price continues to increase after selling the call, as shown in Figure 9.3. It increases to a point where we have a 5 percent or greater return if we sold the LEAPS. At this point, we immediately SLR. We move the strike up one or two increments (two in this case) and buy the Jan 2007 $35.00 @ $3.00. We then sell the current LEAPS to take a profit of $0.40. We have taken profits and reduced capital in the underperforming position by over 50 percent. This capital should be immediately invested elsewhere. We would then generally place a GTC to buy back the problematic call at cost ($0.80).

Step 4: *Stock price declines and the GTC to buy back the call executes.* The GTC order to buy the call at cost executes (see Figure 9.4). In this in-

FIGURE 9.1   Entering a new position at the bottom of a current horizontal cycle.

FIGURE 9.2 A problematic secondary call sale.

stance, the call was held for a period of approximately three weeks. It is important during this time to have patience and wait for time to take its course and for the stock price to fluctuate, allowing the buyback.

Most importantly, during this period of waiting, the SLR has freed the majority of our capital from the position. This capital is now invested in

FIGURE 9.3 Performing an SLR when the LEAPS becomes profitable.

FIGURE 9.4   Stock price declines and the GTC to buy back the call executes.

new productive positions and has been reinvested many times over during the three-week period.

If the stock price continues to move up and does not allow a profitable call buyback, when we are able to sell the current LEAPS for a 5 percent or greater return and the stock is at 75 percent of the current cycle, we will SLR again. We will continue to SLR until the strike price of the LEAPS is equal to the strike price of the call. When the strike prices are equal, we are "against the wall" and can no longer SLR. By this time, we have taken several profits from the LEAPS and have taken out the vast majority of the capital from the position. We will then simply wait for the stock price to decline and time value to erode the buyback cost of the call until it can be bought back at breakeven. Stocks go up and down, but they do not go straight up or straight down.

Step 5: *Sell SLR LEAPS for cost plus 5 percent.* As shown in Figure 9.5, we complete the transaction by selling the SLR LEAPS for cost plus 5 percent. The total profit on the transaction is as follows:

- $0.30 from buyback of original call.
- $0.40 from sale of original LEAPS.
- $0.15 from sale of SLR LEAPS.
- Total = $0.85, or 14.1 percent on original cost of $6.00.

Remember, $3.40 or 57 percent of the $6.00 of capital committed to this position was removed by the SLR. The entire position was open for ap-

FIGURE 9.5 Completing the SLR LEAPS transaction.

proximately one month; however, for three weeks of this month, only $3.00 of capital was committed. This figure effectively brings the return up to around 30 percent on the committed capital of $3.00. This adjustment highlights the value of the SLR technique: Capital can be effectively removed from an underperforming position and committed elsewhere into new, productive positions.

One significant point of note is the secondary call sale that may have been executed at the top of the current horizontal cycle. If this call were executed, the position would not be able to be closed, and we would have applied the SLR again. However, this call should not have been sold. According to the LEAPS secondary call sales rules, a secondary call cannot be sold if the market bid price of the LEAPS is within 10 percent of the GTC sell price. This limitation prevents calls from being sold against positions that are close to an exit. As it is impossible to pick the absolute top of the market, when a call is sold on a position that is close to exit, more often than not, it becomes a hindrance to the position being profitably closed out.

AVERAGING DOWN

Many investment methodologies promote the technique of dollar cost averaging. Dollar cost averaging involves purchasing a certain amount of a stock or fund at regular intervals over time. For example, instead of investing $10,000 in a stock today, invest $2,500 at the end of each quarter over a year.

A modified version of this technique is a valuable defensive technique for LEAPS investors. Occasionally, a LEAPS price will drop significantly over a long period of time. These circumstances may allow you to take advantage of a highly depressed LEAPS price by averaging down.

The four rules for averaging down a LEAPS position are:

1. If the market price of a LEAPS drops significantly to a point where you are able to buy the same LEAPS contract you already own for 15 percent or less of the price you paid for it, then do so. For example, if you own a LEAPS at a cost of $5.00, you would average that position down if you could buy additional contracts at a price of $0.75 (the "average down price").

2. You should buy the number of contracts that brings your average cost (see explanation in "Calculating Adjusted Cost and Average Cost" in the section on rolling out that follows) to a price equal to two times the average down price. For example, if you own a LEAPS at a cost of $5.00, you would average that position down if you could buy additional contracts at a price of $0.75 (the average down price). You should buy the number of contracts that brings your average cost to a value of $1.50 (two times the average down price of $0.75).

3. The 5 percent return calculation for subsequent secondary call sales should be based on *the original contract cost*, not on the average cost of contracts. So, for a buyback on a secondary call sale on a $5.00 LEAPS, you should still attempt to realize a net return of $0.25.

4. Sell the LEAPS at the new average cost plus 5 percent, not the original cost. So, for the preceding example, you should sell the LEAPS for $1.50 plus 5 percent.

Averaging down allows investors to do the following:

- Significantly reduce their average cost in the LEAPS for a relatively small additional capital outlay.
- Significantly increase their LEAPS contracts for a relatively small additional capital outlay.
- Generate significantly higher percentage returns on secondary call sales.
- Exit the position at average cost rather than original cost. This feature has the effect of enabling investors to exit the position at much lower stock prices and, therefore, much quicker.

REPOSITIONING A LEAPS

In the rules for selling secondary calls we established that (1) you cannot sell a call on a LEAPS with a strike price less than the LEAPS and (2) you cannot sell a call on a LEAPS with an expiration longer than the LEAPS.

On rare occasions, a stock may decline significantly to a level where you can no longer sell a call on a position for a minimum 10 percent return without breaching the preceding two rules. If this situation occurs, you must reposition your LEAPS in order to continue generating cash flow from this position.

Repositioning a LEAPS simply means selling the LEAPS you currently own and purchasing a LEAPS with the same expiration one or two strike prices deeper in the money.

Again, you must try not to violate the $10.00 adjusted cost rule; however, on some occasions it may be necessary to do so. If you do violate the $10.00 rule, managing the position with secondary call sales will be more difficult.

Repositioning a LEAPS has the effect of creating more management depth by allowing you to sell lower strike prices that previously would have violated the rule regarding not selling a call on a LEAPS with a strike price less than the LEAPS.

ROLLING OUT

One great advantage of the LEAPS technique is that time is always working more for you than against you. You always sell a call that has a far greater *theta*, or rate of time decay, than the LEAPS you own. To keep time on your side, it is imperative that each year you go through a process called *rolling out*.

As a guide, a one strike price in the money LEAPS with about two years to expiration has a theta value of around –0.003, which means that the LEAPS loses $0.0030 in value each day, or $0.09 per month.

A one strike price in the money LEAPS with a half a year to expiration has a theta value of around –.0042, meaning that the LEAPS loses $0.0042 in value each day, or $0.13 per month.

The objective is to always keep time decay of your LEAPS to a minimum. Rolling out allows you to accomplish this objective by ensuring that there is always at least one year of time value left in the LEAPS.

The Rollout Rules

If an investor is holding a LEAPS that has less than one year to expiration, he or she must sell it and buy another LEAPS relating to the same company. Three guidelines must be followed:

1. A rollout must be conducted on a down day.
2. If your capital position allows, select the same strike price and the furthest out date possible providing that the adjusted cost (discussed later in this section) does not exceed $10.00.
3. If this LEAPS leads to an adjusted cost of more than $10.00 (or if your capital position does not allow you to select the same strike), select the next highest strike price. Continue to raise the strike price until the adjusted cost does not exceed $10.00. Preference is always given to maintaining the lowest strike price possible.

Note that if you raise the strike price of the LEAPS, you will generally have a lower delta value on the LEAPS. This causes a lower delta ratio when selling calls against the LEAPS and also means the stock price must travel higher for you to exit the position at cost plus 5 percent.

Calculating Adjusted Cost and Average Cost

Adjusted cost is a measure of the new cost of your LEAPS after you have rolled out. As an example of how it is calculated, suppose the following conditions exist:

- You hold a Jan 2006 $35.00 LEAPS on JPM at a cost of $5.00.
- You have not been able to exit the position for cost plus 5 percent, but you have been selling and buying back calls to generate cash flow.
- It is now January 2005, and you need to roll out the LEAPS.
- You sell your Jan 2006 $35 LEAPS on JPM for $3.50.
- You buy the Jan 2007 $35 LEAPS on JPM for $8.00.

You figure the adjusted cost as follows:

Adjusted cost = Cost of original − Sell price of original + Cost of new LEAPS
$$= \$5.00 - \$3.50 + \$8.00$$
$$= \$9.50$$

You now must use the adjusted cost of $9.50 for all return calculations. A net 5 percent return on a secondary call sales and buyback is now $9.50 × 0.05 = $0.48. Do not use the original cost of your LEAPS as you now have more capital invested in the position! When selling the LEAPS, also use the adjusted cost of $9.50 plus 5 percent.

Average cost is a measure of new cost of your LEAPS after you have averaged down. Let's use another example to show how this factor is calculated. Suppose the following:

- You hold 10 Jan 2006 $35.00 LEAPS at a cost of $5.00.
- You have not been able to exit the position for cost plus 5 percent, but you have been selling and buying back calls to generate cash flow.
- Following the averaging down rules, you purchase another 46 contracts of the Jan 2006 $35.00 LEAPS on JPM. You purchase this number of contracts as this is the number that will allow you to reduce your average cost down to $1.50 (two times the average down price).

The number of contracts needed to be purchased to reduce the average cost to two times the average down price varies for each position. The number needs to be estimated at first, and then investors can use the following formula to test the accuracy of the estimate. Adjust the number of contracts upwards or downwards as appropriate, until the result of the following formula equals two times the average down price.

Adjusted cost = [(No. original contracts × Cost of original contracts) + (No. new contracts × Cost of new contracts)]/(# Original contracts + No. new contracts)

$$= [(10 \times \$5.00) + (46 \times \$0.75)]/(10 + 46)$$
$$= \$1.50$$

When selling the LEAPS, use the adjusted cost of $1.50 plus 5 percent. However, when performing a secondary call sale, use the original cost of $5.00 when calculating net buyback amounts. For example, a call buyback for a secondary call sale will net a minimum $0.25 or (5 percent of the $5.00 original cost) even though the adjusted cost in this position is now only $1.50. Just one management move with a net buyback return of $0.25 will now allow you to net a return of 16.70 percent.

Thus you can see how averaging down allows realization of much higher returns on an underperforming position.

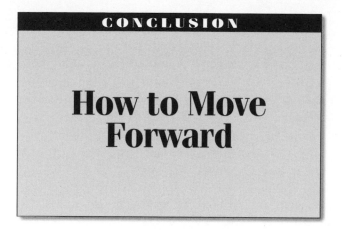

CONCLUSION

How to Move Forward

S ince Compound Stock Earnings was founded in 1999, thousands of investors have been taught the techniques outlined in this book and are now successfully managing their own investments using covered calls. Once comfort and familiarity are gained with the technique, these investors consistently generate monthly returns from their stock investments equivalent to an annual mutual fund return.

This chapter is intended to provide some guidance to those who wish to follow the path of thousands of successful Compound Stock Earnings clients who are now safely and very successfully managing their own stock portfolios.

1. Reread this book until you are confident in your *full and comprehensive* understanding of the concepts and techniques of covered call investing described herein. You should not consider beginning investing if there are any gaps or uncertainties in your understanding. You must be comfortable and confident with *every* concept before placing your hard-earned money at risk.

2. Investigate the support services offered by Compound Stock Earnings such as the 2-Day Intensive Seminar or Covered Call/LEAPS Selections (see Appendix E) and decide which, if any, will enhance your learning and progression. We have found that most investors do not require any support services over the long term, but these services are invaluable to those who are learning the technique.

3. The importance of capital management cannot be overstated for learning investors. Do not invest a significant amount of money while learning the covered call technique. A "significant amount" of money varies for each individual investor. A good "learning stake" is 10–20 percent of the value of your current stock portfolio; or if you do not have a stock portfolio, 10–20 percent of your annual salary. If an investor is gripped with the fear of losing money, it is very difficult to make rational and logical decisions. The learning process is greatly assisted when a smaller amount of capital is at stake.

4. When you are ready to commit funds to the technique, we strongly recommended that all investors begin investing with covered calls and *not* LEAPS. Covered call investing is a superior technique for the learning investor as it is far less complicated and inherently less risky than LEAPS.

5. Invest using the covered call technique with a small learning stake for a minimum of six months before considering progressing to LEAPS. This period will allow you to accumulate some profits in your account, become proficient in both up and down markets, learn from a few mistakes (you cannot develop a new skill without making them), gain some confidence, and gain greater insight into the operation of the markets.

6. Once you have developed a consistent track record of generating returns over a six-month period with covered calls, you are then ready to consider progressing to LEAPS if you wish. Investors should understand that LEAPS investing is a higher risk/higher return strategy when compared to covered calls, and it requires much greater time commitment. A good way to start learning the practical application of the technique is to follow the transactions, management moves, and close-outs being executed by the authors in the Compound Stock Earnings Covered Call/LEAPS Selections service by going to www.compoundstockearnings.com/services.htm.

7. Many investors choose to continue solely with covered call investing, as they are happy with the returns generated and the low time input required. If you would like to progress to LEAPS investing, do so *gradually*. Take 10 percent of your portfolio and place these funds into LEAPS investments for a month or two. Then move another 10 percent to LEAPS investments if you achieve acceptable returns.

8. Do not move more than 20 percent of your portfolio into LEAPS investments until you have a consistent track record over six months of generating returns higher than those realized with your covered call investing.

9. Remember, investing is a long-term wealth-building proposition. Treating it as such and taking the time to learn will greatly increase the likelihood of achieving the desired successful outcomes. Any endeavor worth succeeding in requires aptitude, patience, and perseverance. Investing is no different!

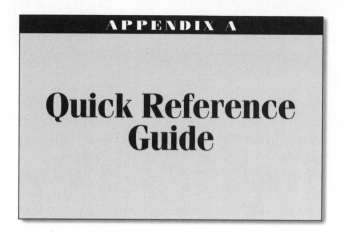

APPENDIX A

Quick Reference Guide

This appendix is best used as a reference. It should not be read to the exclusion of the rest of the book.

COVERED CALLS

Refer to the accompanying flowchart (Figure A.1) that depicts each step in the covered call investment process.

The Rules for Entering New Covered Call Positions in the U.S. Market

A new covered call position involves buying a stock and selling a covered call. The U.S. market has thousands of optionable stocks; therefore investors can be very selective when entering into new covered call positions. The eight rules are as follows:

1. You can only establish new positions on down market days. A down market day is any time when the Dow and the NASDAQ are in the red (trading lower than the close of the previous day).

2. You must always only sell the near month call when entering a transaction.

3. Use the CSE Screener to filter through all available covered call opportunities on the U.S. market.

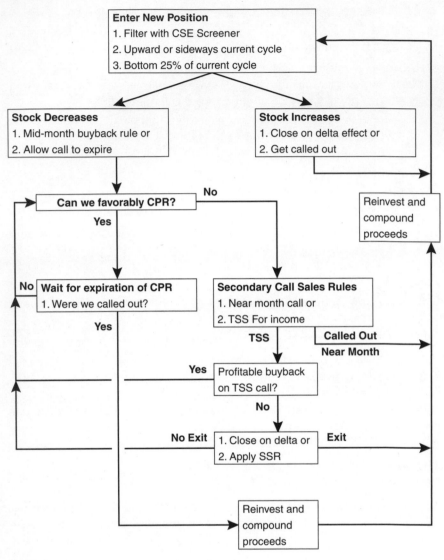

FIGURE A.1 Covered call process flowchart.

4. Select the highest-yielding opportunities presented by the CSE Screener.
5. Ensure that the stock is an upward moving or sideways moving stock.
6. Ensure that the stock adheres to the buying low rule for covered calls.
7. Always give priority to maintaining acceptable levels of diversification between stocks and industries—even if a stock you are already invested in presents an excellent covered call opportunity.
8. Buy the stock first and then immediately sell the call. Do not hesitate. If you buy the stock and wait for a better price for the call, you are no better than a speculator, and you will get burned!

Using the CSE Screener to Select U.S. Covered Calls

The CSE Screener is a proprietary covered call search and filter tool designed, developed, and maintained by Compound Stock Earnings. The CSE Screener allows investors to quickly and easily search the stock market for the highest returning covered call positions that meet specific fundamental and technical requirements. The tool is tailored to accommodate the criteria and rules established in this book for selecting covered call positions.

Anyone who purchases *Covered Calls and LEAPS—A Wealth Option* is entitled to one month's complimentary access to the Covered Call Toolbox (which includes the CSE Screener) by going to www.compoundstockearnings.com/freemonth. Thus readers can actually use the tools while learning about them in this book.

Because the U.S. market is extremely large, you can be very selective in terms of the quality of the companies in which you invest. You should use the following eight parameters to filter U.S. covered call opportunities:

1. Uncalled return of minimum 4 percent.
2. Called return of minimum 4 percent.
3. Price-earnings ratio (PE) of 35 or less.
4. Market capitalization of US$500 million or more.
5. Average broker recommendation of 2.5 or less.
6. An aggregate of the brokers recommending the stock as "Strong Buy" and "Buy" greater than the number of brokers recommending the stock as "Hold."
7. A consensus earnings per share (EPS) estimate for "Next Fiscal Year" forecast to be greater than the consensus EPS estimate for "This Fiscal Year."
8. Stock trading less than 75 percent of its 52-week trading range.

How to Look at a Price Chart

When an investor assesses a price chart, he or she must be able to answer the following four questions:

1. What is the overall trend: upwards, downwards, or sideways?
2. What are the past cycles: upwards, downwards, or sideways?
3. What is the current cycle: upwards, downwards, or sideways?
4. Where are we in the current cycle: the bottom, middle, or top?

Identifying Upward, Downward, and Sideways Moving Stocks in the Context of Covered Calls

Upward moving stocks can be of two types:

1. Stocks in a *generally rising cycle*.
2. Stocks that have had significant price declines in the preceding months and are *currently in an upward cycle*. A stock is currently in an upward cycle if it has (a) substantially broken through the upper line of the declining price cycle and (b) established a new rising price cycle (a cycle with higher tops and higher bottoms).

Downward moving stocks are those that have had significant price declines in the preceding months and are *continuing to decline*. These stocks should be avoided. They have *not* substantially broken through the upper line of the declining price cycle and established a new rising price cycle (a cycle with higher tops and higher bottoms).

Sideways moving stocks are suitable for covered call investment and are characterized by predominantly stable bottoms and tops; that is, the tops and bottoms of the cycle are getting neither higher nor lower.

The Buying Low Rule for Covered Calls

The buying low rule for covered calls exists to ensure that new covered call positions are only entered into in the lower portion of a stock's current price cycle. Investing in stocks that are in the lower portion of the current price cycle increases the likelihood that the stock price will increase after entering into a new position, and therefore, increases the likelihood of being called out at the end of the option month. Being called out at the end of the option month is a primary objective of covered call investing.

The buying low rule for covered calls includes two stipulations:

1. Invest in stocks that are upward moving or sideways moving.

2. Only invest in a stock when it is in the lower 25 percent of the current price cycle. Investing in the lower 25 percent of the cycle makes it more likely that the stock will move up after entering the transaction and, therefore, increases the likelihood of being called out.

The Rules for Investing in Non-U.S. Markets

1. You can establish new positions only on down market days. A down market day is a day when the major market average index for that market is in the red (trading lower than the close of the previous trading day).
2. You must always only sell the near month call when entering a new covered call position.
3. You should assess the universe of optionable stocks for the fundamental and technical data outlined in the U.S. covered call search criteria. Preference should be given to stocks that more fully meet these criteria.
4. You should assess the universe of optionable stocks in the chosen market for both uncalled and called returns and invest in the highest yielding opportunities.
5. Always give priority to maintaining acceptable levels of diversification—never have more than 10 percent of your investment capital in any one stock. Preferably construct a portfolio of between 10 and 20 stocks.
6. Buy the stock first and then immediately sell the call. Do not hesitate. If you buy the stock and wait for a better price for the call, you are no better than a speculator, and you will get burned!

The Mid-Month Rule

Once you have entered into the covered call position or sold a secondary call, all you need to do is have patience and wait for the option's expiration at the end of the month. However, you can decide to be a little more proactive during the month and utilize the mid-month rule, which can have the effect of significantly increasing your returns on the position.

The mid-month technique involves buying back the short call for a profit in the first two weeks of the month. The five rules for implementing this technique are:

1. If you have sold a call for a 5 percent uncalled return or more, the mid-month technique may be considered.
2. If within the first two weeks of the month you are able to buy back the call and lock in an uncalled return of 4 percent for the month, then do so.

3. You then put in a good til canceled (GTC) order to sell the same call for more than you bought it back for.

4. If the GTC order executes, wait until the end of the month to see if you will be called out.

5. If the GTC order does not execute, or if the position is uncalled at expiration, move to the secondary call sales rule.

The Rules for Secondary Call Sales

A secondary call sale is any call sale that occurs after you have bought back the original call or the original call has expired. The six applicable rules are:

1. Secondary calls can only be sold when the markets are in the green (higher than the close of the previous day). For the United States, the markets are in the green when both the Dow Jones Industrial Average and the NASDAQ are trading above the close of the previous day. Foreign markets are in the green when the major market index for that market is trading above the close of the previous day.

2. For the U.S. market, if you can sell a near month call where the uncalled and called returns are both greater than 4 percent, then do so. For foreign markets, if you can sell a near month call where the uncalled and called returns are both greater than 1.5 percent, then do so.

3. If rule 2 isn't applicable, you should use the TSS for income while being sure to adhere to the selling high rule. Move the expiration of the call out to the second to last expiration and sell a call that provides an uncalled return of minimum 10 percent. Do not sell the last expiration of the option series. This must be kept in reserve for defensive techniques.

4. The minimum uncalled return of 10 percent for a TSS for income call sale is based on your purchase price of the stock or the current market value, whichever is higher.

5. The greater the uncalled return generated on the TSS for income call sale, the quicker the call will be bought back as the stock price declines. You may select a lower strike price to allow an easier buyback to the extent the strike price of the call selected plus the call's bid price is greater than the current price of the stock.

6. Once a TSS for income call is sold, it should be bought to close at any time a 5 percent net return can be realized or when the stock reaches 25 percent of the current cycle, whichever occurs first.

The Tethered Slingshot for Income
and the Selling High Rule

The tethered slingshot (TSS) for income and the selling high rule are very important techniques for the covered call writer as they allow consistent generation of income in situations where the stock price is trading below an investor's cost in the stock.

The rules for the TSS for income are embedded in the preceding rules for secondary call sales. These rules state that when a call cannot be sold in the near month that provides both an uncalled and called return of 4 percent or greater, the investor must use the TSS for income. The investor should select the second to last expiration and a strike price call that results in an uncalled return of minimum 10 percent. Before this call can be sold, the investor *must* ensure that the selling high rule has been satisfied. The selling high rule relates to the *timing* of the TSS for income call sale—it is very important that TSS for income calls are sold at the high point of the price cycle.

The *selling high* rule states that secondary call sales using the TSS for income can only be made when a stock is in the upper 75 percent of its current price cycle.

Safely Maximizing TSS for Income Call Sale Opportunities—
Understanding Cycles Within Cycles

Maximizing call sale opportunities means taking advantage of as many movements within the price cycle as possible. To do this, investors must take advantage of short-term cycles while assessing the selling high rule. However, investors must not ignore the long-term cycle when using the TSS for income and selling high rule. Do not sell a call at the bottom of the long-term cycle. Always view the stock initially over a 12-month time frame to understand the long term cycle. Shorter-term cycles can then be assessed. The top of a short-term cycle is often the bottom of the long-term cycle.

The Rules for Selling Calls on Existing
Stock Holdings

1. New calls may only be sold on up market days. For the U.S. market, an up market day is when the Dow Jones Industrial Average and the NASDAQ are in the green (trading higher than the close of the previous day). For foreign markets, an up market day is when the major market average index for that country is in the green (trading higher than the close of the previous day).

2. If the market price of the stock is *higher* than your cost in the stock, both the called and uncalled return calculations should be based on the *current market price* of the stock. If the market price of the stock is

lower than your cost in the stock, all return calculations should be based on *your cost* in the stock.

3. If you have no desire to keep the stock, your objective should be to sell a *near month* call that will provide a satisfactory uncalled and called return. If you can sell a near month call with a resulting uncalled and called return of minimum 2.0 percent for the U.S. market or minimum 1.0 percent for foreign markets, then do so. This minimum return requirement is highly dependant on the volatility of the individual stock. With experience, you will gain a greater understanding of what is a reasonable uncalled and called return for your particular stock holdings.

4. If you cannot satisfy rule 3 or you do not want to be called out of the stock holding, then use the TSS for income while being sure to adhere to the selling high rule.

The 20¢ Rule

If you have a negative called return when an option contract has two weeks to expiration, take the strike price of your call, add the cost of buying back that call (the *ask price*) and subtract the market price of the stock. So:

20¢ rule = Call strike price + Call buyback price (ask) – Stock price

If the 20¢ rule value is equal to $0.20 or less, you are in the danger zone of being called out and you need to take defensive action using the TSS for defense.

Remember, the 20¢ rule is only used in the last two weeks of the option month and only on positions with negative called return. You must monitor such positions carefully during the last two weeks of the option month to make sure you are not in danger of being called out *unprofitably*. If at any time during the last two weeks of the option month you have sold a call that results in a negative called return and the 20¢ rule equals $0.20 or less, you must immediately take defensive action using the TSS for defense.

Tethered Slingshot for Defense

You should implement the TSS for defense immediately if the 20¢ rule has indicated that you are in danger of being called out and that this call out will be unprofitable. The eight rules for using this technique are:

1. Implement the TSS for defense if the 20¢ rule indicates that you are in danger of being called out and that this call out will be unprofitable.

2. Immediately buy back the existing call (this results in a temporary loss).

3. Select the same call strike price but move the expiration date out to the second to last expiration.

4. You have now generated additional covered call income, as the price you received for selling the TSS for defense call is always higher than the cost of buying back the near month. You no longer have a temporary loss.

5. Buy back this new call when the net gain is at least equal to the temporary loss generated in rule 2.

6. You now have a stock with no call obligation, did not get called out, and made additional income every step of the way.

7. You should now be patient and wait for an upswing in the stock price that will allow you to sell a near month call for a minimum of 4 percent uncalled and called return for the U.S. market and 1.5 percent for foreign markets that will allow a positive called return.

8. If the stock reaches 75 percent of the price cycle and does not allow for application of rule 7, go back to the rules for secondary call sales.

Surrogate Stock Replacement

Surrogate stock replacement (SSR) is an invaluable covered call defensive technique. The function of the SSR is to expedite the profitable close-out of a covered call transaction where the following three conditions apply:

1. An investor has used the TSS for income on the position.

2. The stock has continued to move up after selling the TSS for income call. The investor is therefore unable to buy back the TSS for income call due to this buyback being unprofitable.

3. The investor now has a *profit* in the stock position, but is prevented from closing the entire transaction (buying back the call and selling the stock) because doing so would result in an overall transaction loss. In all instances this is due to the loss on buyback of the TSS for income call exceeding the potential profit from selling the stock.

The ten rules for using the SSR technique are:

1. The SSR is to be used on a covered call position where an investor has an open TSS for income call.

2. The investor has a profit in the stock position.

3. The position cannot be closed for a profit, as the loss on buyback of the call is greater than the potential profit from selling the stock. Therefore, if the position is closed out, a net loss for the investor would be created.

4. Use the SSR Worksheet to calculate the net loss in closing the transaction (the SSR Worksheet is part of the Covered Call Toolbox, one month's complementary access to which is available by going to www.compoundstockearnings.com/freemonth). This net loss is the restructure cost.

5. Input various LEAPS contracts into the SSR Worksheet. The SSR usually works better when using the second to last expiration LEAPS, rather than the furthest out LEAPS contract. Start one strike price out of the money and move into the money three or four contracts.

6. Input various near month and two month out call contracts into the SSR Worksheet. Start two strikes out of the money and move into the money two contracts.

7. The SSR should be executed if the SSR Worksheet presents a transaction that has both an uncalled and called return of greater than 2 percent. Preference should be given to the SSR transaction with the highest returns. Preference should also be given to selling the near month call.

8. It is also preferable that the SSR be cash flow positive. Investors with excess capital may still choose to execute the SSR if it is cash flow negative. Optimally, the transaction should generate net cash.

9. If the transactions presented by the SSR Worksheet do not meet the return requirements or cash flow requirements in items (7) and (8), more aggressive investors may choose to enter shorter-term calls into the SSR Worksheet as an alternative to using a LEAPS. Aggressive investors may buy a shorter-term call to construct a SSR if the shorter-term call provides an SSR that meets rules (7) and (8). If buying a shorter-term call:

   (a) Preference must be given to the longest-term call that meets rules (7) and (8).

   (b) An investor must not purchase a call when that call's price consists of more than 15 percent time value. This limit ensures that the investor is purchasing primarily intrinsic value (exercisable value) and will not be affected greatly by time decay in the event that the position is not exited quickly.

   (c) When purchasing a shorter-term call, investors must be aware that in the event the stock begins trading down, the call will need to be rolled out.

10. In the event the call that was shorted in the SSR restructure expires worthless (the position was not called out), the position should be managed like a regular LEAPS position with the following exception:

    (a) The investor should always give preference to selling a near month call if that call will provide a positive called and uncalled return. Remember, the objective of the SSR is not to manage the position for income, but to exit the unproductive position as soon as possible.

Cardiopulmonary Resuscitation

Cardiopulmonary resuscitation (CPR) is an advanced covered call defensive technique that is used to literally resuscitate a fallen stock. The CPR has two typical applications:

1. To dramatically expedite the closing of a new covered call position where the stock price has suffered an immediate decline after entering the transaction. The CPR provides this ability as, in many cases, it allows the investor to lower the strike price of the short call in the near month, yet continue to maintain a positive called return.

2. To generate income and reduce the cost basis in a deeply depressed position. The CPR can effectively be applied where an underperforming stock is now in an upward cycle but the cycle's depth is too shallow to effectively use the TSS for income.

For any given stock position, the construction of a CPR is accomplished as follows:

1. An investor holds a long position of 100 shares of stock.
2. The investor buys one near month (or two month out) call.
3. The investor sells two near month (or two month out) calls with a higher strike price than the call selected in step (2).

CALENDAR LEAPS SPREADS

Refer to Figure A.2, the flowchart that depicts each step in the LEAPS investment process

Calculating the Called Return

The formula for calculating the called return is:

Called return = Strike call – Strike LEAPS – LEAPS price + Call price

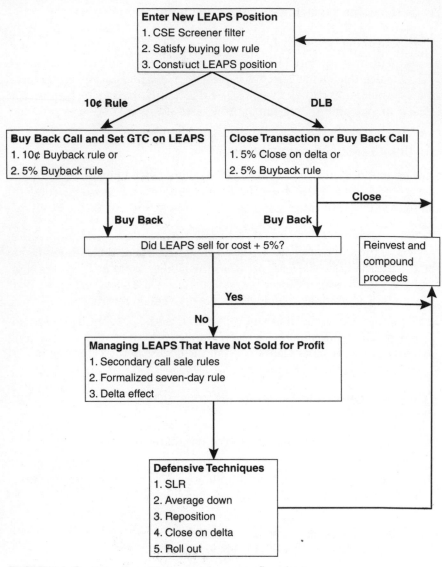

FIGURE A.2   Calendar LEAPS spread process flowchart.

The Rules for Entering New LEAPS Positions

A new calendar LEAPS position involves buying a LEAPS and selling a call. The six rules for entering into new LEAPS positions are:

1. You can only establish new positions on down market days. A down market day is any time when the Dow and the NASDAQ are in the red (trading lower than the close of the previous day).
2. Use the CSE Screener to filter all stocks in the market for the fundamental criteria for LEAPS investments.
3. You must follow the rules for correctly constructing a LEAPS position These rules are imbedded in the CSE Screener.
4. Ensure that the stock adheres to the buying low rule for LEAPS.
5. Always give priority to maintaining acceptable levels of diversification between stocks and industries—even if a stock you are already invested in presents an excellent opportunity.
6. Buy the LEAPS first and then immediately sell the call. Do not hesitate. If you buy the LEAPS and wait for a better price for the call, you are no better than a speculator, and you will get burned!

Parameters for Filtering LEAPS Positions

The eight parameters you should use to filter LEAPS positions are:

1. Uncalled return of minimum 10 percent.
2. Called return of minimum 0 percent.
3. Price-earnings ratio (PE) of 70 or less.
4. Market capitalization of US$5 billion or more.
5. Stock price between $25.00 and $100.00.
6. Average broker recommendation of 2.5 or less.
7. An aggregate of the brokers recommending the stock as "Strong Buy" and "Buy" greater than the number of brokers recommending the stock as "Hold."
8. A consensus earnings per share (EPS) estimate for "Next Fiscal Year" forecast to be greater than the consensus EPS estimate for "This Fiscal Year."

Using Price Charts with the LEAPS Technique

Before entering a new LEAPS position, investors *must* assess the stock's chart. Correct assessment of the price chart is absolutely critical to optimizing returns when using the LEAPS technique. The detailed information provided in the "Using Price Charts" section in Chapter 3 also applies entering a LEAPS position. Remember: If you do not understand a chart, *do not* invest in the stock.

The Buying Low Rule for LEAPS

The buying low rule defines the point in the stock's price cycle at which an investor can enter into new positions or sell secondary calls. It exists to ensure that new LEAPS positions are only constructed on a stock that is in the *low point* of its price cycle. The three rules are:

1. Investment in new LEAPS positions can only be made when a stock's overall or current cycle is increasing or horizontal.
2. Investment in new LEAPS positions can only be made when a stock is in the lower 25 percent of its overall or current price cycle.
3. A stock's price cycle must have at minimum $1.50 of price between the upper and lower lines for a position to be eligible for investment. This third rule ensures that there is enough potential upward movement in the stock price to exit the position.

Constructing a Leaps Position

Selecting a LEAPS

- Because of the delta ratio, you must select a LEAPS that is *one strike price in the money*.
- You may not select a LEAPS that costs more than $10.00; the less it costs, the better. Low cost is necessary to generate leverage. Also, the higher the cost of your LEAPS, the more difficult the position will be to manage in a market downturn.
- The LEAPS selected must have at minimum 12 months to expiration, with the longest-term LEAPS available always given preference.

Selecting the Call

- You must sell a call as soon as you buy a LEAPS. If you wait to get a higher price for the call, you are no better than a speculator and you will get burned!
- You must select a call that results in a positive called return. To make this selection, take the LEAPS strike price and add the cost of the LEAPS and you will arrive at an approximate strike price for the call.

- The call expiration that you select must not be equal to the expiration of the LEAPS. The shortest-term call that meets the requirements for a correct construction should be selected to allow management depth.
- The call selected must combine with the LEAPS selected to have a delta ratio of 1.90 or more.

The Delta Ratio

Delta ratio = LEAPS delta/Call delta

The 10¢ Buyback Rule

The 10¢ buyback rule instructs investors to do two things:

1. Buy back the call at market if the *bid* price of the LEAPS moves to 10¢ above your cost in the LEAPS.
2. Then add the cost of the call buyback to your cost in the LEAPS, add 5 percent to that total, and put in a good til canceled (GTC) order to sell the LEAPS at this price.

The 5% Buyback Rule

The 10¢ buyback rule applies in the event the stock price increases after entering the transaction. Conversely, the 5% buyback rule allows you to take advantage of a downward movement in the stock price after establishing a new position by taking the following two steps:

1. Buy back the call for a net uncalled return of 5 percent if market prices decline.
2. Then add 5 percent to the cost of the LEAPS and place a GTC order to sell the LEAPS at this price.

LEAPS Secondary Call Sales Rules

The eleven rules for selling a secondary call on a LEAPS are as follows:

1. A secondary call can only be sold when the markets are in the green (trading higher than the close of the previous day). The markets are in the green any time when both the Dow Jones Industrial Average and the NASDAQ are trading above the close of the previous day.
2. A secondary call can only be sold after implementing either the 10¢ or 5% buyback rule.

3. A secondary call cannot be sold if the market bid price of the LEAPS is within 10 percent of your GTC sale price.

4. A secondary call can only be sold when the formalized seven-day rule has been satisfied.

5. A secondary call sale should generate a minimum 10 percent uncalled return.

6. The aim is to buy back the call for a net uncalled return of 5 percent.

7. It is preferable to select the same call strike price as the strike price used when the position was established. Simply move the expiration date out in order to maintain a minimum 10 percent uncalled return using the same strike price. This move ensures that the delta ratio remains intact. A call may be sold up to but not exceeding the expiration date of the LEAPS.

8. Preference should always be given to a shorter term call if this call provides the minimum uncalled return requirement of 10 percent (time value erodes more quickly in the investor's favor).

9. If a minimum 10 percent uncalled return with the same strike price cannot be maintained, drop the strike price one increment toward in the money. Preference should always be given to a shorter-term call if this provides the minimum uncalled return requirement of 10 percent.

10. Continue to drop the strike price to generate yield up to the point that the call strike price is equal to the LEAPS strike price. Do not sell a call with a strike price lower than the strike of the LEAPS.

11. In the event that a 10 percent uncalled return cannot be generated without violating rule (10), the LEAPS should be repositioned.

The Formalized Seven-Day Rule

The FSDR encompasses two components:

1. Secondary call sales can only be made when a stock is in the upper 75 percent of its current price cycle.

2. A rising price cycle must have a minimum of $1.50 of price between the upper and lower lines of its price cycle.

The 25 Percent Buyback Rule Exception to FSDR—Declining Cycles
When implementing the FSDR on a declining cycle, investors should *not* aim for a net buyback return of 5 percent. Instead, for larger buyback returns, investors should only buy back the call when the stock reaches the bottom 25 percent of the cycle. The 25% buyback rule leverages

off the fact that the current cycle is *declining*. As such, it is wise to take full advantage of this declining stock price in order to enhance returns.

The Surrogate Leaps Replacement Rules

There are two basic rules for using the surrogate LEAPS replacement (SLR):

1. If the stock price is in the upper 75 percent of the cycle and you are able to sell the original LEAPS for a return of 5 percent or more, then the SLR can be considered.
2. Select the same expiration date; however, move the strike price up one or two increments (preferably not equal to the strike price of the call). Buy this LEAPS and then immediately sell the LEAPS you own.

Once you have taken action based on the rules, there are two distinct scenarios:

1. Stock price continues up. In this scenario you should take advantage of the rising stock price. If you are able to sell the SLR LEAPS for a 5 percent profit, then do so. After selling this LEAPS, you must immediately buy another LEAPS. Simply move the strike price up one increment. You have now performed a second SLR. Continue to take 5 percent profits and SLR the LEAPS to the extent that the strike price of your LEAPS is not higher than the strike price of the call. You can SLR up to the point that the LEAPS and the call have an identical strike price.
2. Stock price declines. In this scenario you should buy back the problematic call, but only when you can exit the call at approximately the cost you sold it for. Once you have bought back the call, go back to the FSDR.

The Averaging Down Rules

The four rules for averaging down a LEAPS position are:

1. If the market price of a LEAPS drops significantly to a point where you are able to buy the same LEAPS contract you already own for 15 percent or less of the price you paid for it, then do so. For example, if you own a LEAPS at a cost of $5.00, you would average that position down if you could buy additional contracts at a price of $0.75 (the "average down price").
2. You should buy the number of contracts that brings your average cost to a price equal to two times the average down price. For example, if

you own a LEAPS at a cost of $5.00, you would average that position down if you could buy additional contracts at a price of $0.75 (the average down price). You should buy the number of contracts that brings your average cost to a value of $1.50 (two times the average down price of $0.75).

3. The 5 percent return calculation for subsequent secondary call sales should be based on *the original contract cost*, not on the average cost of contracts. So, for a buyback on a secondary call sale on a $5.00 LEAPS, you should still attempt to realize a net return of $0.25.

4. Sell the LEAPS at the new average cost plus 5 percent, not the original cost. So, for the preceding example, you should sell the LEAPS for $1.50 plus 5 percent.

The Rollout Rules

If an investor is holding a LEAPS that has less than one year to expiration, he or she must sell it and buy another LEAPS relating to the same company. Three guidelines must be followed:

1. A rollout must be conducted on a down day.

2. If your capital position allows, select the same strike price and the furthest out date possible providing that the adjusted cost does not exceed $10.00.

3. If this LEAPS leads to an adjusted cost of more than $10.00 (or if your capital position does not allow you to select the same strike), select the next highest strike price. Continue to raise the strike price until the adjusted cost does not exceed $10.00. Preference is always given to maintaining the lowest strike price possible.

Foreign Exchange Risk

This appendix is intended solely for investors residing outside of the United States. U.S. investors can disregard this material.

DEFINING FOREIGN EXCHANGE RISK

Transactions involving international stock and options generally introduce *foreign exchange risk*. Foreign exchange risk is the risk that the exchange rate between currencies will change and adversely affect the earnings or value of your portfolio as denominated in your home currency. Foreign exchange risk occurs because instruments listed on foreign markets are generally traded in the *home currency* of that market. For example, if you wish to purchase a U.S. stock or option, you must do so in United States dollars (USD or US$).

The foreign exchange market facilitates the buying and selling of foreign currencies by generally allowing any individual or entity to purchase units of a foreign currency in exchange for the home currency. The *exchange rate* is the market price of one currency against another. For example, 1 USD equals 0.75 Australian dollars (AUD or AU$). Like stock and option prices, exchange rates are generally determined by market forces and are constantly changing.

If you decide to invest in the U.S. markets and you are *not* based in the United States, you will need to be aware of *foreign exchange risk*. If you invest in the U.S. market and are a U.S. resident you are not exposed to foreign exchange risk.

TABLE B.1   Effect of Foreign Exchange Risk

Buy Transaction

Shares Bought	USD Price	Total USD	AUD/USD Rate	AUD Total			
500	$20.00	$10,000	$0.75	$13,333			

Sell Transaction

Shares Sold	USD Price	Total USD	USD Profit	AUD/USD Rate	AUD Total	AUD Profit
500	$20.50	$10,250	$250	$0.77	$13,312	−$22

An example of a non-U.S. investor who invests in the U.S. markets being adversely affected by foreign exchange risk on a simple U.S. stock transaction is given in Table B.1. Notice that the investor bought 500 shares at US$20.00 and sold them at US$20.50, realizing a US$250 profit. However, if the investor converted AUD in order to buy the 500 shares and then converted the USD proceeds of the stock sale back to AUD, he or she may be adversely affected by foreign exchange translation. Because the investor converted AUD to USD at a rate of $0.75 to buy the stock and then converted the USD proceeds to AUD at a rate of $0.77, he or she would actually lose AU$22.00 on the entire transaction.

MANAGING FOREIGN EXCHANGE RISK

Investors using the covered call or LEAPS techniques who are not located in the United States are exposed to foreign exchange risk. Given the long-term compounding focus of the covered call and LEAPS techniques, experience tells us that foreign exchange risk should be viewed more as a potential cost of doing business rather than as a risk of going out of business.

Depending on the level of foreign exchange risk mitigation required by covered call and LEAPS investors, there are four alternative strategies that can be implemented to manage foreign exchange risk.

1. Implement Forward Hedging Strategy

The most comprehensive of all foreign exchange risk management methods, implementing forward hedging leads to the virtual elimination of foreign exchange risk. This method involves the use of future or option contracts to hedge foreign exchange conversions.

Experience indicates that such a strategy is highly complicated to implement with the covered call and LEAPS techniques due to the uncertainty in the timing of future USD capital and earnings flows. Forecasting future earnings and capital flows and constructing complicated hedging strategies to accommodate these flows only serves to detract from what should be an investor's primary focus: generating and compounding cash flow. A forward hedging strategy is simply not appropriate for this type of investing as its benefits do not outweigh its costs.

2. Convert to USD and Back to Home Currency for Each Transaction

A second method simply involves converting your home currency as required when purchasing new positions. Investors would then convert back to the home currency when profits are realized or capital is freed up by exiting an existing position.

This method has proven ineffective for the covered call and LEAPS technique. Both covered call and LEAPS investors aim to generate returns of around 5 percent per transaction. This small return target can easily be eroded by relatively minor foreign exchange movements. For example, a 5 percent USD return can easily be eroded to just a 1 percent or 2 percent home currency return due to a small movement in the USD/home currency exchange rate.

Additionally, investors using this risk management technique find themselves regularly buying and selling currency—possibly numerous times a day for LEAPS investors. Apart from detracting from the investor's primary focus of generating and compounding cash flow, this technique also serves to significantly increase transaction costs.

3. Use Home Currency as Collateral for USD

A third method involves using deposited home currency as collateral for borrowed USD. For example, if an investor deposited AU$10,000 and the AUD/USD exchange rate was 0.75, then this investor would be able to invest in U.S. stocks or options to a value of US$7,500. Investors then receive interest at the prevailing AUD cash rate on the Australian dollar balance over a predetermined sum by the broker (see broker's web site for current balance limits) and pay interest on the borrowed USD balance at the prevailing U.S. interest rate.

Along with method 4, using home currency as collateral for USD is one of two preferred methods for managing foreign exchange risk. It allows investors to realize profits in USD and accumulate and compound these profits in USD. This method is also particularly beneficial when the interest rate differential between the home currency and the USD is significant. This method results in a profit to the investor when credit interest paid by the broker is greater than debit interest charged by the broker.

One disadvantage of this technique is the need for investors to provision for the potential of decreased buying power resulting from a devaluation of the home currency against the USD. Under the conditions of a devaluating home currency, a fully invested portfolio may be subject to margin calls due to a lack of collateral to fund the negative USD balance. In a climate of a devaluing home currency, investors should instead consider using method 4.

4. Convert to USD and Remain in USD

A fourth method involves converting your home currency to USD as you invest your capital in the U.S. market. Investors would then simply accumulate profits in USD and use these USD to invest in more positions to compound the asset base. The accumulated USD balance is only translated back to the home currency when an investor wishes to remove money from the account.

Along with method 3, converting to and remaining in USD is one of the preferred methods for managing foreign exchange risk.

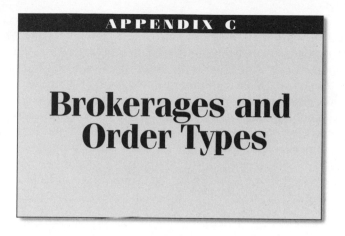

Brokerages and Order Types

SELECTING A BROKERAGE HOUSE

The significance of brokerage commissions should not be ignored. An investor's choice of brokerage house has a large impact on overall profitability.

Whether you are investing in covered calls or LEAPS, you must use a *discount broker*. Discount brokers have cheaper rates of brokerage/commission because they provide an execution only service (they do not provide research or advice). Both covered call and LEAPS investors make a significant number of transactions each month and realize small profits on each of these transactions. Therefore, transaction costs have a very high bearing on profitability with this method of investing.

Again, the impact of different commission structures at various brokerage houses is very significant and should not be ignored. Not selecting a competitively priced broker is no different than ignoring the operating expenses in a traditional business.

If you are investing in the U.S. market, there are several discount brokers very suitable for this type of investing. *Deep* discount brokers are even better, as they have extremely cheap commissions, so small that commissions *needn't be accounted for* when considering profits on trades. For example, one industry-leading deep discount broker charges commissions of just $0.75 per 100 shares and $0.75 per option contract—with no minimum trade size! If an investor buys 100 shares of a $30.00 stock, this is a $3,000 investment. The commission for this stock purchase and the sale of one option contract would total just $1.50, or 0.05 percent of the invested capital. This is a remarkable rate of commission, and, for all intents and purposes, the trade is practically *commission free*.

The brokerage industry is constantly evolving with new online players entering the market and existing brokerage houses regularly making changes to trading platforms and commission structures. The current industry best brokers for using this technique can be found at www .compoundstockearnings.com/brokers. We highly recommend that investors use one of these brokers because trading platforms and transaction costs have a dramatic effect on profitability.

COMMON ORDERS USED IN ONLINE BROKERAGE PLATFORMS

There are four basic kinds of orders that investors can use with the covered call and LEAPS techniques. The first two of the following relate to price execution and the second two pertain to order duration.

1. Limit (LMT). A limit order is one that is price specific, for example, buy 100 C shares at $45.00. The order will not be filled unless it can be filled at a price of $45.00 or less. Limit orders are the safest way to buy or sell a stock or option, and they should be used as often as possible.

2. Market (MKT). A market order is one that is not price specific, for example, buy 100 C shares at market. The order will be filled at the best price available in the market; a price is *not* guaranteed.

3. Good til Canceled (GTC). A GTC order will sit in the market until the investor who placed it cancels it or it executes. For example, a GTC limit order to buy 100 C shares at $45.00 will sit in the market until the shares can be bought at $45.00 or the investor cancels the order.

4. Day Order (DAY). A day order will only sit in the market until the end of the trading day it was transmitted. For example, a day order to buy 100 C shares at limit of $45.00 will be purged from the market at the end of the day if it has not executed.

CONDITIONAL ORDERS AND THE 10¢ AND 5% RULES

Conditional orders are an invaluable tool for LEAPS investors utilizing the 10¢ rule who are not able to monitor the market continuously throughout the trading day. These orders allow investors to place an order into the market that is conditional on certain events occurring, for example a stock or option trading at a certain price.

LEAPS investors can use conditional orders to automate the process of buying back a call under the 10¢ and 5% buyback rules. Thus they can conduct their LEAPS investing for only a few hours a day, rather than being at the computer for the entire day waiting for situations to arise. Take the following new position for example:

- Long 2 JPM Jan 2007 $35.00 LEAPS @ $5.00
- Short 2 JPM Dec 2005 $40.00 Calls @ $1.00

Conditional orders allow investors to place an order to take care of the 10¢ buyback rule as follows:

- Buy back Dec 2005 $40.00 call at market if bid price of Jan 2007 $35.00 LEAPS reaches $5.10.

A simple limit order also allows investors to take care of the 5% buyback rule as follows:

- Buy back Dec 2005 $40.00 call at limit of $0.75.

By using the conditional order format, investors can ensure the rules are being followed without sitting at the computer all day. Compound Stock Earnings recommended brokers accommodate conditional orders.

CREDIT SPREADS AND THE DELTA LOW BRIDGE

Credit spreads are an invaluable tool for delta low bridge (DLB) investors who are not able to monitor the market continuously throughout the trading day. These orders allow investors to place an order into the market that will execute when a certain price spread can be realized on the sale and buyback of two option contracts.

For example, take the following DLB investment:

- Long 2 JPM Jan 2007 $35.00 LEAPS @ $5.00
- Short 2 JPM Dec 2005 $40.00 Calls @ $1.00

Credit spread orders allow an investor to place an order into the market that will allow the call to be bought back and the LEAPS to be simultaneously sold when the investor can realize a predetermined profit. In this case, the predetermined profit would be the LEAPS cost plus 5 percent, or $5.00 \times 0.05 = 0.25. The credit spread order system will execute the buyback of the call and the simultaneous sale of the LEAPS if a credit difference of $0.25 can be realized in the market.

Investors can also place a limit order into the market to take care of the 5 percent profitable buyback of the call if the market price drops.

As with conditional orders, credit spread orders can allow the DLB investor to follow the rules without being at the computer throughout the entire trading day.

Using ETFs and HOLDRs for Diversification

For all intents and purposes exchange-traded funds (ETFs) and Holding Company Depositary Receipts (HOLDRs) trade and operate just like normal stocks. However, they differ from normal stocks as they represent the performance of an industry or an index. This feature is an advantage in that it makes ETFs and HOLDRs great tools for diversification.

For example, you can construct a LEAPS spread on a stock called the "DIA" that tracks the price of the Dow Jones Industrial Average. For all intents and purposes, if you buy the DIA you are actually investing in the Dow Jones Index. The Dow is an index of the most significant companies listed on the New York Stock Exchange. Alternatively, you can buy a stock called the "XLF," which provides you with exposure to U.S. companies in the financial sector. Thus, if you want to add a financial company to your portfolio you may elect to invest directly in JP Morgan, or, alternatively, you may wish to invest in the XLF, which will give you exposure to JP Morgan and a whole host of other financial companies. This diversification will decrease your portfolio risk.

The disadvantage, however, is that you will not have the liberty of screening the finance companies within the Dow and the S&P 500 and selecting a company that has a low PE and a very high broker rating.

ETFs and HOLDRs are particularly helpful for investors using the LEAPS technique with limited capital resources as they allow diversification between different companies and industries with the purchase of only a few positions. Be sure to remember that you need to treat them as just another stock.

Here are some ETFs and HOLDRs that you may wish to use with the LEAPS technique:

DIA	Dow Jones Industrial Average tracking stock
QQQQ	NASDAQ 100 tracking stock
XLB	Material Select Sector SPDR
XLE	Energy Select Sector SPDR
XLF	Financial Select Sector SPDR
XLI	Industrial Select Sector SPDR
XLK	Technology Select Sector SPDR
XLP	Consumer Staples Select Sector SPDR
XLU	Utilities Select Sector SPDR
XLV	Health Care Sector SPDR
HLY	Consumer Discretionary Select Sector SPDR
BDH	Broadband HOLDRs Trust
HHH	Internet HOLDRs Trust
IAH	Internet Architect HOLDRs Trust
OIH	Oil Services HOLDRs Trust
PPH	Pharmaceutical HOLDRs Trust
RKH	Regional Bank HOLDRs Trust
RTH	Retail HOLDRs Trust
SMH	Semiconductor HOLDRs Trust
SWH	Software HOLDRs Trust
TTH	Telecom HOLDRs Trust
UTH	Utilities HOLDRs Trust
WMH	Wireless HOLDRs Trust

The LEAPS technique works very well using both individual stocks and also ETFs and HOLDRs.

APPENDIX E

Compound Stock Earnings Support Services

www.compoundstockearnings.com

Compound Stock Earnings is an investment education resource operated by the authors of this book, Joseph Hooper and Aaron Zalewski. Since its inception in 1999, Compound Stock Earnings has grown to become the definitive education and information resource for the covered call technique.

Through its web site, www.compoundstockearnings.com, Compound Stock Earnings provides a host of services ranging from search and filter tools like the CSE Screener, to daily covered call and LEAPS selections sent by e-mail to clients, to the 2-Day Intensive Seminar. The impetuses of the services are to provide investors with the critical *information and education* needed to be successful in the business of writing covered calls.

Details of Compound Stock Earnings support services can be found at http://www.compoundstockearnings.com/services.htm. Services offered at the time of writing include the following.

COVERED CALL TOOLBOX

All investors who purchase *Covered Calls and LEAPS—A Wealth Option* are entitled to one month's complimentary access to the Covered Call Toolbox by going to www.compoundstockearnings.com/freemonth. This access provides investors with an opportunity to actually use the tools while learning about them in this book.

The Covered Call Toolbox includes the CSE Screener for both covered calls and LEAPS, the SSR and CPR Worksheets, and the Option Chains tools that have been discussed in this book. These tools are indispensable to the covered call and LEAPS investor. The CSE Screener is particularly essential because it dramatically improves the ability of covered calls and LEAPS investors to quickly find, qualify, and construct positions. Given the many thousands of stocks in the market, it is almost impossible for investors to manually filter stocks to find the best positions. The CSE Screener performs this function quickly and accurately with real time prices.

COVERED CALL/LEAPS SELECTIONS

Covered Call/LEAPS Selections subscribers receive real time, covered call and LEAPS transactions e-mailed directly to them. The service is unique in that the selections are generally trades we are executing in our own accounts or funds. They are not broker-style recommendations where we have no financial interest in the transaction performing well.

A Covered Call/LEAPS Selections subscription is an ideal way for clients to see firsthand the practical application of the covered call and LEAPS technique in terms of timing, position construction, and management.

THE 2-DAY INTENSIVE SEMINAR

The 2-Day Intensive Seminar is held at selected times in selected cities throughout the country. It is also offered online through an audiovisual link over the Internet to allow investors to attend the seminar without the inconvenience and expense of travel.

The most vital function of the 2-Day Intensive Seminar is to illustrate the practical application of the rules and techniques for covered call/LEAPS investing. It explains, elaborates on, and provides examples of every topic contained in *Covered Calls and LEAPS—A Wealth Option*. The seminar also covers new techniques or adaptations of rules that come about due to the ever-changing conditions of the market.

For investors who need hands-on classroom-style explanation and instruction on the covered call and LEAPS technique, the 2-Day Intensive Seminar is invaluable.

THE MASTER CLASS DVD

The Master Class was an advanced two-day seminar on both covered calls and LEAPS. It was a unique seminar in that it was taught by four of the most successful, long-term Compound Stock Earnings clients, each of whom uses advanced adaptations and interpretations of the techniques presented in this book—developed through years of their own individual use of the technique. The four client presenters each taught half a day of the two-day seminar, covering exactly what they do to produce superior returns using the covered call or LEAPS technique. The topics included covered calls on blue-chip stocks, covered call selection and management strategies (including the advanced SSR and CPR techniques), and adaptations of the LEAPS technique.

The presenters' backgrounds are diverse, including a professional fund manager using the covered call technique, an ex-investment banker who is now a full-time investor using the covered call technique, and two retired investors who have built their accounts using covered calls and now use the technique as their sole source of income in retirement.

The Master Class was recorded in its entirety in high-definition DVD. For those who want to be taught advanced techniques from actual Compound Stock Earnings clients who have consistently returned in excess of 60 percent annually in their accounts, the Master Class DVD is the ultimate resource.

THE COW REPORT

Every Saturday morning, our covered call experts sift through all of the week's e-mail correspondence from Compound Stock Earnings clients across the world and compile the most interesting questions and comments into a weekly e-newsletter, the Compound Stock Earnings Cow Report. All investors who purchase *Covered Calls and LEAPS—A Wealth Option* are entitled to lifetime access to the Cow Report by going to www.compound stockearnings.com/cowreport.

WHERE TO FIND SERVICES

All services are available through our web site at www.compoundstock earnings.com/services.htm.

Glossary

American option (or expiration) An option that may be exercised at any time prior to its expiration. The majority of stock options traded on American and international options exchanges are American-style options. The covered call technique involves the use of American style-options only.

at the money An option where the stock price is trading at the exercise price. For example, a $15.00 call option would be considered at the money if the stock price is $15.00. In practical terms, market participants also describe an option as at the money when the stock price is close to the exercise price of the option. So if an option's strike price is $15.00 and the stock price is, for example, $14.90 or $15.10, it would be deemed as being *at the money*.

averaging down A modified version of the traditional dollar cost averaging technique. Used to significantly reduce the average cost of a LEAPS position.

buying to close Closing a short stock or option position.

calendar LEAPS Selling a call option and owning a LEAPS on the same underlying stock for cover. See also *LEAPS*.

called return The sum of the uncalled return plus the profit or loss you make if your call is exercised (called out) divided by your cost in the stock. If you are called out, you have to deliver the stock you own at the exercise price of the call. See also *uncalled return*.

call option An option that gives the holder the right, but not the obligation, to buy a stock at a certain price up to a certain date. Call options are used by speculators who expect an increase in the price of the underlying asset.

call out (or called out) The result of an option that an investor has sold being exercised by an option buyer. In the case of stock options, results in the option seller being required to deliver the underlying stock at the exercise price of the option.

cardiopulmonary resuscitation (CPR) An advanced covered call defensive technique used to expedite the close of a fallen covered call position or to generate income on deeply depressed stock.

cash settlement   There are two types of settlement styles for exchange-traded options—physical settlement and cash settlement. Cash settled options give the owner the right to receive a cash payment based on the difference between the underlying asset price at the time of the option's exercise and the exercise price of the option. The majority of stock options are physically settled while the majority of index options are cash settled. See also *physical settlement*.

closing transaction   A transaction where an option buyer makes an offsetting sale of an identical option or an option seller makes an offsetting purchase of an identical option. The effect of the transaction is that the number of contracts the investor is exposed to is decreased.

conditional orders   Orders placed into the market on the condition that certain events occur, for example, a stock or option trading at a specified price.

covered call   Selling a call option and owning the underlying stock for cover.

calendar LEAPS   A technique for selling a call option while owning a LEAPS on the same underlying stock for cover. See also *LEAPS*.

credit spread   A closing order that executes when a predetermined price spread can be realized on the sale and buyback of two option contracts on the same underlying security. Most commonly used with the DLB technique. See also *delta low bridge*.

CSE Screener   A proprietary online search engine used to assist in identifying the best covered call and calendar LEAPS transactions in the U.S. market.

delta   The rate of change of the option price with respect to the price of the underlying stock. It is a measure of how much an option's price will increase or decrease for an incremental increase or decrease in the stock price. For example, an option with a delta of 0.60 means that when the stock price changes by an amount, the option price will change by 60 percent of that amount. Thus, if the stock price increases by $1.00, then the option will increase in price by $0.60 (60 percent of the stock price's increase).

delta low bridge (DLB)   An alternative LEAPS technique similar to the 10¢ rule LEAPS technique. The primary difference between the two techniques is DLB investors do not buy back the short call under the 10¢ rule if the stock price rises after entering a transaction. Instead DLB investors exit the entire transaction on the delta effect. See also *DLB index; 10¢ buyback rule*.

delta ratio   A measure of the interaction between the LEAPS delta and the call delta: Delta ratio = LEAPS delta/Call delta.

derivative   A financial instrument whose price depends directly on the value of an underlying security, index, debt instrument, commodity, or other financial instrument.

dividend   A distribution of earnings to shareholders usually paid quarterly in the form of cash.

DLB index   A calculation for any given LEAPS position of the percentage a stock price must rise in order for the position to exit on the delta effect with the desired minimum 5 percent return.

Dow (the)   Short for the Dow Jones Industrial Average, which is a stock index. It is the price of a collection of 30 blue-chip industrial companies listed on the New York Stock Exchange (NYSE). It provides a measure of how the blue-chip stock market is performing.

downward moving stock   A stock whose upper line of the price channel is at a gradient less than horizontal; a stock making lower tops and lower bottoms. A downward trending stock.

earnings per share   A company's earnings divided by the number of ordinary shares.

European option (or expiration)   An option that may be exercised only on its expiration date. The majority of stock options traded on American and international options exchanges are American-style options. The covered call technique involves the use of American-style options only.

exchange-traded fund (ETF)   A basket of stocks that is bought and sold on the stock exchange as if it were a single stock. An ETF typically represents a particular sector of the economy or a particular index.

exercise   See *call out*.

52-week range   Refers to the lowest and highest price a company's stock has traded for during the past year.

foreign exchange risk   The risk that the exchange rate between currencies will change and adversely affect the earnings or value of a portfolio as denominated in an investor's home currency.

formalized seven-day rule (FSDR)   A technique used to assist in identifying the timing of secondary call sales on a LEAPS position. See also *secondary call*.

good til canceled (GTC)   An order to buy or sell a stock or option that remains in effect until it is executed or canceled by the investor who placed it.

HOLDRs   Acronym for Holding Company Depositary Receipts. Listed on the American Stock Exchange (AMEX), HOLDRs are securities that represent an investor's ownership in the common stock or American Depositary Receipt of specified companies in a particular industry. Similar to an ETF.

in the money   An option that has intrinsic value, where the owner of the option stands to profit by exercising his or her right under the contract. For a call option to be in the money, the stock price must be higher than the strike price. For example, a $15.00 call option is in the money when the stock price is greater than $15.00. See also *intrinsic value*.

intrinsic value   The exercisable value of an option, which is the difference between the stock price and the exercise price. The value an option owner could realize by exercising an option and selling the stock in the market at the current market price. Intrinsic value cannot be negative.

LEAPS   Acronym for long-term equity anticipation securities. They are simply long-term options. They have exactly the same standardized characteristics as a normal option but with a long-term expiration. Contracts with one year or more of time value and a January 200x expiration are known as LEAPS.

limit order   An order designed to fill only at a specified price or better.

liquidity   Market liquidity refers to the ability to quickly buy or sell a stock or option without causing a significant movement in the price.

long position   An overall buy position in a stock or option.

market order   An order designed to fill at the best price currently available in the market.

market value   The value of the portfolio if it were immediately liquidated for cash at current market prices.

NASDAQ   A U.S. stock market that lists approximately 3,300 companies; heavily weighted with technology companies.

opening transaction   A transaction where an option buyer or seller establishes a new position or increases an existing position as either a buyer or a seller. The effect of the transaction is that the number of contracts/shares the investor is exposed to is increased.

option   A financial instrument and contract that gives the holder the right, but not the obligation, to buy or sell a financial asset at a certain price up to a certain date.

option chain   A list of all standardized options available for a particular stock or index.

option contract   Unlike stocks, options are referred to in contracts. Each contract relates to a certain number of shares in the underlying asset—this number changes depending on which exchange the option trades on. In the United States, option contracts generally relate to 100 shares.

out of the money   An option that has no intrinsic value, where the owner of the option does not stand to profit by exercising his or her right under the contract. For a call option to be out of the money, the stock price must be lower than the strike price. For example, a $15.00 call option is out of the money when the stock price is below $15.00.

PE (price-earnings) ratio   A stock's market price divided by its earnings per share. A PE ratio of a stock is used to measure how cheap or expensive the stock price is.

physical settlement   There are two types of settlement styles for exchange-traded options—physical settlement and cash settlement. Physical settlement options give the owner the right to receive physical delivery of the underlying asset when the option is exercised. The majority of stock options are physically settled while the majority of index options are cash settled. See also *cash settlement*.

put option   An option that gives the holder the right, but not the obligation, to *sell* a stock at a certain price up to a certain date. Put options are used by speculators who expect a decrease in the price of the underlying asset.

premium   The price of an option; the amount of money the buyer pays for the rights and the seller receives for the obligations granted by the contract. Expressed on a per share basis.

price channel or cycle   The price trend that a stock is trading in. Identified by the trading range between two parallel lines.

rollout   A technique used in LEAPS investing in which the investor sells an existing contract and repurchases another contract on the same underlying security with greater time to expiration.

S&P 500   Short for the Standard & Poor's 500, which is an index of the 500 largest publicly traded U.S. corporations and is often considered representative of the stock market in general. The majority of the companies included in the index are listed on the New York Stock Exchange (NYSE).

secondary call   Any call that is sold subsequent to the call that was originally sold when entering a covered call or LEAPS position.

short position   An overall sell position in a stock or option.

sideways moving stock   A stock whose lower line of the price channel is at a gradient approximately equal to horizontal; a stock making relatively equal tops and bottoms. A sideways trending stock.

surrogate LEAPS replacement (SLR)   A LEAPS technique used when an investor sells a call under the FSDR and the stock price continues to move up, preventing a profitable call buyback. It allows investors to reduce capital in the position and realize profits on a LEAPS by taking advantage of a rising stock price—without unprofitably buying back the short call.

surrogate stock replacement (SSR)   An advanced covered call defensive technique used to remedy a TSS for income call that cannot be bought back for a profit. See also *tethered slingshot for defense*; *TSS for income*.

10¢ buyback rule   A means for LEAPS investors to expedite the buyback of the call if the stock price is moving up and then to sell the LEAPS for a profit if the stock price continues up. This rule facilitates the close of the transaction.

tethered slingshot for defense (TSS)   A covered call defensive technique used to prevent an unprofitable call out.

time value   The portion of an option's price that exceeds the exercisable value.

TSS for income   A covered call management technique used to generate income when the stock price has declined after entry.

20¢ rule   A means for investors to determine whether an investment is in danger of being called out and if it is, therefore, necessary to implement the TSS for defense to prevent being called out. The 20¢ rule value = Call strike price + Call buyback price (ask) − Stock price. If the 20¢ rule value is equal to $0.20 or less, the danger zone of being called out exists and defensive action using the TSS for defense must be taken.

uncalled return   Also known as the "percentage return" or "yield," it is simply the premium received on the call sale divided by the cost of the stock or LEAPS. See also *called return*.

underlying asset   The asset that an option (or other derivative security) derives its value from. For example, the underlying asset of an IBM stock option is IBM stock.

upward moving stock   A stock whose lower line of the price channel is at a gradient greater than horizontal; a stock making higher tops and higher bottoms. An upward trending stock.

Disclaimer and Legal Information

Disclaimers

All information presented by Compound Stock Earnings, Inc., and/or Compound Stock Earnings Seminars, Inc., by its directors, employees, contractors, and consultants in seminars, Web sites, literature, verbal opinion or e-mail or through any other medium provides general information only. All references to international and USA securities are made using historical data and are for educational purposes only. No trading suggestions of any kind are made nor should be implied. In presenting the material, neither Compound Stock Earnings, Inc., and/or Compound Stock Earnings Seminars, Inc., nor its directors, employees, contractors, and consultants has taken into consideration any individual's investment objectives, financial situation, or particular needs. All recipients of general information furnished by Compound Stock Earnings, Inc., and/or Compound Stock Earnings Seminars, Inc., should seek independent professional advice as to the suitability of any investment strategy to their personal financial profile and goals.

Compound Stock Earnings, Inc., and/or Compound Stock Earnings Seminars, Inc., seminars, Web sites, literature, or e-mail or any other communications are provided by Compound Stock Earnings, Inc., and/or Compound Stock Earnings Seminars, Inc., on an "as is" basis. Compound Stock Earnings, Inc., and/or Compound Stock Earnings Seminars, Inc., makes no representations or warranties of any kind, express or implied, as to the operation of the Web site or the information, content, materials, or products included in seminars, Web sites, literature, verbal opinion or e-mail or in any other communication. To the full extent permissible by law, Compound Stock Earnings, Inc., and/or Compound Stock Earnings Seminars, Inc., disclaims all warranties, express or implied, including, but not limited to, implied warranties of merchantability and fitness for a particular purpose. Compound Stock Earnings, Inc., and/or Compound Stock Earnings Seminars, Inc., will not be liable for any damages of any kind arising from the use of information furnished through seminars, Web sites, or literature or through any other medium, including, but not limited to, direct, indirect, incidental, punitive, and consequential damages.

While content is based on information from sources that are considered reliable, Compound Stock Earnings, Inc., and/or Compound Stock Earnings Seminars,

Inc., its directors, employees, contractors, and consultants do not represent, warrant, or guarantee, expressly or implied, that the information presented is complete or accurate. Additionally, no responsibility is accepted to inform you of any matter that subsequently comes to its notice, which may affect any of the information contained in this document. Compound Stock Earnings, Inc., and/or Compound Stock Earnings Seminars, Inc., their officers or employees may at any time have a position, either long, short, or in a derivative, in any of the financial instruments discussed herein.

Risk and Liability

Compound Stock Earnings, Inc., and/or Compound Stock Earnings Seminars, Inc., its directors, employees, contractors, and consultants specifically disclaim any liability, whether based in contract, tort, strict liability, or otherwise, for any direct, indirect, incidental, consequential, or special damages arising out of or in any way connected with seminars, Web sites, literature, verbal opinion, or e-mail or any other communications or the information or material available from or through it even if Compound Stock Earnings, Inc., and/or Compound Stock Earnings Seminars, Inc., has been advised of the possibility of such damages, including liability in connection with mistakes or omissions in, or delays in transmission of, information to or from the user, interruptions in telecommunications connections to the site, or viruses.

Compound Stock Earnings, Inc., and/or Compound Stock Earnings Seminars, Inc., limits any liability that cannot be excluded to restoring the service, resupplying the material, or refunding any amount paid to Compound Stock Earnings, Inc., and/or Compound Stock Earnings Seminars, Inc., for the service or material. Any or all products or services provided by Compound Stock Earnings, Inc., and/or Compound Stock Earnings Seminars, Inc., may be modified over time.

All financial instruments including equity and derivative securities involve risk. Financial market participants must satisfy suitability requirements outlined by relevant brokers in order to trade financial instruments. Transacting in financial instruments is inherently risky and uncertain. Past results are not indicative of future performance.

None of the information and data contained in or communicated by seminars, Web sites, literature, e-mail, verbal opinion or through any other medium, constitutes a recommendation to purchase or sell a security, or to provide investment advice.

The information presented by Compound Stock Earnings, Inc., and/or Compound Stock Earnings Seminars, Inc., its directors, employees, contractors, and consultants in seminars, Web sites, literature, or verbal opinion or through any other medium is provided for general informational purposes. The materials are not a substitute for obtaining professional advice from a qualified person, firm, or corporation. Consult the appropriate professional advisor for more complete and current information. Compound Stock Earnings, Inc., and/or Compound Stock Earnings Seminars, Inc., is not engaged in rendering any legal, taxation, or other professional service by furnishing these general information materials.

Compound Stock Earnings, Inc., and/or Compound Stock Earnings Seminars, Inc., makes no representations or warranties about the accuracy or completeness of the information contained on this Web site or associated literature or through any other medium. Any links provided to other server sites are offered as a matter of convenience and in no way are meant to imply that Compound Stock Earnings, Inc., and/or Compound Stock Earnings Seminars, Inc., endorses, sponsors, promotes, or is affiliated with the owners of or participants in those sites, or endorses any information contained on those sites, unless expressly stated.

Use of Information

Compound Stock Earnings, Inc., and/or Compound Stock Earnings Seminars, Inc., is the copyright owner of all text and graphics contained on or in Compound Stock Earnings, Inc., and/or Compound Stock Earnings Seminars, Inc.'s Web sites, e-mails, seminar materials, or any other associated literature except as otherwise indicated. Other parties' trademarks and service marks that may be referred to herein are the property of their respective owners. You may print a copy of the information furnished on the Compound Stock Earnings, Inc., and/or Compound Stock Earnings Seminars, Inc., Web site or e-mails for your personal use only, but you may not reproduce or distribute the text or graphics to others or substantially copy the information on your own server, or link to this Web site, without prior written permission of Compound Stock Earnings, Inc., and/or Compound Stock Earnings Seminars, Inc.

Permission to use and reproduce documents and related graphics available from seminars, Web sites, or literature or through any other medium can only be granted by Compound Stock Earnings, Inc., and/or Compound Stock Earnings Seminars, Inc., in writing and if so will only be granted provided that: 1. the copyright notice appears in all copies and that both the copyright and this permission notice appear; 2. use and reproduction of documents and related graphics is limited to personal, noncommercial use; 3. no documents or related graphics, including logos, are modified in any way; and 4. no graphics, including logos, are used separate from accompanying text. Use or reproduction for any other purpose without the prior written consent of Compound Stock Earnings, Inc., is expressly prohibited by law, and may result in civil and criminal penalties. Compound Stock Earnings, Inc., and/or Compound Stock Earnings Seminars, Inc., reserves the right to revoke any given authorization at any time in writing, at which point any such use must be discontinued immediately.

Violators will be prosecuted to the maximum extent possible.

Applicable Law

The Compound Stock Earnings, Inc., Web site is created and controlled by Compound Stock Earnings, Inc., and Compound Stock Earnings Seminars, Inc., in Texas, United States of America. As such, the laws of Texas and the United States of America will govern these disclaimers, and terms and conditions, without giving effect to any principles of conflicts of laws. We reserve the right to make changes to our site and these disclaimers, and terms and conditions at any time.

Privacy Policy

Compound Stock Earnings, Inc., and/or Compound Stock Earnings Seminars, Inc., is committed to safeguarding your privacy. Please read the following statement to understand how your personal information will be treated while using the Compound Stock Earnings, Inc., and Compound Stock Earnings Seminars, Inc., Web site.

If you have any questions regarding our privacy statement, please feel free to contact us by e-mail at sylvia@compoundstockearnings.com.

Gathering of Information

Voluntary Submission

Compound Stock Earnings, Inc., and/or Compound Stock Earnings Seminars, Inc., does not collect personally identifying information about any individual Compound Stock Earnings, Inc., Web site user except when knowingly provided by such individual. For example, we may ask you for information when you register to receive information or to book attendance at a seminar. You always have the option not to provide the information we request. If you choose not to provide the information we request, you can still visit most of the Compound Stock Earnings, Inc., Web site, but you may be unable to access certain options and services.

A cookie is a data file that certain Web sites write to your computer's hard drive when you visit such sites. A cookie file can contain information, such as a user identification code, that the site uses to track the pages you have visited. Compoundstockearnings.com uses cookies solely to track user traffic patterns throughout the Compoundstockearnings.com Web site and to allow you access to "member only" sections of the site. We use this data on an anonymous basis and we do not correlate this information with personal data of any user.

Most Web site browsers automatically accept cookies, but you can usually change your browser settings to display a warning before accepting a cookie, or to refuse all cookies. However, if you choose to disable the receipt of cookies from our Web site, you may not be able to use certain features of the site.

Compoundstockearnings.com Web servers automatically collect information about a site user's IP address, browser type, and referrer by reading this information from the user's browser (information provided by every user's browser). This information is collected in a database and used—in an aggregated, anonymous manner—in our internal analysis of traffic patterns within our Web site. This information is automatically logged by most Web sites.

About the DVD

INTRODUCTION

This appendix provides you with information on the contents of the DVD that accompanies this book.

SYSTEM REQUIREMENTS

- A computer with DVD player and appropriate software installed OR
- A stand-alone DVD player attached to a television monitor

   Note: the DVD is compatible with all NTSC DVD players

WHAT'S ON THE DVD

The following sections provide a summary of the software and other materials you'll find on the DVD.

Content

This companion DVD contains two video presentations on executing covered calls and LEAPS transactions.

Playing the DVD on a PC

In the event the DVD does not automatically load on your PC:

- Open *My Computer*.
- With your mouse, right click on the DVD drive.

- Open *Properties.*
- Open the *AutoPlay* tab.
- Using the drop down menu, select *Video Files.*
- Select the DVD player.
- Click on *Apply.*
- Put the *Covered Calls and LEAPS* DVD into the disc drive.

The video should now load automatically.

CUSTOMER CARE

If you have trouble with the DVD, please call the Wiley Product Technical Support phone number at (800) 762-2974. Outside the United States, call (317) 572-3994. You can also contact Wiley Product Technical Support at **http://support.wiley.com**. John Wiley & Sons will provide technical support only for installation and other general quality control items. For technical support on the applications themselves, consult the program's vendor or author.

To place additional orders or to request information about other Wiley products, please call (877) 762-2974.

Index

For more information regarding the DVD, see the About the DVD section on page 221.

John Wiley & Sons, Inc.